A HISTORY OF T

BY
Gregory of Tours

Translated by Ernest Brehaut

INTRODUCTION

The *History of the Franks* by Gregory, bishop of Tours, is an historical record of great importance. The events which it relates are details of the perishing of the Roman Empire and the beginning of a great modern state and for these events it is often the sole authority. However although Gregory was relating history mainly contemporaneous or recent, we must allow largely for error and prejudice in his statements of fact. It is rather as an unconscious revelation that the work is of especial value. The language and style, the intellectual attitude with which it was conceived and written, and the vivid and realistic picture, unintentionally given, of a primitive society, all combine to make the *History of the Franks* a landmark in European culture. After reading it the intelligent modern will no longer have pleasing illusions about sixthcentury society.

Gregory's life covers the years from 538 to 594. He was a product of central Gaul, spending his whole life in the Loire basin except for brief stays elsewhere. [*note: Besides Clermont and Tours in which cities Gregory spent most of his life we hear of stays at Poitiers, Saintes, Bordeaux, Riez, Cavaillon, Vienne, Lyons, Chalon-sorSaône, ChâlonssurMarne, Rheims, Soissons, Metz, Coblentz, Braine, Paris, Orleans. Monod,* Sources de l'histoire Mérovingienne, *p. 37.*] The river Loire may be regarded as the southern limit of Frankish colonization and Gregory therefore lived on the frontier of the barbarians. He was born and grew up at Clermont in Auvergne, a city to which an inexhaustibly fertile mountain valley is tributary. In this valley his father owned an estate. Its wealth brought Clermont much trouble during the disorderly period that followed the breakup of Roman rule, and Gregory gives a hint of the eagerness which the Frankish kings felt to possess this country [*note: Childebert the elder is represented as saying:* Velim unquam Arvernam Lemanem quae tantae jocunditatis gratia refulgere dicitur, oculis cernere. *H. F. III: 9.*]

After 573 Gregory lived at Tours in the lower Loire valley. This city with its pleasant climate and moderately productive territorial background had more than a local importance in this age. It lay on the main thoroughfare between Spain and Aquitania and the north. Five Roman roads centered in it and the traffic of the Loire passed by it. The reader of Gregory's history judges that sooner or later it was visited by every one of importance at the time. It was here that the Frankish influences of the north and the Roman influences of the south had their chief contact. However the natural advantages of Tours at this time were surpassed by the supernatural ones. Thanks to the legend of St. Martin this conveniently situated city had become "the religious metropolis" of Gaul. St. Martin had made a great impression on his generation. [*note: In France, including Alsace and Lorraine, there are at the present time three thousand six hundred and seventyfive churches dedicated to St. Martin, and four hundred and twentyfive villages or hamlets are named after him. C. Bayet, in Lavisse,* Histoire de France, *221, p. 16*]
A Roman soldier, turned monk and then bishop of Tours, he was a man of heroic character and force. He had devoted himself chiefly to the task of Christianizing the *pagani* or rural population of Gaul and had won a remarkable ascendancy over the minds of a superstitious people, and this went on increasing for centuries after his death. The center of his cult was his tomb in the great church built a century before Gregory's time just outside the walls of Tours. This was the chief point of Christian pilgrimage in Gaul, a place of resort for the healing of the sick and the driving out of demons, and a sanctuary to which many fled for protection. [*note: . C. Bayet, in Lavisse,* Histoire de France, *21, pp. 13 ff.*] In a time of dense superstition and political and social disorder this meant much in the way of securing peace, influence, and wealth, and it was to the strategic advantage of the office of bishop of Tours as well as to his own aggressive character that Gregory owed his position as the leading prelate of Gaul.

Gregory does not neglect to tell us of his family connections and status in society. [***note:*** *Monod, op. cit. pp. 25 ff. See pp. 13, 84, 109,0, 140.*] He belonged to the privileged classes. Of his father's family he tells us that "in the Gauls none could be found better born or nobler," and of his mother's that it was "a great and leading family." On both his father's and his mother's side he was of senatorial rank, a distinction of the defunct Roman empire which still retained much meaning in central and southern Gaul. But the great distinction open at this time to a Gallo-Roman was the powerful and envied office of bishop. Men of the most powerful families struggled to attain this office and we can therefore judge of Gregory's status when he tells us proudly that of the bishops of Tours from the beginning all but five were connected with him by ties of kinship. We hear much of Gregory's paternal uncle Gallus, bishop of Auvergne, under whom he probably received his education and entered the clergy, and of his granduncle Nicetius, bishop of Lyons, and of his greatgrandfather Gregory, bishop of Langres, in honor of whom Gregory discarded the name of Georgius Florentinus which he had received from his father. Entering on a clerical career with such powerful connections he was at the same time gratifying his ambitions and obeying the most strongly felt impulse of his time.

In spite of all these advantages, under the externals of Christianity Gregory was almost as superstitious as a savage. His superstition came to him straight from his father and mother and from his whole social environment. He tells us that his father, when expecting in 534 to go as hostage to king Theodobert's court, went to "a certain bishop" and asked for relics to protect him. These were furnished to him in the shape of dust or " sacred ashes " and he put them in a little gold case the shape of a peapod and wore hem about his neck, although he never knew the names of the saints whose relics they were. According to Gregory's account the miraculous assistance given to his father by these relics was a common subject of family conversation. After his death the relics passed to Gregory's mother, who on one occasion . extinguished by their help a great fire that had got started in the straw stacks on the family estate near Clermont. While on a horseback journey from Burgundy to Auvergne Gregory himself happened to be wearing these same relics. A fearful thunderstorm threatened the party, but Gregory "drew the beloved relics from his breast and lifted them up against the cloud, which at once separated into two parts and passed on the right and left, and after that did no harm to them or any one else." In spite of himself Gregory could not help being somewhat elated at the incident and he hinted to his companions that his own merit must have had something to do with it. "No sooner were the words spoken than my horse shied suddenly and threw me heavily on the ground; and I was so shaken that I could scarcely get up. I understood that my vanity was the cause of it, and it was a lesson to me to be on my guard against the spur of pride. And if thereafter I happened to have the merit merely to behold miracles of the saints I would say distinctly that they had been worked by God's grace through faith in the saints." [***note:*** Gloria Martyrum, *c.83*].

The number of miracles at which Gregory " assisted " was great. A picturesque and significant one is the following: "It happened once that I was journeying to visit my aged mother in Burgundy. And when passing through the woods on the other side of the river Bèbre we came upon highwaymen. They cut us off from escape and were going to rob and kill us. Then I resorted to my usual means of assistance and called on St. Martin for help. And he came to my help at once and efficiently, and so terrified them that they could do nothing against us. And instead of causing fear they were afraid, and were beginning to flee as fast as they could. But I remembered the apostle's words that our enemies ought to be supplied with food and drink, and told my people to offer them drink. They wouldn't wait at all, but fled at top speed. One would think that they were being clubbed along or were being hurled along involuntarily faster than their horses could possibly go", [***note:*** De Virtut. S. Mart. *I, 36.*]

The reality of this incident need not be doubted. The highwaymen were as superstitious as Gregory, probably more so. When they found what they had against them they fled in a panic. The peculiar wording of the last sentence makes it seem likely that Gregory for his part thought that the highwaymen had demons to help them and that these in their urgent flight before the superior " virtue " of St. Martin were responsible for the appearance he describes. Of Gregory's education and literary training we receive scanty details. At the age of eight he was beginning to learn to read.[*note:* Vitae Patram, *VIII, 3.*] The books he read were naturally the Scriptures and works of Christian writers and his contact with pagan literature of the classical period must have been slight; he appears to have read Virgil and Sallust's *Catiline* but probably did not go beyond these. [*note: Bonnet, Le Latin de Gregoire de Tours, pp. 4876*]. His attitude toward pagan literature was the conventional one of his age,-fear of the demonic influences embodied in it; [*note: Speaking of Jupiter, Mercury, Minerva, Venus, a character in the* Vitae Patrum, *XVII, says,* Nolite, o, viri, nolite eos invocare, non sunt enim dii isti sed daemones.] he expresses it thus: "We ought not to relate their lying fables lest we fall under sentence of eternal death." [*note: Gloria Martyrum, Pref.*] Among Christian writers Sulpicius Severus, Prudentius, Sidonius Apollonaris, and Fortunatus were the only ones to exercise a genuine influence on his style.

The question has been much discussed whether sixthcentury education in Gaul included a knowledge of the liberal arts. Gregory gives us no definite information on the point. It is true that he is explicit as to his own case. He says, " I was not trained in grammar or instructed in the finished style of the heathen writers, but the influence of the blessed father Avitus, bishop of Auvergne, turned me solely to the writings of the church." [*note: Vitae Patrum, II, Pref.*] Gregory does indeed mention Martianus Capella's work on the seven liberal arts and seems to have had some notion of the scope of each one, [*note: See p. 240. (i.e. Book X.16)*] but in the face of his repeated confessions of ignorance of the most elementary of them as well as the actual proof of ignorance which he constantly gives, the conclusion must be that they were not included in his education. As to the general situation the only evidence is furnished by Gregory's famous preface in which he declares that "liberal learning is declining or rather perishing in the Gallic cities," and no one could be found sufficiently versed in the liberal arts to write the *History of the Franks* as it ought to be written. We may feel certain that Gregory's idea of the qualifications for historical writing were not high; correct spelling, knowledge of the rules of grammar, rhetoric, and dialectic as laid down in the textbooks would be sufficient. But, as he tells us, no person so qualified could be found to undertake the task. Again we hear of bishops who were illiterate. It is plain that the trend of the evidence is all in one direction, namely that in Gaul by this time the liberal arts had disappeared from education.

Gregory's Latin presents many problems. Its relation to sixth-century linguistic development is not well understood although it has been closely scrutinized. Gregory's vocabulary does not show the decadence that might be expected. It is extremely rich and varied and contains a moderate number of Celtic, Germanic, and Hunnish additions. Old Latin words, however, often have new and unexpected meanings. In the field of grammar the situation is different. Judged by anything like a classical standard Gregory is guilty of almost every conceivable barbarity. He spells incorrectly, blunders in the use of the inflections, confuses genders, and often uses the wrong case with the preposition. In addition he is very awkward in handling the Latin verb: the different voices, tenses, and modes are apt to look alike to him. His constructions too, are frequently incorrect. In all this he seems very erratic, he may use the correct form ten times and then give us something entirely different. No method has so far been traced in his vagaries.
Gregory's literary style is as peculiar as his language. It is often vigorous and direct, giving realistic and picturesque delineations of events. Within his limitations he well understood the complexity of human motives and actions, and now and then he shows a trace of humor.

However, offending elements often appear; sometimes his realism verges on a brutal plainness. He is also by no means free from literary affectation; indeed by his choice of expressions, his repetitions and unnatural arrangement of words, he is almost always striving for effect. In his day the tradition of literary workmanship was quite dead but it would seem as if its ghost tortured Gregory. On the whole his literary style is uncouth, awkward, and full of rude surprises.

There are wellmarked variations in the style. At times we have the conventionalized jargon of the church, in which Gregory was proficient and which was always in the back of his mind ready to issue forth when other inspiration failed. At the opposite extreme from this is the easy, clear narrative in which the popular tales, both Frankish and Roman, are often recited. It is believed that in some of these we have a version of epic recitals of Frankish adventures. Then there are the passages, like the baptism of Clovis [***note:****l See p. 40 (i.e. Book II:30-31).]* or the tale of the two lovers, which Gregory labored to make striking. These do not offend; they are so naïvely overdone that they are merely amusing.

In the light of these conclusions, objectively reached, [***note:*** *They are substantially the conclusions of Bonnet in* Le Latin de Gregoire de Tours, *Paris, 1890.*], as to Gregory's language and style, how shall we interpret the confessions in regard to them which he repeatedly makes? In these confessions there are two leading notions: first, that he is without qualifications to write in the literary style; second, that the popular language can be more widely understood. The inference is always therefore that Gregory writes in the language of the day. This, however, cannot be so. A language spoken by the people would have something organic about it, and it would not defy as Gregory's does the efforts of scholars to find its usages. It would be simpler than the literary language and probably as uniform in its constructions. We must decide then that Gregory's self-analysis is a mistaken one, correct in the first part but not in the second. He knew he could not write the literary language but in spite of this he made the attempt, and the result is what we have, a sort of hybrid, halfway between the popular speech and the formally correct literary language.

In the Epilogue of the *History of the Franks* written in 594, the year of Gregory's death, he gives us a list of his works: "I have written ten books of *History,* seven of *Miracles,* one on the *Lives of the Fathers,* a commentary in one book on the *Psalms,* and one book on the *Church Services [****note:*** *See p. 247 (Book X: 31.) In the Arndt and Brusch edition in the* Monumenta Germania Historica *we have all these titles included. The commentary on the* Psalms *however is in a fragmentary condition, and the Lives of the Fathers appears as one of eight books of* Miracles. *The book on* Church Services *is there entitled* Account of the Movements of the Stars as they ought to be observed in performing the Services. *It is really a brief astronomical treatise the purpose of which was in the absence of clocks to guide the church services at night.]* These works represent two sides of Gregory's experience,-his profession, and his relations with the Merovingian state.

In the former sphere the overshadowing interest was the miraculous. We have eight books devoted to miracles and it may be said that as a churchman Gregory never got very far away from them. It is idle to discuss the question whether he believed in them or not. It is more to the point to attempt to appreciate the part they played in the thought and life of the time. They were considered as the most significant of phenomena. They seemed a guarantee that the relations were right between the supernatural powers on the one hand and on the other the men who possessed the "sanctity" to work miracles and those who had the faith or merit to be cured or rescued by them. Gregory's eight books of *Miracles* were thus a register of the chief interest of his day, with an eye of course to its promotion, and it is much more remarkable that he wrote a *History of the Franks* than that he compiled this usually wearisome array of impossibilities.

A brief glance at the practical situation that lay back of the four books which Gregory devotes to the miracles wrought by St. .Martin will be enlightening. The cult of St. Martin was a great organized enterprise at the head of which Gregory was placed. In the sixth century St. Martin's tomb was a center toward .which the crippled, the sick, and those possessed by demons flowed as if by gravity from a large territory around Tours. The cures wrought there did much " to strengthen the faith." They passed from mouth to mouth and brought greater numbers to the shrine and it was to aid this process that the four books of St. Martin's miracles were written. Gregory is here a promoter and advertiser. To get at the practical side of the situation we have only to remember that St. Martin's tomb was the chief place of healing among the shrines of Gaul, and that the shrines of the sixth century stood for the physicians, hospitals, drugs, patent medicines, and other healing enterprises of the twentieth.

The History of the Franks is Gregory's chief work. It was written in three parts. The first, comprising books IIV, begins with the creation, and after a brief outline of events enters into more detail with the introduction of Christianity into Gaul. Then follow the appearance of the Franks on the scene of history, their conversion, the conquest of Gaul under Clovis, and the detailed history of the Frankish kings down to the death of Sigibert in 575. At this date Gregory had been bishop of Tours two years. The second part comprises books V and VI and closes with Chilperic's death in 584. During these years Chilperic held Tours and the relations between him and Gregory were as a rule unfriendly. The most eloquent passage in the *History of the Franks is* the closing chapter of book VI, in which Chilperic's character is unsympathetically summed up. The third part comprises books VIIX. It comes down to the year 591 and the epilogue was written in 594, the year of Gregory's death. The earlier part of the work does not stand as it was first written; Gregory revised it and added a number of chapters. It will be noticed that from the middle of the third book on, Gregory was writing of events within his own lifetime, and in the last six books, which are of especial value, of those that took place after he became bishop. For the earlier part of the work he depended on various chronicles, histories and local annals, and also on oral tradition. [***note:*** *The list given by Manitius is as follows: Chronicles of Jerome Victor, Sulpicius Severus; history of Orosius; church history of EusebiusRufinus; Life of St. Martin by Sulpicius Severus; letters of Sidonius Apollinaris and Ferreolus writings of Avitus; histories of of Renatus Profuturus Frigeridus and Sulpicius Alexander (not elsewhere known), annals of of Arles, Angers, Burgundy.* Geschichte der Lateinischen Litteratur.]

For the task undertaken by Gregory in the *History of the Franks* no one else was so well qualified His family connections were such as to afford him every opportunity of knowing the occurrences of central Gaul, while his position as bishop of Tours with all that it entailed brought him into touch with almost every person and matter of interest throughout the country. His frequent journeys and wide acquaintance, his leadership among the bishops, and his personal relations with four kings, Sigibert, Chilperic, Gunthram,and Childebert and also with most of the leading Franks, gave him unsurpassed opportunities for learning what was going on. Perhaps his most realistic notions of the working of Frankish society were obtained in dealing with the political refugees who sought- refuge in St. Martin's church. Though these people must have always been interesting to talk with, they were the cause of some of Gregory's most harrowing and at the same time informing experiences. This varied contact with the world about him made Gregory what every reader feels him to be, a vivid and faithful delineator of his time.

The *History of the Franks* must not be looked upon as a secular history. The old title, *Ecclesiastical History of the Franks, is* a better one descriptively. It is written not from the point of view of the GalloRoman or the Frank, but solely from that of the churchman, almost that of the bishop. Gregory does not take a tone of loyalty to the Frankish kings, much less of inferiority. His attitude toward them is cold unless they are zealous supporters of the church, and he speaks with the utmost disgust of their civil wars, which seemed to him absolute madness in view of the greater war between the good and evil supernatural powers. [*note: Book III, Pref, and IV Pref.*] On the other hand his loyalty to his worthy fellowbishops is often proved. No doubt the words he quotes from Paulinus expressed his own feelings: "Whatever evils there may be in the world, you will doubtless see the worthiest men as guardians of all faith and religion." [*note: Book II:13, Cf. V:11*] Everywhere we can read in the lines and between the lines Gregory's single-minded devotion to the church and above all to the cult of St. Martin.

The great value of Gregory's writings is that we get in them an intimate view of sixthcentury ideas. At first sight, perhaps, we seem to have incongruous elements which from the modern viewpoint we cannot bring into harmony with one another. Credulity and hardheaded judgment appear side by side. How could Gregory be so shrewd and worldlyminded in his struggle with Chilperic and at the same time show such an appetite for the miraculous? How could he find it necessary to preface his history, as no other historian has done, with an exact statement of his creed? And how could he relate Clovis's atrocities and then go on to say, "Every day God kept laying his enemies low before him and enlarging his kingdom because he walked with right heart before him and did what was pleasing in his eyes"? These apparently glaring incongruities must have some explanation.

The reason why they have usually passed as incongruities is perhaps that it is difficult for us to take an unprejudiced view of religious and moral phenomena that are in the direct line of our cultural descent. If we could regard the Franks and GalloRomans as if they were alien to us, living, let us say, on an island of the southern Pacific, and believing and practising a religion adapted to their general situation, the task of understanding the *History of the Franks* would become easier. It is really a primitive society with a primitive interpretation of life and the universe with which we have to deal.

Look at the conception of religion held by Gregory. It seems most explicable, not by the creed he thrusts at us or by any traditional elements interpreted in a traditional sense, but by the living attitude toward the supernatural which he held. Two words are always recurring in his writings; *sanctus* and *virtus*, [*note: Nunc autem cognovi quod magna est virtus eius beati Martini. Nam ingrediente me atrium domus. Vidi virum senem exhibentem arborem in manu sua, quae mox extensis ramis omne atrium texit. Ex ea emm unus me adtigit ramus, de cuius ictu turbatus corrui.* Book VII:42] the first meaning sacred or holy, and the second the mystic potency emanating from the person or thing that is sacred. These words have in themselves no ethical meaning and no humane implications whatever. They are the keywords of a religious technique and their content is wholly supernatural. In a practical way the second word is the more important. It describes the uncanny, mysterious power emanating from the supernatural and affecting the natural. The manifestation of this power may be thought of as a contact between the natural and the supernatural in which the former, being an inferior reality, of course yielded. These points of contact and yielding are the miracles we continually hear of. The quality of sacredness and the mystic potency belong to spirits, in varying degrees to the faithful, and to inanimate objects. They are possessed by spirits, acquired by the faithful, and transmitted to objects.

There was also a false mystic potency. It emanated from spirits who were conceived of as alien and hostile, and, while it was not strong as the true "virtue," natural phenomena yielded before it and it had its own miracles, which however were always deceitful and malignant in purpose. This "virtue" is associated with the devil, demons, soothsayers, magicians, pagans and pagan gods, and heretics, and through them is continually engaged in aggressive warfare on the true " virtue." [***note:*** *See pp. 38 (Book II:28), 162 (Book VI:35), 185 (Book VII:44), 205 (Book IX:3).*]

For the attainment of the true mystic potency asceticism was the method. This was not a withdrawal from lower activities of life to gain more power for higher activities, but it was undertaken m contempt of life, and in the more thoroughgoing cases the only restraint was the desire to avoid selfdestruction, which was forbidden. Almost every known method of self-denial and self mortification was practised. Humility of mind was insisted on as an always necessary element. Fasting was part of the prescribed method. The strength of the motive behind asceticism may be judged from the practice of immuring, [***note:*** *For an objective account of immuring as the climax of religious practice see Vol II, chap. I, Sven Hedin's* Trans-Himalaya, *1909. The following is his account of an immured monk who was brought out from his cell after a long time. "He was all bent up together and as small as a child and his body was nothing but a lightgray parchment like skin and bones. His eyes had lost their color, were quite bright and blind. His hair hung round his head in uncombed matted locks and was pure white. His body was covered only by a rag for time had eaten away his clothing and he had received no new garments. He had a thin unkempt beard, and had never washed himself all the time or cut his nails."*] several specimens of which are related by Gregory. In this the ascetic was shut in a cell and the door walled up and only a narrow opening left to hand in a scanty supply of food. Here he was to remain until he died. Such men were regarded as having the true "virtue" in the highest degree. In reality their life must have made them distinctly inferior in all the ordinary virtues of a natural existence. [***note:*** *pp, 147-150 (Book VI:6), 158 (Book VI:28), 198-199 (Book: VIII:34)*]

As asceticism was the method by which mystic potency was attained, so miracles were the product, and the proof that it had been acquired. Of course in theory the main object of the mystic was to assimilate himself to the supernatural and not expressly to work miracles. Still to society in general the miracles were the important thing. In the first place they served the immediate purpose for which a miracle might be needed, healing the sick or driving out a demon or something of the sort; in the second place they encouraged society by evidencing the fact that things in general were right and that their spiritual leaders had the right "medicine." Incredulity is not to be expected in such a situation. The miracle played an integral part in the life-theory of the time. It was the proof of religion and it did not need to be proved itself. Furthermore many miracles were real; for example, the cessation of a pain or natural recovery from a sickness would be regarded as a miracle.

Some mention should be made of the transmissibility of the mystic potency. The case of St. Martin is a good example. During his lifetime he acquired this power in a large degree. When he died on November 8, 397, at a village halfway between Tours and Poitiers, the inhabitants of these cities were all ready to fight for his body, when the people of Tours managed to secure it by stealth. This was because of the sanctity and mystic "virtue" inherent in it. It was carried to Tours and buried there and proved the greatest asset of the city. The mystic potency resided in the tomb and the area about it, and was transmitted to the dust accumulated on it, the wine and oil placed on it for the purpose, and was carried in these portable forms to all parts of Gaul. Gregory himself, for example, carried relics of St. Martin on his journeys and records that they kept his boat from sinking in the river Rhine.

The system of superstition just outlined is the greater and more real part of Gregory's religion. There was the right mystery and the wrong mystery; and both were of a low order; men had to deal with capricious saints and malignant demons. It was a real, live, local religion comparable with that of savages. By the side of this and intertwined with it the elements of traditional Christianity in a more or less formalized and ritualized shape were retained. Here the great stress was laid on the creed, not, however, that it amounted to anything in Gregory's mind as a creed. He was no theologian. His acceptance of it and insistence on it was ritualistic. However, although he accepted it as he tells us with *pura credulitas,* [***note:*** *Book I:Pref*] that is, without a critical thought, it was not mere formality. He felt, no doubt, that it was a sort of mystic formula, especially the Trinitarian part of it,-for putting men into the right relation with the supernatural. If they believed in the creed they had the right "medicine"; if they did not, they had not.

This system of superstition was not calculated to nourish delicate moral sensibilities. Life had gone too far back to the primitive word applied to the adept in this religion was *sanctus* and it indicated not moral excellence at all but a purely mystic quality. The "virtue" which this person possessed was mystic potency, which was not moral but a supernatural force. The orthodox of course called the saint good, but this was merely because they were on the same side, just as Cicero for example six centuries before called members of his political party the *boni.* Gregory's moral praise or blame is distributed in the same way. When he praises a man we must look for the service done by this man to the church, and when he blames one we must look in like manner for the opposite. Outside of the interests of the orthodox group Gregory is not morally thinskinned; he shared in the brutality of his contemporaries, as we can see in many recitals. His portrait of Clovis throws no false light back on Gregory. Clovis was a champion and favorite of the right supernatural powers in their fight with the wrong ones, and any occasional atrocities he committed in the struggle were not only pardonable but praiseworthy. [***note:*** *See pp. 47-50 (Book II:40-43)*].

Secular activities and the state of mind just indicated could not coexist in the same society. We have noticed already how education was desecularized. It is of interest to note also what had happened to the secular professions of medicine and law.

The profession of medicine had almost completely disappeared. It is true indeed that we hear of a few physicians. For example when Austrechild, king Gunthram's wife, was dying, she accused her two physicians of having given her "potions" that were proving fatal, and asked the king to take an oath to have them executed. He did so and kept his word and Gregory remarks with what seems excessive moderation, " Many wise men think that this was not done without sin." [***note:*** *p 130 (Book V;34)*] Again we hear of Gregory's own illness, when he sent for a physician. He soon decided that "secular means could not help the perishing," and sent for some dust from St. Martin's tomb which he put in water and drank, and was soon cured. [***note:*** *De Virtut. S. Martin, II.1*] Such tales indicate the status of the medical profession.

The truth was that the condition of the people's minds made the profession an impossibility. Disease was looked upon as supernatural. The sick man thought he had a better chance if he called the priest rather than the doctor. Gregory tells us of Vulfilaic, who was suddenly covered from head to foot with angry pimples; he rubbed himself with oil consecrated at St. Martin's tomb, and they speedily disappeared. He reasoned that if they had been driven away by St. Martin, they had plainly been sent by the devil. [note: p. 196 (book VIII:154)] This meant to him that the whole thing was supernatural and that the true mystic power had driven out the false which had caused the trouble.

Perhaps this was not the reasoning in every case, but at any rate, the people went to the shrines and churches to be healed. In some cases the diagnosis was quite clear as with a patient at Limoges. The priest put holy oil on his head and " the demon went down into his finger-nail; seeing this the priest poured oil on the finger and soon the skin burst, blood flowed from the place, and the demon thus took his departure. [***note:*** *Glor.Conf. c.9*]

Such practices were not isolated or unusual, but typical. Mystical healing was adjusted to an everyday basis, as many "cases " cited by Gregory indicate. Many, like the following are found: "Charigisil, king Clothar's secretary, whose hands and feet were made helpless by a humor, came to the holy church, and devoting himself to prayer for two or three months, was visited by the blessed bishop [*note: St. Martin*] and had the merit to obtain health in his crippled limbs. He was later *domesticus* of the king I have mentioned, and did many kindnesses to the people of Tours and the officials of the holy church." An analysis of this record reveals the typical elements, with the exception of fasting which is usually mentioned. The miraculous properties of St. Martin were thus reinforced by change of scene, prolonged treatment, and a rigorous mental and physical regimen.

With such a state of mind prevailing no rivals of the clergy in the healing art were to be found except among those healers who used a "virtue" of another kind-the false virtue of the magicians and demons; the few physicians who remained were not real competitors.

The administration of justice was also affected by the same causes which brought about the disappearance of medicine There was little inducement to look for evidence when an appeal could be made to superstitious fear. Hence the importance of the oath. Gregory himself, when he was charged with slandering queen Fredegunda, had to take oath to his innocence on three altars We have also other appeals to the supernatural in the trial by combat and the ordeal. Another interference in the domain of law was a peculiar one; holy men seemed to have a particular desire to set prisoners free. Gregory himself begs them off. We heal of one dead bishop whose body sank like lead on the street before the jail and could not be moved until all in the jail were let loose. [*note: De Virtut. S. Martin., I, 21, 25.*] Another holy man tried to secure the pardon of a notorious criminal and falling, brought him back to life after he was executed.

In the *History of the Franks* attention is given from time to time to natural phenomena. With few exceptions these passages deal with prodigies. Gregory tells for example of the prodigies of the year 587. Most of them are given from his own personal observation. [*note: Book IX:5*] Mysterious marks which could not be deleted in any way appeared on dishes; vines made a new growth and bore deformed fruit in the month of October after the vintage; at the same time fresh leaves and fruits appeared on fruit trees; rays of light were seen in the north. In addition Gregory mentions from hearsay that snakes had fallen from the clouds, and that a village with its inhabitants and dwellings had disappeared entirely. He goes on to say, "Many other signs appeared such as usually announce a king's death or the destruction of a country." In the same way he tells us of the signs preceding plagues. Sometimes he relates the prodigies without giving any sequel to them. In one case he says, " I do not know what these prodigies foretold." It is evident that the idea which Gregory had of the phenomena of nature was such as to prevent his giving any intelligent attention to them. The supernatural came between him and objective realities in such a way as to prevent the latter from having a natural effect upon his mind.

The inhibiting and paralyzing force of superstitious beliefs penetrated to every department of life, and the most primary and elementary activities of society were influenced. War, for example, was not a simple matter of a test of strength and courage, but supernatural matters had to be taken carefully into consideration. When Clovis said of the Goths in southern Gaul, "I take it hard that these Arians should hold a part of the Gauls; let us go with God's aid and conquer them and bring the land under our dominion," [*note: see p. 45 (Book II:37)*] he was not speaking in a hypocritical or arrogant manner but in real accordance with the religious sentiment of the time. What he meant was that the Goths, being heretics, were at once enemies of the true God and inferior to the orthodox Franks in their supernatural backing. Considerations of duty, strategy, and self-interest all reinforced one another in Clovis's mind. However, it was not always the orthodox side that won. We hear of a battle fought a few years before Gregory became bishop of Tours between king Sigibert and the Huns, [*note: Book IV:29*] in which the Huns " by the use of magic arts caused various false appearances to arise before their enemies and overcame them decisively. " It is very plain that one exceedingly important function of the leader of a sixthcentury army was to keep the right relation with the supernatural powers. Clovis is represented as heeding this necessity more than any other Frankish king. [**note:** *pp 3638 (Book II:22-29), 40 (Book II:31), 45 (Book II: 37), 5354 (Book II: Pref)*]

It is clear that in the sixthcentury state of mind in Gaul nothing was purely secular. As far as possible all secular elements had been expelled. Men did not meet the objective realities of society and of nature as they were; there was a superstitious interpretation for everything. The hope in such a condition of things lay only in unconscious developments which might break through the closed system of thought before the latter realized that it was on the defensive. The most promising element in the situation was the Frankish state. Apparently the Frankish kingship was not to any large extent a magicoreligious institution, but simply a recent development arising out of the conquest. As an institution it was not grounded in the superstitious past, and the cold hostility of the bishops kept it from the development usual in a benighted society. To this chance we may perhaps attribute a momentous result; in it lay the possibility and promise of a secular state.

In the case of King Chilperic we apparently have a premature development in this direction. We must read between the lines when Gregory speaks of him. Gregory calls him "the Nero and Herod of our time," and loads him with abuse. He ridicules his poems, and according to his own story overwhelms him with an avalanche of contempt when he ventures to state some new opinions on the Trinity. The significant thing about Chilperic was this, that he had at this time the independence of mind to make such a criticism, as well as the hard temper necessary to fight the bishops successfully. "In his reign," Gregory tells us, "very few of the clergy reached the office of bishop." Chilperic used often to say: "Behold our treasury has remained poor, our wealth has been transferred to the churches; there is no king but the bishops; my office has perished and passed over to the bishops of the cities." [**note:** *see p. 166 (Book VI: 46)*] Chilperic was thus the forerunner of the secular state in France.
E. B.

History of the Franks

PREFACE

With liberal culture on the wane, or rather perishing in the Gallic cities there were many deeds being done both good and evil: the heathen were raging fiercely; kings were growing more cruel; the church. attacked by heretics, was defended by Catholics; while the Christian faith was in general devoutly cherished, among some it was growing cold; the churches also were enriched by the faithful or plundered by traitors-and no grammarian skilled in the dialectic art could be found to describe these matters either in prose or verse; and many were lamenting and saying: "Woe to our day, since the pursuit of letters has perished from among us and no one can be found among the people who can set forth the deeds of the present on the written page." Hearing continually these complaints and others like them I [have undertaken] to commemorate the past, order that it may come to the knowledge of the future; and although my speech is rude, I have been unable to be silent as to the struggles between the wicked and the upright; and I have been especially encouraged because, to my surprise, it has often been said by men of our day, that few understand the learned words of the rhetorician but many the rude language of the common people. I have decided also that for the reckoning of the years the first book shall begin with the very beginning of the world, and I have given its chapters below.

BOOK I

IN CHRIST'S NAME HERE END THE CHAPTERS OF THE FIRST BOOK

HERE BEGINS THE FIRST BOOK OF THE HISTORIES

As I am about to describe the struggles of kings with the heathen enemy, of martyrs with pagans, of churches with heretics, I desire first of all to declare my faith so that my reader may have no doubt that I am Catholic. I have also decided, on account of those who are losing hope of the approaching end of the world, to collect the total of past years from chronicles and histories and set forth clearly how many years there are from the beginning of the world. But I first beg pardon of my readers if either in letter or in syllable I transgress the rules of the grammatic art in which I have not been fully instructed, since I have been eager only for this, to hold fast, without any subterfuge or irresolution of heart, to that which we are bidden in the church to believe, because I know that he who is liable to punishment for his sin can obtain pardon from God by untainted faith.

I believe, then, in God the Father omnipotent. I believe in Jesus Christ his only Son, our Lord God, born of the Father, not created. [I believe] that he has always been with the Father, not only since time began but before all time. For the Father could not have been so named unless he had a son; and there could be no son without a father. But as for those who say: "There was a time when he was not," [**note:** *A leading belief of Arian Christology.*] I reject them with curses, and call men to witness that they are separated from the church. I believe that the word of the Father by which all things were made was Christ. I believe that this word was made fresh and by its suffering the world was redeemed, and I believe that humanity, not deity, was subject to the suffering. I believe that he rose again on the third day, that he freed sinful man, that he ascended to heaven, that he sits on the right hand of the Father, that he will come to judge the living and the dead. I believe that the holy Spirit proceeded from the Father and the Son, that it is not inferior and is not of later origin, but is God, equal and always coeternal with the Father and the Son, consubstantial in its nature, equal in omnipotence, equally eternal in its essence, and that it has never existed apart from the Father and the Son and is not inferior to the Father and the Son. I believe that this holy Trinity exists with separation of persons, and one person is that of the Father, another that the Son, another that of the Holy Spirit. And in this Trinity confess that there is one Deity, one power, one essence. I believe that the blessed Mary was a virgin after the birth as she was a virgin before. I believe that the soul is immortal but that nevertheless it has no part in deity. And I faithfully believe all things that were established at Nicæa by the three hundred and eighteen bishops. But as to the end of the world I hold beliefs which I learned from our forefathers, that Antichrist will come first. An Antichrist will first propose circumcision, asserting that he is Christ; next he will place his statue in the temple at Jerusalem to be worshipped, just as we read that the Lord said: "You shall see the abomination of desolation standing in the holy place." But the Lord himself declared that that day is hidden from all men, saying: "But of that day and that hour knoweth no one not even the anger in heaven, neither the Son, but the Father alone." Moreover we shall here make answer to the heretics [**note:** *the Arians*] who attack us, asserting that the Son is inferior to the Father since he is ignorant of this day. Let them learn then that Son here is the name applied to the Christian people, of whom God says: "I shall be to them a father and they shall be to me for sons." For if he had spoken these words of the onlybegotten Son he would never have given the angels first place. For he uses these words: "Not even the angels in heaven nor the Son," showing that he spoke these words not of the only-begotten but of the people of adoption. But our end is Christ himself, who will graciously bestow eternal life on us if we turn to him.

As to the reckoning of this world, the chronicles of Eusebius bishop of Cæsarea, and of Jerome the priest, speak clearly, an they reveal the plan of the whole succession of years.

Orosius too, searching into these matters very carefully, collects the whole number of years from the beginning of the world down to his own time. Victor also examined into this in connection with the time of the Easter festival. And so we follow the works of the writers mentioned above and desire to reckon the complete series of years from the creation of the first man down to our own time, if the Lord shall deign to lend his aid. And this we shall more easily accomplish if we begin with Adam himself.

1.

In the beginning the Lord shaped the heaven and the earth in his Christ, who is the beginning of all things, that is, in his son; and after creating the elements of the whole universe, taking a frail clod he formed man after his own image and likeness, and breathed upon his face the breath of life and he was made into a living soul. And while he slept a rib was taken from him and the woman, Eve, was created. There is no doubt that this first man Adam before he sinned typified the Redeemer. For as the Redeemer slept in the stupor of suffering and caused water and blood to issue from his side, he brought into existence the virgin and unspotted church, redeemed by blood, purified by water, having no spot or wrinkle, that is, washed with water to avoid a spot, stretched on the cross to avoid a wrinkle. These first human beings, who were living happily amid the pleasant scenes of Paradise, were tempted by the craft of the serpent. They transgressed the divine precepts and were cast out from the abode of angels and condemned to the labors of the world.

2.

Through intercourse with her companion the woman conceived and bore two sons. But when God received the sacrifice of the one with honor, the other was inflamed with envy; he rushed on his brother, overcame and killed him, becoming the first parricide by shedding a brother's blood.

3.

Then the whole race rushed into accursed crime, except the just Enoch, who walked in the ways of God and was taken up from the midst by the Lord himself on account of his uprightness, and reed from a sinful people. For we read: " Enoch walked with the Lord, and he did not appear for God took him."

4.

And so the Lord, being angered against the iniquities of the people who did not walk in his ways, sent a flood, and by its waters destroyed every living soul from the face of the earth; only Noah, who was most faithful and especially belonged to him and bore the stamp of his image, he saved in the ark, with his wife and those of his three sons, that they might restore posterity. Here the heretics upbraid us because the holy Scripture says that the Lord was angry. Let them know therefore that our God is not angry like a man; for he is aroused in order to inspire fear; he drives away to summon back; he is angry in order to amend. Furthermore I have no doubt that the ark typified the mother church. For passing amidst the waves and rocks of this world it protects us in its motherly arms from threatening ills, and guards us with its holy embrace and protection.

Now from Adam to Noah are ten generations, namely: Adam, Seth, Enos, Cainan, Malalehel, Jareth, Enoch, Mattusalam, Lamech, Noah. In these ten generations 2242 years are included.

The book Joshua clearly indicates that Adam was buried in the land of Enacim, which before was called Hebron.

5.

Noah had after the flood three sons, Shem, Ham and Japheth. From Japheth issued nations, and likewise from Ham and from Shem. And, as ancient history says, from these the human race was scattered under the whole heaven. The first-born of Ham was Cush. He was the first inventor of the whole art of magic and of idolatry, being instructed by the devil. He was the first to set up an idol to be worshipped, at the instigation of the devil, and by his false power he showed to men stars and fire falling from heaven. He passed over to the Persians. The Persians called him Zoroaster, that is, living star. They were trained by him to worship fire, and they reverence as a god the man who was himself consumed by the divine fire.

6.

Since men had multiplied and were spreading over all the earth they passed out from the East and found the grassy plain of Senachar. There they built a city and strove to raise a tower which should reach the heavens. And God brought confusion both to their vain enterprise and their language, and scattered them over the wide world, and the city was called Babyl, that is, confusion, because there God had confused their tongues. This is Babylonia, built by the giant Nebron, son of Cush. As the history of Orosius tells, it is laid out foursquare on a very level plain. Its wall, made of baked brick cemented with pitch, is fifty cubits wide, two hundred high, and four hundred and seventy stades in circumference. A stade contains five agripennes. Twenty-five gates are situated on each side, which make in all one hundred. The doors of these gates, which are of wonderful size, are cast in bronze. The same historian tells many other tales of this city, and says: "Although such was the glory of its building still it was conquered and destroyed."

[7. Abraham, who is described as "the beginning of our faith." 8. Isaac, Esau, Jacob, Job. 9. The twelve patriarchs, the story of Joseph, and the coming out of Egypt to the crossing of the Red Sea.]

10.

Since many authorities have made varying statements about this crossing of the sea I have decided to give here some information concerning the situation of the place and the crossing itself. The Nile flows through Egypt, as you very well know, and waters it by its flood, from which the inhabitants of Egypt are named Nilicolæ. And many travelers say its shores are filled at the present time with holy monasteries. And on its bank is situated, not the Babylonia of which we spoke above, but the city of Babylonia in which Joseph built wonderful granaries of squared stone and rubble. [*note: The pyramids, apparently*] They are wide at the base and narrow at the top in order that the wheat might be cast into them through a tiny opening, and these granaries are to be seen at the present day. From this city the king set out in pursuit of the Hebrews with armies of chariots and a great infantry force. Now the stream mentioned above coming from the east passes in a westerly direction towards the Red Sea; and from the west a lake or arm of the Red Sea juts out and stretches to the east, being about fifty miles long and eighteen wide. [*note: Gregory's geography is mixed*] And at the head of this lake the city of Clysma is built, not on account of the fertility of the soil, since there is nothing more barren, but because of the harbor, since ships coming from the Indias lie there for the convenience of the harbor; and the wares purchased there are carried through all Egypt. Toward this arm the Hebrews hastened through the wilderness, and they came to the sea itself and encamped, finding fresh water. It was it this place, shut in by the wilderness as well as by the sea, that they encamped, as it is written: "Pharaoh, hearing that the sea and the wilderness shut them in and that they had no way by which they could go, set out in pursuit of them." And when they were close upon them and the people cried to Moses, he stretched out his wand over the sea, according to the command of the Deity, and it was divided, and they walked on dry ground, and, as the Scripture says, they crossed unharmed under Moses' leadership, a wall of water on either hand, to that shore which is before Mount Sinai, while the Egyptians were drowned. And many tales are told of this crossing, as I have said. But we desire to insert in this account what we have learned as true from the wise, and especially from those who have visited the place. They actually say that the furrows which the wheels of the chariots made remain to the present time and are seen in the deep water as far as the eye can trace them. And if the roughness of the sea obliterates them in a slight degree, when the sea is calm they are divinely renewed again as they were. Others say that they returned to the very bank where they had entered, making a small circuit through the sea. And others assert that all entered by one way; and a good many, that a separate way opened to each tribe, giving this evidence from the Psalms: "Who divided the Red Sea in parts." [Ps. 135:13] But these parts ought to be understood according to the spirit and not according to the letter. For there are many parts in this world, which is figuratively called a sea. For all cannot pass to life; equally or by one way. Some pass in the first hour, that is those who are born anew by baptism and are able to endure to the departure from this life unspotted by any defilement of the flesh. Others in the third hour, plainly those who are converted later in life; others in the sixth hour, being those who hold in check the heat of wanton living. And in each of these hours, as the evangelist relates, they are hired for the work of the Lord's vineyard, each according to his faith. These are the parts in which the passage is made across this sea. As to the opinion that upon entering the sea they kept close to the shore and returned, these are the words which the Lord said to Moses: "Let them turn back and encamp before Phiahiroth which is between Magdalum and the sea before Belsephon." There is no doubt that this passage of the sea and the pillar of cloud typified our baptism, according to the words of the blessed Paul the apostle: "I would not, brethren, have you ignorant that our fathers were all under the cloud and all baptized unto Moses in the cloud and in the sea." And the pillar of fire typified the holy Spirit. Now from the birth of Abraham to the going forth of the children of Israel from Egypt and the crossing of the Red Sea, which was in the eightieth year of Moses, there are reckoned four hundred and sixty-two years.

[11. The Israelites spend forty years in the wilderness. 12. From the crossing of the Jordan to David. 13. Solomon. 14. Division of the kingdom into Judæa and Israel. 15. The captivity. 16. From the captivity to the birth of Christ.]

17.

In order not to seem to have knowledge of the Hebrew race alone [**note:** *Gregory's purpose is not realized*] we shall tell what the remaining kingdoms were in the time of the Israelites. In the time of Abraham Ninus ruled over the Assyrians; Eorops over the Sitiones; among the Egyptians it was the sixteenth government, which they call in their own tongue dynasty. In Moses' time lived Trophas, seventh king of the Argives; Cecrops, first in Attica; Cencris, who was overwhelmed in the Red Sea, twelfth among the Egyptians; Agatadis, sixteenth among the Assyrians; Maratis was ruler of the Sicionii. . . [**note:** *Jerome's Chronicle was the source for the history summarized here. It is dear that Gregory had not much sense of the historical perspective in spite of a list of states Which might impress his audience. He passes directly from "Servius the sixth king of Rome " to Julius Caesar the founder of the empire.*]

[**18.** Beginning of the Roman empire; founding of Lyons, a city afterwards ennobled by the blood of martyrs. **19.** Birth of Christ. **20.** Christ's crucifixion. **21.** Joseph is imprisoned and escapes miraculously. **22.** James fasts from the death of the Lord to the resurrection **23.** The day of the Lord's resurrection is the first, not the seventh. **24.** Pilate transmits an account of Christ to Tiberius. The end of Pilate and of Herod. **25.** Peter and Paul are executed at Rome by order of Nero, who later kills himself. **26.** The martyrs, Stephen, James and Mark; burning of Jerusalem by Vespasian; death of John. **27.** Persecution under Trajan. **28.** The rise of heresy. Further persecutions. **29.** The martyrs of Lyons. Irenæus, second bishop, converts the whole city. His death and that of vast numbers," of whom Gregory knows of forty-eight.]

30.

Under the emperor Decius many persecutions arose against the name of Christ, and there was such a slaughter of believers that they could not be numbered. Babillas, bishop of Antioch, with his three little sons, Urban, Prilidan and Epolon, and Xystus, bishop of Rome, Laurentius, an archdeacon, and Hyppolitus, were made perfect by martyrdom because they confessed the name of the Lord. Valentinian and Novatian were then the chief heretics and were active against our faith, the enemy urging them on. At this time seven men were ordained as bishops and sent into the Gauls to preach, as the history of the martyrdom of the holy martyr Saturninus relates. For it says: " In the consulship of Decius and Gratus, as faithful memory recalls, the city of Toulouse received the holy Saturninus as its first and greatest bishop." These bishops were sent: bishop Catianus to Tours; bishop Trophimus to Arles; bishop Paul to Narbonne; bishop Saturninus to Toulouse; bishop Dionisius to Paris; bishop Stremonius to Clermont, bishop Martial to Limoges.

And of these the blessed Dionisius, bishop of Paris, after suffering divers pains in Christ's name, ended the present life by the threatening sword. And Saturninus, already certain of martyrdom said to his two priests: "Behold, I am now to be offered as a victim and the time of my death draws near. I ask you not to leave me at all before I come to the end." But when he was seized and was being dragged to the capitol he was abandoned by them and was dragged alone. And so when he saw that he was abandoned he is said to have made this prayer; "Lord Jesus Christ, grant my request from holy heaven, that this church may never in all time have the merit to receive a bishop from among its citizens." And we know that to the present it has been so in this city. And he was tied to the feet of a mad bull, and being sent headlong from the capitol he ended his life. Catianus, Trophimus, Stremonius, Paul and Marcial lived in the greatest sanctity, winning people to the church and spreading the faith of Christ among all, and died in peace, confessing the faith. And thus the former by martyrdom as well as the latter by confession, left the earth and were united in the heavens.

31.

One of their disciples went to the city of Bourges and carried to the people the news of Christ the lord as the saviour of all. A few of them believed and were ordained priests and learned the ritual of psalmsinging, and were instructed how to build a church and how they ought to observe the worship of the omnipotent God. But as they had small means for building as yet, the citizens asked for the house of a certain man to use for a church. But the Senators and the rest of the better class of the place were at that time, devoted to the heathen religion and the believers were of the poor, according to the word of the Lord with which he reproached the Jews saying; "Harlots and publicans go into the kingdom of God before you." And they did not obtain the house from the person from whom they asked it, but they found a certain Leocadius, [*note: Gregory's paternal grandmother was Leocadia, who traced her descent from Vectius Epagatus See* Historia Francorum *ed. Arndt, Introd. p. 4, in Monumenta*

Germaniae Historica The story related above was from Gregory's family tradition.] the first senator of the Gauls, who was of the family of Vectius Epagatus, who, we have said above, suffered in Lyons in Christ's name. And when they had made known to him at the same time their petition and their faith he answered; " If my own house in the city of Bourges were worthy of this work I would not refuse to offer it." And when they heard this they fell at his feet and offered three hundred gold pieces on a silver dish and said the house was very worthy of this mystery. And he accepted three gold pieces from them for a blessing and kindly returned the rest, although he was yet entangled in the error of idolatry, and he became a Christian and made his house a church. This is now the first church in the city of Bourges, built with marvelous skill and made illustrious by the relics of Stephen, the first martyr.

32.

Valerian and Gallienus received the Roman imperial power in the twentyseventh place, and set on foot a cruel persecution of the Christians. At that time Cornelius brought fame to Rome by his happy death, and Cyprian to Carthage. In their time also Chrocus the famous king of the Alemanni raised an army and overran the Gauls. This Chrocus is said to have been very arrogant. And when he had committed a great many crimes he gathered the tribe of the Alemanni, as we have stated,-by the advice, it is said, of his wicked mother,-and overran the whole of the Gauls, and destroyed from their foundations all the temples which had been built in ancient times. And coming to Clermont he set on fire, overthrew and destroyed that shrine which they call Vasso Galatæ in the Gallic tongue. It had been built and made strong with wonderful skill. And its wall was double, for on the inside it was built of small stone and on the outside of squared blocks. The wall had a thickness of thirty feet. It was adorned on the inside with marble and mosaics. The pavement of the temple was also of marble and its roof above was of lead.

[**33.** Martyrs of Clermont. **34.** The bishop of Gévaudan is maltreated by the Alemanni.]

35.

Under Diocletian, who was emperor of Rome in the thirty-third place, a cruel persecution of the Christians was kept up for four years, at one time in the course of which great numbers of Christians were put to death, on the sacred day of Easter, for worshipping the true God. At that time Quirinus, bishop of the church of Sissek, [***note:*** *In Hungary*] endured glorious martyrdom in Christ's name. The cruel pagans cast him into a river with a millstone tied to his neck, and when he had fallen into the waters he was long supported on the surface by a divine miracle, and the waters did not suck him down since the weight of crime did not press upon him. And a multitude of people standing around wondered at the thing, and despising the rage of the heathen they hastened to free the bishop. He saw this and did not permit himself to be deprived of martyrdom, and raising his eyes to heaven he said: "Jesus lord, who sittest in glory at the right hand of the Father, suffer me not to be taken from this course, but receive my soul and deign to unite me with thy martyrs in eternal peace." With these words he gave up the ghost, and his body was taken up by the Christians and reverently buried.

36.

Constantine was the thirty-fourth emperor of the Romans, and he reigned prosperously for thirty years. In the eleventh year of his reign, when peace had been granted to the churches after the death of Diocletian, our blessed patron Martin was born at Sabaria, a city of Pannonia, of heathen parents, who still were not of the lowest station. This Constantine in the twentieth year of his reign caused the death of his son Crispus by poison, and of his wife

Fausta by means of a hot bath, because they had plotted to betray his rule. In his time the venerated wood of the Lord's cross was found, through the zeal of his mother Helen on the information of Judas, a Hebrew who was called Quiriacus after baptism. The historian Eusebius comes down to this period in his chronicle. The priest Jerome continues it from the twenty-first year of Constantine's reign. He informs us that the priest Juvencus wrote the gospels in verse at the request of the emperor named above.

[**37.** James of Nisibis and Maximin of Trèves. **38.** Hilarius bishop of Poitiers.]

39.

At that time our light arose and Gaul was traversed by the rays of a new lamp, that is, the most blessed Martin then began to preach in the Gauls, and he overcame the unbelief of the heathen, showing among the people by many miracles that Christ the Son of God was the true God. He destroyed heathen shrines, crushed heresy, built churches, and while he was glorious for many other miracles, he completed his title to fame by restoring three dead men to life. At Poitiers, in the fourth year of Valentinian and Valens, Saint Hilarius passed to heaven full of sanctity and faith, a priest of many miracles; for he too is said to have raised the dead.

[**40.** Melania's journey to Jerusalem.]

41.

After the death of Valentinian, Valens, who succeeded to the undivided empire, gave orders that the monks be compelled to serve in the army, and commanded that those who refused should be beaten with clubs. After this the Romans fought a very fierce battle in Thrace, in which there was such slaughter that the Romans fled on foot after losing their horses, and when they were being cut to pieces by the Goths, and Valens was fleeing with an arrow wound, he entered a small hut, the enemy closely pursuing, and the little dwelling was burned over him. And he was deprived of the burial he desired. And thus the divine vengeance finally came for shedding the blood of the saints. Thus far Jerome; from this period the priest Orosius wrote at greater length.

[**42.** The pious emperor Theodosius. **43.** The emperor Maximus with capital at Trèves. **44.** Urbicus, second bishop of Clermont, and his wife. **45.** Hillidius, third bishop of Clermont, and his miracles. **46.** Nepotian and Arthemius, fourth and fifth bishops of Clermont. **47.** Legend of the two lovers of Clermont.]

48. In the second year of the reign of Arcadius and Honorius, Saint Martin, bishop of Tours, departed this life at Candes, a village of his diocese, and passed happily to Christ in the eighty-first year of his life and the twenty-sixth of his episcopate, a man full of miracles and holiness, doing many services to the infirm He passed away at midnight of the Lord's day, in the consulship of Atticus and Cæsarius. Many heard at his passing away the sound of psalm-singing in heaven, which I have spoken of at greater length in the first book of his *Miracles.* Now as soon as the saint of God fell sick at the village of Candes, as we have related, the people of Poitiers came to be present at his death, as did also the people of Tours. And when he died, a great dispute arose between the two peoples. For the people of Poitiers said: "As a monk, he is ours; as an abbot, he belonged to us; we demand that he be given to us. Let it be enough for you that when he was a bishop on earth you enjoyed his conversation, ate with him, were strengthened by his blessings and cheered by his miracles. Let all that be enough for you. Let us be permitted to carry away his dead body." To this the people of Tours replied: "If you say that the working of his miracles is enough for us, let us tell you that while he was placed among you he worked more miracles than he did here. For, to pass over most of them, he raised two dead men for you, and one for us; and as he used often to say himself, there was more virtue in him before he was bishop than after. And so it is necessary that he complete for us after death what he did not finish in his lifetime. For he was taken away from you and given to us by God. If a custom long established is kept, a man shall have his tomb by God's command in the city in which he was ordained. And if you desire to claim him because of the right of the monastery, let us tell you that his first monastery was at Milan." While they were arguing in this way the sun sank and night closed in. And the body was placed in the midst, and the doors were barred and the body was guarded by both peoples, and it was going to be carried off by violence by the people of Poitiers in the morning. But omnipotent God was unwilling that the city of Tours should be deprived of its protector. Finally at midnight the whole band from Poitiers were overwhelmed with sleep and no one remained out of this multitude to keep watch. Then when the people of Tours saw that they had fallen asleep they seized on the clay of the holy body and some thrust it out the window and others received it outside, and placing it in a boat they went down the river Vienne with all their people and entered the channel of the Loire, and made their way to the city of Tours with great praises and plentiful psalm-singing, and the people of Poitiers were waked by their voices, and having no treasure to guard they returned to their own place greatly crestfallen. And if any one asks why there was only one bishop, that is, Litorius, after the death of bishop Gatianus to the time of Saint Martin, let him know that for a long time the city of Tours was without the blessing of a bishop, owing to the resistance of the heathen. For they who lived as Christians at that time celebrated the divine office secretly and in hiding. For if any Christians were found by the heathen they were punished with stripes or slain by the sword.

Now from the suffering of the Lord to the passing of Saint Martin, 412 years are included.

HERE ENDS THE FIRST BOOK CONTAINING 5597 YEARS WHICH ARE RECKONED FROM THE BEGINNING OF THE WORLD TO THE DEATH OF THE HOLY BISHOP MARTIN.

BOOK II
HERE BEGIN THE CHAPTERS OF THE SECOND BOOK

HERE END THE CHAPTERS

HERE BEGINS THE SECOND BOOK

FOLLOWING the order of time we shall mingle together in our tale the miraculous doings of the saints and the slaughters of the nations. I do not think that we shall be condemned thoughtlessly if we tell of the happy lives of the blessed together with the deaths of the wretched, since it is not the skill of the writer but the succession of times that has furnished the arrangement. The attentive reader, if he seeks diligently, will find in the famous histories of the kings of the Israelites that under the just Samuel the wicked Phineas perished, and that under David, whom they called Stronghand, the stranger Goliath was destroyed. Let him remember also in the time of the great prophet Elias, who prevented rains when he wished and when he pleased poured them on the parched ground, who enriched the poverty of the widow by his prayer, what slaughters of the people there were, what famine and what thirst oppressed the wretched earth. Let him remember what evil Jerusalem endured in the time of Hezekiah, to whom God granted fifteen additional years of life. Moreover under the prophet Elisha, who restored the dead to life and did many other miracles among the peoples, what butcheries, what miseries crushed the very people of Israel. So too Eusebius, Severus and Jerome in their chronicles, and Orosius also, interwove the wars of kings and the miracles of the martyrs. We have written in this way also, because it is thus easier to perceive in their entirety the order of the centuries and the system of the years down to our day. And so, leaving the histories of the writers who have been mentioned above, we shall describe at God's bidding what was done in the later time.

1.

After the death of the blessed Martin, bishop of Tours, a very great and incomparable man, whose miracles fill great volumes in our possession, Bricius succeeded to the bishopric. Now this Bricius, when he was a young man and the saint was yet living in the body, used to lay many traps for him, because he was often accused by Saint Martin of following the easy way. And one day when a sick man was looking for the blessed Martin in order to get medicine from him he met Bricius, at this time a deacon, in the square, and he said to him in a simple fashion: "Behold I am seeking the blessed man, and I don't know where he is or what he is doing." And Bricius said: "If you are seeking for that crazy person look in the distance; there he is, staring at the sky in his usual fashion, as if he were daft." And when the poor man had seen him and got what he wanted, the blessed Martin said to the deacon: " Well, Bricius, I seem to you crazy, do I? " And when the latter, in confusion at this, denied he had said so, the saint replied: "Were not my ears at your lips when you said this at a distance? Verily I say unto you that I have prevailed upon God that you shall succeed to the bishop's office after me, but let me tell you that you will suffer many misfortunes in your tenure of the office. Bricius on hearing this laughed and said: "Did I not speak the truth that he uttered crazy words?" Furthermore, when he had attained to the rank of priest, he often attacked the blessed man with abuse. But when he had become bishop by the choice of the citizens, he devoted himself to prayer. And although he was proud and vain he was nevertheless considered chaste in his body. But in the thirty-third year after his ordination there arose against him a lamentable ground for accusation. For a woman to whom his servants used to give his garments to be washed, one who had changed her garb on the pretext of religion, conceived and bore a child. Because of this the whole population of Tours arose in wrath and laid the whole blame on the bishop, wishing with one accord to stone him. For they said: "The piety of a holy man has too long been a cover for your wantonness. But God does not any longer allow us to be polluted by kissing your unworthy hands." But he denied the charge forcibly. "Bring the infant to me," said he. And when the infant, which was thirty days old was brought, the bishop said to it: "I adjure you in the name of Jesus Christ, son of omnipotent God, to declare publicly to all if I begot you." And the child said. "It is not you who's my father" When the people asked him to inquire who was the father, the bishop said: "That is not my affair. I was troubled in so far as the matter concerned me; inquire for yourselves whatever you want." Then they asserted that this had been done by magic arts, and arose against him in a conspiracy, and dragged him along, saying: "You shall not rule us any longer under the false name of a shepherd." And to satisfy the people he placed red-hot coals in his cloak and drawing it close to him he walked as far as the tomb of the blessed Martin along with throngs of the people. And when the coals were cast down before the tomb his robe was seen to be unburned. And he said: "Just as you see this robe uninjured by the fire, so too my body is undefiled by union with a woman." And when they did not believe but denied it, he was dragged, abused, and cast out, in order that the words of the saint might be fulfilled: "Let me tell you that you will suffer many misfortunes in your episcopate." When he was cast out they appointed Justinian to the office of bishop. Finally Bricius went to see the pope of the city of Rome, weeping and wailing and saying: "Rightly do I suffer this because I sinned against a saint of God and often called him crazy and daft; and when I saw his miracles I did not believe." And after his departure the people of Tours said to their bishop: " Go after him and attend to your own interest, for if you do not attack him, you shall be humiliated by the contempt of us all." And Justinian went forth from Tours and came to Vercelli, a city of Italy, and was smitten by a judgment of God and died in a strange country. The people of Tours heard of his death, and persisting in their evil course, they appointed Armentius in his place. But bishop Bricius went to Rome and related to the pope all that he had endured. And while he remained at the apostolic see he often celebrated the solemn ceremony of the mass, weeping for the wrong he had done to the saint of God. In the seventh year he left Rome and by the authority of that pope purposed to return to Tours. And when he came to the village called Mont-Louis at the sixth milestone from the city, he resided there. Now Armentius was seized with a fever and died at midnight. This was at once revealed to bishop Bricius in a vision, and he said to his people: "Rise quickly, so that we may go to bury our brother, the bishop of Tours." And when they came and entered one gate of the city, behold they were carrying his dead body out by another. And when he was buried, Bricius returned to the bishop's chair and lived happily seven years after. And when he died in the forty-seventh year of his episcopate, Saint Eustochius, a man of magnificent holiness, succeeded him.

2.

After this the Vandals left their own country and burst into the Gauls under king Gunderic. And when the Gauls had been thoroughly laid waste they made for the Spains. The Suebi, that is, Alamanni, following them, seized Gallicia. Not long after a quarrel arose between the two peoples, since they were neighbors And when they had gone armed to the battle, and were already at the point of fighting, the king of the Alemanni said: "Why are all the people involved in war? Let our people, I pray, not kill one another in battle, but let two of our warriors go to the field in arms and fight with one another. Then he whose champion wins shall hold the region without strife." To this all the people agreed, that the whole multitude might not rush on the edge of the sword. In these days king Gunderic had died and in his place Thrasamund held the kingdom. And in the conflict of the champions the side of the Vandals was overcome, and, his champion being slain, Thrasamund promised to depart, and so, when he had made the necessary preparations for the journey, he removed from the territories of Spain.

About the same time Thrasamund persecuted the Christians, and by torture and different sorts of death tried to force all Spain to consent to the perfidy of the Arian sect. And it so happened that a certain maiden bound by religious vows was brought to trial. She was very rich and of the senatorial nobility according to the ranking of the world, and what is nobler than all this, strong in the catholic faith and a blameless servant of Almighty God. And when she was brought before the eyes of the king he first began to coax her with kind words to be baptized again. And when she repelled his venomous shaft by the armor of the faith, the king commanded that wealth be taken from her who already in her heart possessed the kingdom of paradise, and later that she should be tortured without hope of this life. Why make a long story? After long examinations, after losing the treasure of earthly riches, when she could not be forced to attack the blessed Trinity she was led against her will to be rebaptized. And when she was being forcibly immersed in that filthy bath and was crying loudly; "I believe that the Father and the holy Spirit are of one substance With the Son," when she said this she stained the water with a worthy ointment [***note:*** *For* qua sanguine cuncta infecit *read* digne aquas unguine infecit. *See Bonnet, Le Latin de Gregoire de Tours, p. 457.*], that is, she defiled it with excrement. Then she was ; taken to the examination according to the law, and after the needle, flame and claw, she was beheaded for Christ the lord. After this the Vandals crossed the sea, the Alemanni following as far as Tangier, and were dispersed throughout all Africa and Mauritania.

[3. Persecutions of Catholics by Arians under the Vandal king Honeric of Africa. **4.** The same, under the Gothic king Athanaric of Spain. **5.** Journey of Bishop Aravatius of Tongres to Rome thait he might avert by prayer the threatened invasion of the Huns. But there he learns that "it was sanctioned in the council of the Lord that the Huns must come into the Gauls and ravage them." He: returns to Tongres and dies.]

6. Now the Huns left Pannonia and, as certain say, on the very watchnight of holy Easter arrived at the city of Metz, after devastating the country, and gave the city over to burning, slaying the people with the edge of the sword and killing the very priests of the Lord before the holy altars. And there remained in the city .no place unburned except the oratory of the blessed Stephen, the deacon and first martyr. And I do not hesitate to tell what I have heard from certain persons about this oratory. For they say that before these enemies came, a man of the faith saw in a vision the blessed levite Stephen as if conferring with the holy apostles Peter and Paul, and speaking as follows about this disaster: " I beg you, my lords, to prevent by your intercession the burning of the city of Metz by the enemy, because there is a place in it in which the relics of my life on earth are preserved; rather let the people learn that I have some influence with God. But if the wickedness of the people has grown too great, so that nothing else can be done except deliver the city to burning, at least let this oratory not be consumed." And they replied to him: " Go in peace, beloved brother, your oratory alone the fire shall not burn. But as for the city shall not prevail, because the sentence of the will of the Lord has already gone out over it. For the sin of the people has grown great, and the outcry of their wickedness ascends to the presence of God; therefore this city shall be burned with fire." Whence it is certain that it was by the intercession of these that when the city was burned the oratory remained unharmed.

7.

And Attila king of the Huns went forth from Metz and when he had crushed many cities of the Gauls he attacked Orleans and strove to take it by the mighty hammering of battering rams. Now at that time the most blessed Annianus was bishop in the city just mentioned, a man of unequaled wisdom and praiseworthy holiness, whose miracles are faithfully remembered among us. And when the people, on being shut in, cried to their bishop, and asked what they were to do, trusting in God he advised all to prostrate themselves in prayer, and with tears to implore the ever present aid of God in their necessities. Then when they prayed as he had directed, the bishop said: "Look from the wall of the city to sec whether God's mercy yet comes to your aid." For he hoped that by God's mercy Ætius was coming, to whom he had recourse before at Arles when he was anxious about the future. But when they looked from the wall, they saw no one. And he said: "Pray faithfully, for God will free you this day." When they had prayed he said: "Look again." And when they looked they saw no one to bring aid. He said to them a third time: "If you pray faithfully, God comes swiftly." And they besought God's mercy with weeping and loud cries. When this prayer also was finished they looked from the wall a third time at the old man's command, and saw afar off a cloud as it were arising from the earth. When they reported this the bishop said: "It is the aid of the Lord." Meanwhile, when the walls were now trembling from the hammering of the rams and were just about to fall, behold, Ætius came, and Theodore, king of the Goths and Thorismodus his son hastened to the city with their armies, and drove the enemy forth and defeated him. And so the city was freed by the intercession of the blessed bishop, and they put Attila to flight. And he went to the plain of Moirey and got ready for battle. And hearing this, they made manful preparations to meet him....

Ætius with the Goths and Franks fought against Attila. And the latter saw that his army was being destroyed, and escaped by flight. And Theodore, king of the Goths, was slain in the battle. Now let no one doubt that the army of Huns was put to flight by the intercession of the bishop mentioned above. And so Ætius the patrician, along with Thorismodus, won the victory and destroyed the enemy. And when the battle was finished, Ætius said : to Thorismodus: "Make haste and return swiftly to your native land, for fear you lose your father's kingdom because of your brother." The latter, on hearing this, departed speedily with the intention of anticipating his brother, and seizing his father's throne first. At the same time Ætius by a stratagem caused the king of the Franks to flee. When they had gone, Ætius took the spoils of the battle and returned victoriously to his country with much booty. And Attila retreated with a few men. Not long after Aquileia was captured by the Huns and burned and altogether destroyed. Italy was overrun and plundered. Thorismodus, whom we have mentioned above, overcame the Alans in battle, and was himself defeated later on by his brothers, after many quarrels and battles, and put to death.

[8. The history of Renatus Frigeridus is quoted for the character of Ætius and an account of his death.]

9.

The question who was the first of the kings of the Franks is disregarded by many writers. Though the history of Sulpicius Alexander tells much of them, still it does not name their first king, but says that they had dukes. However, it is well to relate what he says of them. For when he tells that Maximus, losing all hope of empire, remained within Aquileia, almost beside himself, he adds: "At that time the Franks burst into the province of Germany under Genobaud, Marcomer, and Sunno, their dukes, and having broken through the boundary wall they slew most of the people and laid waste the fertile districts especially, and aroused fear even in Cologne. And when word was carried to Trèves, Nanninus and Quintinus, the military officers to whom Maximus had intrusted his infant son and the defense of the Gauls, assembled an army and met at Cologne. Now the enemy, laden with plunder after devastating the richest parts of the provinces, had crossed the Rhine, leaving a good many of their men on Roman soil all ready to renew their ravages. An attack upon these turned to the advantage of the Romans, and many Franks perished by the sword near Carbonnière. And when the Romans were consulting after their success whether they ought to cross into Francia, Nanninus said no, because he knew the Franks would not be unprepared and would doubtless be stronger in their own land. And since thi displeased Quintinus and the remainder of the officers, Nanninus returned to Mayence, and Quintinus crossed the Rhine with his army near the stronghold of Neuss, and at his second camp from the river he found dwellings abandoned by their occupants and great villages deserted. For the Franks pretended to be afraid and retired into the more remote tracts, where they built an abattis on the edge of the woods. And so the cowardly soldiers burned all the dwellings, thinking that to rage against them was the winning of victory, and they passed a wakeful night under the burden of their arms. At the first glimmer of dawn they entered the wooded country under Quintinus as commander of the battle, and wandered in safety till nearly midday, entangling themselves in the winding paths. At last, when they found everything solidly shut up by great fences, they struggled to make their exit into the marshy fields which were adjacent to the woods, and the enemy appeared here and there, and sheltered by trunks of trees or standing on the abattis as if on the summit of towers, they sent as if from engines a shower of arrows poisoned by the juices of herbs, so that sure death followed even superficial wounds inflicted in places that were not mortal. Later the army was surrounded by the enemy in greater number, and it eagerly rushed into the open places which the Franks had left unoccupied. And the horsemen were the first to plunge into the morasses, and the bodies of men and animals fell indiscriminately together, and they were overwhelmed by their own confusion. The foot soldiers also who had escaped the hoofs of the horses were impeded by the mud, and extricated themselves with difficulty, and hid again in panic in the woods from which they had struggled a little before. And so the ranks were thrown into disorder and the legions cut in pieces. Heraclius, tribune of the Jovinians, and nearly all the officers were slain, when night and the lurking places of the woods offered a safe escape to a few." This he narrated in the third book of his History.

And in the fourth book, when he tells of the killing of Victor son of Maximus, the tyrant, he says: "At that time Carietto and Sirus who had been appointed in place of Nanninus, were absent in the province of Germany with the army opposed to the Franks". And a little later when the Franks had taken booty from Germany, he added: "Arbogastes, wishing no further delay, warned Cæsar that the punishment due must be exacted from the Franks, unless they speedily restored all the plunder they had taken the previous year when the legions were destroyed, and delivered up the instigators of the war to be punished for their treachery in breaking the peace." He related that this had been done under the leadership of dukes and says further: "A few days later he held a hasty conference with Marcomer and Sunno, princes [*note: 'Regalabus'*] of the Franks and required hostages of them as usual, and then retired to Treves to spend the winter." But when he calls them princes, we do not know whether they were kings or held in the place of kings. Still the same writer, when he told of the hard straits of the emperor Valentinian, added this: "While events of various sorts were taking place in the East throughout Thrace, the public order was disturbed in Gaul. Valentinian the emperor was shut up in Vienne in the palace, and reduced almost below the position of a private person, and the military command was given over to the Frankish allies, and even the civil offices fell under the control of Arbogast's faction, and no one of all the oathbound soldiery was found to dare to heed the familiar speech or obey the command of the emperor." Then he says: "In the same year Arbogast pursued with heathenish hate the princes of the Franks, Sunno and Marcomer, and hastened to Cologne in the depth of winter, since he knew that all the retreats of Francia could be safely penetrated and ravaged with fire when the woods, left bare and dry by the fall of the leaves, could not conceal men lying in ambush. And so he gathered an army and crossed the Rhine, and devastated the country of the Brictori, near the bank, and also the district which the Chamavi inhabit, and no one met him any where, except that a few of the Ampsivarii and Chatti appeared with Marcomer as duke on the ridges of distant hills." At another time this writer, no longer mentioning dukes and princes, openly asserts that the Franks had a king, and without mentioning his name he says: " Then the tyrant Eugenius undertook a military expedition, and hastened to the Rhine to renew in the customary way the old alliances with the kings of the Alemanni and the Franks and to threaten the barbarian nations at that time with a great army." So much the historian mentioned above wrote about the Franks.

Renatus Profuturus Frigeridus, whom we have already mentioned, in his story of the capture and destruction of Rome by the Goths, says: "Meantime when Goare had gone over to the Romans, Respendial, king of the Alamanni, turned the army of his people from the Rhine, since the Vandals were getting the worse of the war with the Franks, having lost their king Godegisil, and about 20,000 of the army, and all the Vandals would have been exterminated if the army of the Alamanni [*note: Alamanni for Alani*] had not come to their aid in time." It is surprising to us that when he names the kings of the other nations he does not name the king of the Franks as well. However, when he says that Constantine, after seizing imperial power, commanded his son Constantius to come to him from the Spains, he speaks as follows: "The tyrant Constantine summoned from the Spains his son Constans, also a tyrant, in order to consult with him about their general policy; and so Constans left at Saragossa his court and his wife, and gave Gerontius charge over all in the Spains, and hastened to his father without breaking his journey. And when they met, many days passed and there was no danger from Italy, and Constantine gave himself up to gluttony and urged his son to return to Spain. And while Constans was sending his troops forward, being still with his father, news came from Spain that Maximus, one of his clients, had been given imperial authority by Gerontius, and was securing a following of the barbarians. Alarmed at this, they sent Edobeccus forward to the German tribes, and Constans and Decimus Rusticus, now a prefect,-he had been master of the offices,-hastened to the Gauls, with the intention of presently returning to Constantine with the Franks and Alamanni and all the soldiers."

Again, when he writes that Constantine was being besieged, he uses these words: "The fourth month of the siege of Constantine was scarcely yet under way, when news came suddenly from farther Gaul that Iovinus had assumed royal state, and was threatening the besiegers with the Burgundians, Alamanni, Franks, Alans, and all his army. So the attack on the walls was hastened, the city opened its gates, and Constantine surrendered. He was sent hastily into Italy, and was slain at the river Mincio by assassins sent to meet him by the emperor." And a little later the same writer says: "At the same time Decimus Rusticus, prefect of the tyrants, Agrœtius, one of the chief secretaries of Jovinus, and many nobles, were captured in Auvergne by the commanders of Honorius and cruelly put to death. The city of Trèves was plundered and burnt in a second inroad of the Franks." And when .Asterius had been made a patrician by an imperial letter, he adds this: "At the same time Castinus, count of the bodyguard, undertook an expedition against the Franks and was sent into the Gauls." This is what these have told of the Franks. And the `historian Horosius says in the seventh book of his work: "Stilico gathered the nations, crushed the Franks, crossed the Rhine, wandered through the Gauls, and made his way as far as the Pyrenees."

This is the evidence that the historians who have been named have left us about the Franks, and they have not mentioned kings. Many relate that they came from Pannonia and all dwelt at first on the bank of the Rhine, and then crossing the Rhine they passed into Thuringia, and there among the villages and cities appointed longhaired kings over them from their first or, so to speak, noblest family. This title Clovis' victories afterwards made a lasting one, as we shall see later on. We read in the Fasti Consulares that Theodomer, king of the Franks, son of Richimer, and Ascyla his mother, were once on a time slain by the sword. They say also that Chlogio, a man of ability and high rank among his people, was king of the Franks then, and he dwelt at the stronghold of Dispargum which is within the borders of the Thuringians. And these parts, that is, towards the south, the Romans dwelt as far as the Loire. But beyond the Loire the Goths were in control; the Burgundians also, who belonged to the sect of the Arians, dwelt across the Rhone in the district which is adjacent to the city of Lyons. And Chlogio sent spies to the city of Cambrai, and : they went everywhere, and he himself followed and overcame the : Romans and seized the city, in which he dwelt for a short time, and he seized the land as far as the river Somme. Certain authorities assert that king Merovech, whose son was Childeric, was of the family of Chlogio.

10.

Now this people seems to have always been addicted to heathen worship, and they did not know God, but made themselves images of the woods and the waters, of birds and beasts and of the other elements as well. They were wont to worship these as God and to offer sacrifice to them. O ! would that that terrible voice had touched the fibers of their hearts which spoke through Moses to the people saying, "Thou shalt have no other gods before me. Thou shalt not make unto thee any graven image nor worship any likeness of anything that is in heaven or on earth or in the water; thou shalt not make them and shalt not worship them." . . .

And in Isaiah he speaks a second time: "I am the first, and I am the last, and besides me there is no god and creator whom I do not know. They that fashion a graven image are all of them vanity, and the things that they delight in shall not profit them. They are themselves witnesses of what they are, that they do not see nor have understanding, and they are confounded in them. Behold all his fellows shall be put to shame, for the workmen are of men. On the coals and with hammers did he form it, and he worked it with his strong arm. In like manner, too, the carpenter fashioned it with compasses, and made the likeness of a man as if of a comely man dwelling in a house. He hewed down the wood, he worked and made a graven image, and worshipped it as a god, he fastened it with nails and hammers so that it should not fall to pieces. They are carried because they cannot walk; and the remainder of the wood is prepared by men for the hearth and they are warmed. And from another he made a god, and a graven image for himself. He bends before it and worships it and prays, saying: 'Deliver me, for thou art my god. I burned half of it with fire; and baked bread upon its coals; I baked flesh and ate, and from the residue I shall make an idol, I shall worship before a wooden trunk; part of it is ashes.' The foolish heart worshipped it, and did not deliver his soul. And he does not say: 'Perhaps there is a lie in my right hand?'" The nation of the Franks did not understand at first; but it understood later, as the following history relates.

[11. Avitus, citizen of Clermont, emperor of Rome, and bishop of Placentia.]

12.

Childeric was excessively wanton and being king of the Franks he began to dishonor their daughters. And they were angry with him on this account and took his kingdom from him. And when he learned that they wished also to kill him he hastened to Thuringia, leaving there a man who was dear to him to calm their furious tempers; he arranged also for a sign when he should be able to return to his country, that is, they divided a gold piece between them and Childeric took one half and his friend kept the other part, saying: " Whenever I send you this part and the joined parts make one coin, then you shall return securely to your native place." Accordingly Childeric went off to Thuringia and remained in hiding with king Basinus and Basina his wife. The Franks, after he was driven out, with one accord selected as king Egidius, whom we have mentioned before as the commander of the troops sent by the republic. And when he was in the eighth year of his reign over them that faithful friend secretly won the good will of the Franks and sent messengers to Childeric with the part of the divided coin which he had kept, and Childeric learned by this sure sign that he was wanted by the Franks, and returned from Thuringia at their request and was restored to his kingdom. Now when these princes were reigning at the same time, the Basina whom we have mentioned above left her husband and came to Childeric. And when he asked anxiously for what reason she had come so far to see him it is said that she answered: " I know your worth," said she, "and that you are very strong, and therefore I have come to live with you. For let me tell you that if I had known of any one more worthy than you in parts beyond the sea I should certainly have sought to live with him." And he was glad and united her to him in marriage. And she conceived and bore a son and called his name Clovis. He was a great and distinguished warrior.

[13. Artemius, bishop of Clermont, is succeeded by Venerandus and he by Rusticus.]

14.

In the city of Tours after the death of bishop Eustochius in the 17th year of his episcopate, Perpetuus was ordained fifth bishop after the blessed Martin. And when he saw that miracles were being worked continually at Saint Martin's tomb, and that the chapel which had been built over it was a tiny one, he judged it unworthy of such miracles, and moving it away he built there great church which remains to the present day, situated 550 paces from the city. It is 160 feet long and 60 wide and 45 high to the vault; it has 32 windows in the part around the altar, 20 in the nave; 41 columns; in the whole building 52 windows, 120 columns; 8 doors, three in the part around the altar and five in the nave. The feast of the church is given sanctity by a triple virtue: that is, the dedication of the temple, the transfer of the body of the saint, and his ordination as bishop. This feast you shall observe four days before the Nones of July, and remember that his burial is the third day before the Ides of November. And if you celebrate these faithfully, you will merit the protection of the blessed bishop both in the present life and that to come. And since the ceiling of the former chapel was of choice workmanship the bishop thought it unworthy that this work should perish, and he built another church in honor of the blessed apostles Peter and Paul in which he placed the ceiling. He built many other churches which remain to the present time in Christ's name.

[15. Eufronius, bishop of Autun, who "piously sent the block of marble which is placed above the holy tomb of the blessed Martin."]

16.

Now after the death of the bishop Rusticus, saint Namatius became the eighth bishop of Clermont. He undertook the task of building the older church which is still standing and is contained within the walls of the city, one hundred and fifty feet in length, sixty in width,-that is, the nave,-fifty in height to the vault, with a round apse in front and on each side aisles finely built, the whole building is laid out in the form of a cross; it has forty-two windows, seventy columns, eight doors. The fear of God is in it and a great brightness is seen, and in the spring a very pleasant fragrance as if of spices is perceived there by the devout. It has near the altar walls of variegated work adorned with many kinds of marble. The blessed bishop on finishing the building in the twelfth year, sent priests to Bologna in Italy, to procure relics of saints Agricola and Vitalis, who we know very certainly were crucified in the name of Christ our God.

17.

His wife built the church of Saint Stephen in the outskirts of the city. And wishing to adorn it with colors she used to carry a book in her bosom, reading the histories of ancient times and describing to the painters what they were to represent on the walls. It happened one day that while she sat in the church and read, a certain poor man came to pray, and seeing her in black clothing, already an old woman, he thought she was one of the needy, and he took out part of a loaf and put it in her lap and went off. But she did not disdain the gift of the poor man who did not know her, but took it and thanked him and put it away, and setting it before her at meals used it as holy bread until it was used up.

18.

Now Childeric fought at Orleans and Odoacer came with the Saxons to Angers. At that time a great plague destroyed the people. Egidius died and left a son, Syagrius by name. On his death Odoacer received hostages from Angers and other places. The Britanni were driven from Bourges by the Goths, and many were slain at the village of Déols. Count Paul with the Romans and Franks made war on the Goths and took booty. When Odoacer came to Angers, king Childeric came on the following day, and slew count Paul, and took the city. In a great fire on that day the house :of the bishop was burned.

19.

After this war was waged between the Saxons and the ; Romans; but the Saxons fled and left many of their people to be slain, the Romans pursuing. Their islands were captured and » ravaged by the Franks, and many were slain. In the ninth month of that year, there was an earthquake. Odoacer made an alliance with Childeric, and they subdued the Alamanni, who had overrun that part of Italy.

20.

Euric, king of the Goths, in the 14th year of his reign, placed duke Victorius in command of seven cities. And he went at once to Clermont, and desired to add it to the others, and writings concerning this exist to the present. He gave orders to set up at the church of Saint Julian the columns which are placed there. He gave orders to build the church of Saint Laurentius and saint Germanus at the village of Licaniacus. He was at Clermont nine years. He brought charges against Euchirius, a senator, whom he ordered to be put in prison and taken out at night, and after having him bound beside an old wall he ordered the wall to be pushed over upon him. As for himself, since he was overwanton in his love for women and was afraid of being killed by the people of Auvergne, he fled to Rome, and there was stoned to death because he wished to practise a similar wantonness. Euric reigned four years after Victorius's death, and died in the twentyseventh year of his reign There was also at that time a great earthquake.

[21. Bishop Eparchius of Clermont finds his church at night full of demons.]

22.

The holy Sidonius was so eloquent that he generally improvised what he wished to say without any hesitation and in the clearest manner. And it happened one day that he went by invitation to a fête at the church of the monastery which we have mentioned before, and when his book, by which he had been wont to celebrate the holy services, was maliciously taken away, he went through the whole service of the fête improvising with such readiness that he was admired by all, and it was believed by the bystanders that it was not a man who had spoken there but an angel. And this we have set forth more fully in the preface of the book which we have composed about the masses written by him. Being a man of wonderful holiness and, as we have said, one of the first of the senators, he often carried silver dishes away from home, unknown to his wife, and gave them to poor people. And whenever she learned of it, she was scandalized at him, and then he used to give the value to the poor and restore the dishes to the house.

[23. Terrible fate of priests who rebelled against their bishop. 24. In time of famine in Burgundy Ecdicius feeds more than four thousand persons. 25. The Gothic king Evatrix persecutes the Christians in southwestern Gaul. 26. A bishop being "suspected by the Goths " is carried a captive into Spain.]

27. After these events Childeric died and Clovis his son reigned in his stead. In the fifth year of his reign Siagrius, king of the Romans, son of Egidius, had his seat in the city of Soissons which Egidius, who has been mentioned before, once held. And Clovis came against him with Ragnachar, his kinsman, because he used to possess the kingdom, and demanded that they

make ready a battlefield. And Siagrius did not delay nor was he afraid to resist. And so they fought against each other and Siagrius, seeing his army crushed, turned his back and fled swiftly to king Alaric at Toulouse. And Clovis sent to Alaric to send him back, otherwise he was to know that Clovis would make war on him for his refusal. And Alaric was afraid that he would incur the anger of the Franks on account of Siagrius, seeing it is the fashion of the Goths to be terrified, and he surrendered him in chains to Clovis' envoys. And Clovis took him and gave orders to put him under guard, and when he had got his kingdom he directed that he be executed secretly.; At that time many churches were despoiled by Clovis' army, since he was as yet involved in heathen error. Now the army had taken from a certain church a vase of wonderful size and beauty, along with the remainder of the utensils for the service of the church. And the bishop of the church sent messengers to the king asking that the vase at least be returned, if he could not get back any more of the sacred dishes. On hearing this the king said to the messenger: "Follow us as far as Soissons, because all that has been taken is to be divided there and when the lot assigns me that dish I will do what the father [***note:*** papa. *The word was used in the early Middle Ages in unrestricted, informal sense, and applied widely to bishops. Cf. Du Cange,* Glossariam] asks." Then when he came to Soissons and all the booty was set in their midst, the king said: "I ask of you, brave warriors, not to refuse to grant me in addition to my share, yonder dish," that is, he was speaking of the vase just mentioned. In answer to the speech of the king those of more sense replied: " Glorious king, all that we see is yours, and we ourselves are subject to your rule. Now do what seems wellpleasing to you; for no one is able to resist your power." When they said this a foolish, envious and excitable fellow lifted his battleax and struck the vase, and cried in a loud voice: " You shall get nothing here except what the lot fairly bestows on you." At this all were stupefied, but the king endured the insult with the gentleness of patience, and taking the vase he handed it over to the messenger of the church, nursing the wound deep in his heart. And at the end of the year he ordered the whole army to come with their equipment of armor, to show the brightness of their arms on the field of March. And when he was reviewing them all carefully, he came to the man who struck the vase, and said to him "No one has brought armor so carelessly kept as you; for neither your spear nor sword nor ax is in serviceable condition." And seizing his ax he cast it to the earth, and when the other had bent over somewhat to pick it up, the king raised his hands and drove his own ax into the man's head. "This," said he, "'is what you did at Soissons to the vase." Upon the death of this man, he ordered the rest to depart, raising great dread of himself by this action./ He made many wars and gained many victories In the tenth year of his reign he made war on the Thuringi and brought them under his dominion.

28.

Now the king of the Burgundians was Gundevech, of the family of king Athanaric the persecutor, whom we have mentioned before. He had four sons; Gundobad, Godegisel, Chilperic and Godomar. Gundobad killed his brother Chilperic with the sword, and sank his wife in water with a stone tied to her neck. His two daughters he condemned to exile; the older of these, who became a nun, was called Chrona, and the younger Clotilda. And as Clovis often sent embassies to Burgundy, the maiden Clotilda was found by his envoys. And when they saw that she was of good bearing and wise, and learned that she was of the family of the king, they reported this to King Clovis, and he sent an embassy to Gundobad without delay asking her in marriage. And Gundobad was afraid to refuse, and surrendered her to the men, and they took the girl and brought her swiftly to the king. The king was very glad when he saw her, and married her, having already by a concubine a son named Theodoric.

29.

He had a first-born son by queen Clotilda, and as his wife wished to consecrate him in baptism, she tried unceasingly to persuade her husband, saying: "The gods you worship are nothing, and they will be unable to help themselves or any one else. For they are graven out of stone or wood or some metal. And the names you have given them are names of men and not of gods, as Saturn, who is declared to have fled in fear of being banished from his kingdom by his son; as Jove himself, the foul perpetrator of all shameful crimes, committing incest with men, mocking at his kinswomen, not able to refrain from intercourse with his own sister as she herself says: *Jovisque et soror et conjunx.* What could Mars or Mercury do? They are endowed rather with the magic arts than with the power of the divine name. But he ought rather to be worshipped who created by his word heaven and earth, the sea and all that in them is out of a state of nothingness, who made the sun shine, and adorned the heavens with stars, who filled the waters with creeping things, the earth with living things and the air with creatures that fly, at whose nod the earth is decked with growing crops, the trees with fruit, the vines with grapes, by whose hand mankind was created, by whose generosity all that creation serves and helps man whom he created as his own." But though the queen said this the spirit of the king was by no means moved to belief, and he said: "It was at the command of our gods that all things were created and came forth, and it is plain that your God has no power and, what is more, he is proven not to belong to the family of the gods." Meantime the faithful queen made her son ready for baptism; she gave command to adorn the church with hangings and curtains, in order that he who could not moved by persuasion might be urged to belief by this mystery. The boy, whom they named Ingomer, died after being baptized, still wearing the white garments in which he became regenerate. At this the king was violently angry, and reproached the queen harshly, saying: " If the boy had been dedicated in the name of my gods he would certainly have lived; but as it is, since he was baptized in the name of your God, he could not live at all." To this the queen said: "I give thanks to the omnipotent God, creator of all, who has judged me not wholly unworthy, that he should deign to take to his kingdom one born from my womb. My soul is not stricken with grief for his sake, because I know that, summoned from this world as he was in his baptismal garments, he will be fed by the vision of God."

After this she bore another son, whom she named Chlodomer at baptism; and when he fell sick, the king said: "It is impossible that anything else should happen to him than happened to his brother, namely, that being baptized in the name of your Christ, should die at once." But through the prayers of his mother, and the Lord's command, he became well.

30.

The queen did not cease to urge him to recognize the true God and cease worshipping idols. But he could not be influenced in any way to this belief, until at last a war arose with the Alamanni, in which he was driven by necessity to confess what before he had of his free will denied. It came about that as the two armies were fighting fiercely, there was much slaughter, and Clovis's army began to be in danger of destruction. He saw it and raised his eyes to heaven, and with remorse in his heart he burst into tears and cried: "Jesus Christ, whom Clotilda asserts to be the son of the living God, who art said to give aid to those in distress, and to bestow victory on those who hope in thee, I beseech the glory of thy aid, with the vow that if thou wilt grant me victory over these enemies, and I shall know that power which she says that people dedicated in thy name have had from thee, I will believe in thee and be baptized in thy name. For I have invoked my own gods but, as I find, they have withdrawn from aiding me; and therefore I believe that they possess no power, since they do not help those who obey them. I now call upon thee, I desire to believe thee only let me be rescued from my adversaries." And when he said thus, the Alamanni turned their backs, and began to disperse in flight. And when they saw that their king was killed, they submitted to the

dominion of Clovis, saying: "Let not the people perish further, we pray; we are yours now."
And he stopped the fighting, and after encouraging his men, retired in peace and told the
queen how he had had merit to win the victory by calling on the name of Christ. This
happened in the fifteenth year of his reign.

31.

Then the queen asked saint Remi, bishop of Rheims, to summon Clovis secretly, urging him to
introduce the king to the word of salvation. And the bishop sent for him secretly and began to
urge him to believe in the true God, maker of heaven and earth, and to cease worshipping
idols, which could help neither themselves nor any one else. But the king said: "I gladly hear
you, most holy father; but there remains one thing: the people who follow me cannot endure to
abandon their gods; but I shall go and speak to them according to your words." He met with
his followers, but before he could speak the power of God anticipated him, and all the people
cried out together:/ "O pious king, we reject our mortal gods, and we are ready to follow the
immortal God whom Remi preaches." This was reported to the bishop, who was greatly
rejoiced, and bade them get ready the baptismal font. The squares were shaded with tapestried
canopies, the churches adorned with white curtains, the baptistery set in order, the aroma of
incense spread, candles of fragrant odor burned brightly, and the whole shrine of the baptistery
was filled with a divine fragrance: and the Lord gave such grace to those who stood by that
they thought they were placed amid the odors of paradise. And the king was the first to ask to
be baptized by the bishop. Another Constantine advanced to the baptismal font, to terminate
the disease of ancient leprosy and wash away with fresh water the foul spots that had long
been borne. And when he entered to be baptized, the saint of God began with ready speech:
"Gently bend your neck, Sigamber; worship what you burned; burn what you worshipped."
The holy bishop Remi was a man of excellent wisdom and especially trained in rhetorical
studies, and of such surpassing holiness that he equalled the miracles of Silvester. For there is
extant a book of his life which tells that he raised a dead man. And so the king confessed all-
powerful God in the Trinity, and was baptized in the name of the Father, Son and holy Spirit,
and was anointed with the holy ointment with the sign of the cross of Christ. And of his army
more than 3000 were baptized. His sister also, Albofled, was baptized, who not long after
passed to the Lord. And when the king was in mourning for her, the holy Remi sent a letter of
consolation which began in this way: "The reason of your mourning pains me, and pains me
greatly, that Albofled your sister, of good memory, has passed ; away. But I can give you this
comfort, that her departure from the world was such that she ought to be envied rather than e
mourned." Another sister also was converted, Lanthechild by name, who had fallen into the
heresy of the Arians, and she confessed that the Son and the holy Spirit were equal to the
Father, and was anointed.

32.

At that time the brothers Gundobad and Godegisel were kings of the country about the Rhone
and the Saône together With the province of Marseilles. And they, as well as their people
belonged to the Arian sect. And since they were fighting with each other, Godegisel, hearing
of the victories of King Clovis, sent an embassy to him secretly, saying: "If you will give me
aid in attacking my brother, so that I may be able to kill him in battle or drive him from the
country, I will pay you every year whatever tribute you yourself wish to impose." Clovis
accepted this offer gladly, and promised aid whenever need should ask. And at a time agreed
upon he marched his army against Gundobad. On hearing of this, Gundobad, who did not
know of his brother's treachery, sent to him, saying: " Come to my assistance, since the Franks
are in motion against us and are coming to our country to take it. Therefore let us be united
against a nation hostile to us lest because of division we suffer in turn what other peoples have

suffered." And the other said: "I will come with my army, and will give you aid." And these three, namely, Clovis against Gundobad and Godegisel, were marching their armies to the same point, and they came with all their warlike equipment to the strong hold named Dijon. And they fought on the river Ouche, and Godegisel joined Clovis, and both armies crushed the people of Gundobad. And he perceived the treachery of his brother, whom he had not suspected, and turned his back and began to flee, hastening along the banks of the Rhone, and he came to the city of Avignon. And Godegisel having won the victory, promised to Clovis a part of his kingdom, and departed quietly and entered Vienne in triumph as if he now held the whole kingdom. King Clovis increased his army further, and set off after Gundobad to drag him from his city and slay him. He heard it, and was terrified, and feared that sudden death would come to him. However he had with him Aridius, a man famed for energy and wisdom, and he sent for him and said: "Difficulties wall me in on every side, and I do not know what to do, because these barbarians have come upon us to slay us and destroy the whole country." To this Aridius answered: "You must soften the fierceness of this man in order not to perish. Now if it is pleasing in your eyes, I will pretend to flee from you and to pass over to his side, and when I come to him, I shall prevent his harming either you or this country. Only be willing to do what he demands of you by my advice, until the Lord in his goodness deigns to make your cause successful." And Gundobad said: "I will do whatever you direct." When he said this, Aridius bade him goodby and departed, and going to King Clovis he said: "Behold I am your humble servant, most pious king, I come to your protection, leaving the wretched Gundobad. And if your goodness condescends to receive me, both you and your children shall have in me a true and faithful servant." Clovis received him very readily, and kept him by him, for he was entertaining in storytelling, ready in counsel, just in judgment, and faithful in what was put in his charge. Then when Clovis with all his army sat around the walls of the city, Aridius said: "O King, if the glory of your loftiness should kindly consent to hear the few words of my lowliness, though you do not need counsel, yet I would utter them with entire faithfulness, and they will be advantageous to you and to the cities through which you purpose to go. Why," said he, "do you keep your army here, when your enemy sits in a very strong place? If you ravage the fields, lay waste the meadows, cut down the vineyards, lay low the oliveyards, and destroy all the produce of the country, you do not, however, succeed in doing him any harm. Send an embassy rather and impose tribute to be paid you every year, so that the country may be safe and you may rule forever over a tributary. And if he refuses, then do whatever pleases you." The king took this advice, and commanded his army to return home. Then he sent an embassy to Gundobad, and ordered him to pay him every year a tribute. And he paid it at once and promised that he would pay it for the future.

33.

Later he regained his power, and now contemptuously refused to pay the promised tribute to king Clovis, and set his army in motion against his brother Godegisel, and shut him up in the city of Vienne and besieged him. And when food began to be lacking for the common people, Godegisel was afraid that the famine would extend to himself, and gave orders that the common people be expelled from the city. When this was done, there was driven out, among the rest, the artisan who had charge of the aqueduct. And he was indignant that he had been cast out from the city with the rest, and went to Gundobad in a rage to inform him how to burst into the city and take vengeance on his brother. Under his guidance an army was led through the aqueduct, and many with iron crowbars went in front, for there was a vent in the aqueduct closed with a great stone, and when this had been pushed away with crowbars, by direction of the artisan, they entered the city, and surprised from the rear the defenders who were shooting arrows from the wall. The trumpet was sounded in the midst of the city, and the besiegers seized the gates, and opened them and entered at the same time, and when the people between these two battle lines were being slain by each army, Godegisel sought refuge in the church of the heretics, and was slain there along with the Arian bishop. Finally the Franks who were with Godegisel gathered in a tower. But Gundobad ordered that no harm should be done to a single one of them, but seized them and sent them in exile to king Alaric at Toulouse, and he slew the Burgundian senators who had conspired with Godegisel. He restored to his own dominion all the region which is now called Burgundy. He established milder laws for the Burgundians lest they should oppress the Romans.

[34. King Gundobad is converted to the doctrine of the Trinity but will not confess it in public. The writings of bishop Avitus are described.]

35.

Now when Alaric, king of the Goths, saw Clovis conquering nations steadily, he sent envoys to him saying: "If my brother consents, it is the desire of my heart that with God's favor we have a meeting." Clovis did not spurn this proposal but went to meet him. They met in an island of the Loire which is near the village of Amboise in the territory of Tours, and they talked and ate and drank together, and plighted friendship and departed in peace. Even at that time many in the Gauls desired greatly to have the Franks as masters.

36.

Whence it happened that Quintian, bishop of Rodez, was driven from his city through illwill on this account. For they said: "It is your desire that the rule of the Franks be extended over this land." A few days later a quarrel arose between him and the citizens, and the Goths who dwelt in the city became suspicious when the citizens charged that he wished to submit himself to the control of the Franks; they took counsel and decided to slay him with the sword. When this was reported to the man of God he rose in the night and left the city of Rodez with his most faithful servants and went to Clermont. There he was received kindly by the holy bishop Eufrasius, who had succeeded Aprunculus of Dijon, and he kept Quintian with him, giving him houses as well as fields and vineyards, and saying: "The wealth of this church is enough to keep us both; only let the charity which the blessed apostle preaches endure among the bishops of God." Moreover the bishop of Lyons bestowed upon him some of the possessions of the church which he had in Auvergne. And the rest about the holy Quintian, both the plottings which he endured and the miracles which the Lord deigned to work through him, are written in the book of his life.

37

Now Clovis the king said to his people: "I take it very hard that these Arians hold part of the Gauls. Let us go with God's help and conquer them and bring the land under our control. Since these words pleased all, he set his army in motion and made for Poitiers where Alaric was at that time. But since part of the host was passing through Touraine, he issued an edict out of respect to the blessed Martin that no one should take anything from that country except grass for fodder, and water. But one from the army found a poor man's hay and said: "Did not the king order grass only to be taken, nothing else ? And this," said he, " is grass. We shall not be transgressing his command if we take it." And when he had done violence to the poor man and taken his hay by force, the deed came to the king. And quicker than speech the offender was slain by the sword, and the king said: "And where shall our hope of victory be if we offend the blessed Martin ? . It would be better for the army to take nothing else from this country." The king himself sent envoys to the blessed church saying: "Go, and perhaps you will receive some omen of victory :. from the holy temple." Then giving them gifts to set up in the holy place, he said: "If thou, O Lord, art my helper, and hast determined to surrender this unbelieving nation, always striving against thee, into my hands, consent to reveal it propitiously at the entrance to the church of St. Martin, so that I may know that thou wilt deign to be favorable to thy servant." Clovis' servants went on their way according to the king's command, and drew near to the place, and when they were about to enter the holy church, the first singer, without any pre-arrangement, sang this response: "Thou hast girded me, O Lord, with strength unto the battle; thou hast subdued under me those that rose up against me, and hast made mine enemies turn their backs unto me, and thou hast utterly destroyed them that hated me." On hearing this singing they thanked the Lord, and paying their vow to the blessed confessor they joyfully made their report to the king. Moreover, when he came to the river Vienne with his army, he did not know where he ought to cross. For the river had swollen from the rains. When he had prayed to the Lord in the night to show him a ford where he could cross, in the morning by God's will a hind of wonderful size entered the river before them, and when it passed over the people saw where they could cross. When the king came to the neighborhood of Poitiers and was encamped some distance off, he saw a ball of fire come out of the church of Saint Hilarius and pass, as it were, over him, to show that, aided by the light of the blessed confessor Hilarius, he should more boldly conquer the heretic armies, against which the same bishop had often fought for the faith. And he made it known to all the army that neither there nor on the way should they spoil any one or take any one's property.

There was in these days a man of praiseworthy holiness, the abbot Maxentius, who had become a recluse in his own monastery in Poitou because of his fear of God. We have not put the name of the monastery in this account because the place is called to the present day *Cellula sancti Maxentii.* And when his monks saw a division of the host approaching the monastery, they prayed to the abbot to come forth from his cell to consult with them. And as he stayed, they were panic-stricken and opened the door and dragged him from his cell. And he hastened boldly to meet the enemy to ask for peace. And one of them drew out his sword to launch a stroke at his head, and when he had raised his hand to his ear it became rigid and the sword fell. And he threw himself at the feet of the blessed man, asking pardon. And the rest of them seeing this returned in great fear to the army, afraid that they should all perish together. The man's arm the holy confessor rubbed with consecrated oil, and made over it the sign of the cross and restored it to soundness. And owing to his protection the monastery remained uninjured. He worked many other miracles also, and if any one diligently seeks for them he will find them all in reading the book of his Life. In the twenty-fifth year of Clovis.

Meantime king Clovis met with Alaric, king of the Goths, in the plain of Vouillé at the tenth milestone from Poitiers, and while the one army was for fighting at a distance the other tried to come to close combat. And when the Goths had fled as was their custom, king Clovis won the victory by God's aid. He had to help him the son of Sigibert the lame, named Chloderic. This Sigibert was lame from a wound in the leg, received in a battle with the Alemanni near the town of Zulpich. Now when the king had put the Goths to flight and slain king Alaric, two of the enemy suddenly appeared and struck at him with their lances, one on each side. But he was saved from death by the help of his coat of mail as well as by his fast horse. At that time there perished a great number of the people of Auvergne, who had come with Apollinaris and the leading senators. From this battle Amalaric, son of Alaric, fled to Spain and wisely seized his father's kingdom Clovis sent his son Theodoric to Clermont by way of Albi and Rodez. He went, and brought under his father's dominion the cities from the boundaries of the Goths to the limit of the Burgundians. Alaric reigned twentytwo years. When Clovis had spent the winter in Bordeaux and taken all the treasures of Alaric at Toulouse, he went to Angoulême. And the Lord gave him such grace that the walls fell down of their own accord when he gazed at them. Then he drove the Goths out and brought the city under his own dominion. Thereupon after completing his victory he returned to Tours, bringing many gifts to the holy church of the blessed Martin.

38.

Clovis received an appointment to the consulship from the emperor Anastasius, and in the church of the blessed Martin he clad himself in the purple tunic and chlamys, and placed a diadem on his head. Then he mounted his horse, and in the most generous manner he gave gold and silver as he passed along the way which is between the gate of the entrance [of the church of St. Martin] and the church of the city, scattering it among the people who were there with his own hand, and from that day he was called consul or *Augustus.* Leaving Tours he went to Paris and there he established the seat of his kingdom. There also Theodoric came to him.

[**39.** Licinius was bishop of Tours at the time of Clovis' visit. His travels.]

40.

When King Clovis was dwelling at Paris he sent secretly to the son of Sigibert saying: "Behold your father has become an . old man and limps in his weak foot. If he should die," said he, 'Of due right his kingdom would be yours together with our friendship." Led on by greed the son plotted to kill his father. And when his father went out from the city of Cologne and crossed the Rhine and was intending to journey through the wood Buchaw, as he slept at midday in his tent his son sent assassins in against him, and killed him there, in the idea that he would get his kingdom But by God's judgment he walked into the pit that he had cruelly dug for his father. He sent messengers to king Clovis to tell about his father's death, and to say: "My father is dead, and I have his treasures in my possession, and also his kingdom. Send men to me, and I shall gladly transmit to you from his treasures whatever pleases you." And Clovis replied: "I thank you for your good will, and I ask that you show the treasures to my men who come, and after that you shall possess all yourself." When they came, he showed his father's treasures. And when they were looking at the different things he said: "It was in this little chest that my father used to put his gold coins. " " Thrust in your hand, " said they, "to the bottom, and uncover the whole." When he did so, and was much bent over, one of them lifted his hand and dashed his battleax against his head, and so in a shameful manner he incurred the death which he had brought on his father. Clovis heard that Sigibert and his son had been slain, and came to the place and summoned all the people, saying: " Hear what has happened. When I," said he, "was sailing down the river Scheldt Cloderic, son of my kinsman, was in pursuit of his own father asserting that I wished him killed. And when his father was fleeing through the forest of Buchaw, he set highwaymen upon him, and gave him over to death, and slew him. And when he was opening the treasures, he was slain himself by some one or other. Now I know nothing at all of these matters. For I cannot shed the blood of my own kinsmen, which it is a crime to do. But since this has happened, I give you my advice, if it seems acceptable; turn to me, that you may be under my protection." They listened to this, and giving applause with both shields and voices, they raised him on a shield, and made him king over them. He received Sigibert's kingdom with his treasures, and placed the people, too, under his rule. For God was laying his enemies low every day under his hand, and was increasing his kingdom, because he walked with an upright heart before him, and did what was pleasing in his eyes.

41.

After this he turned to Chararic. When he had fought with Siagrius this Chararic had been summoned to help Clovis, but stood at a distance, aiding neither side, but awaiting the outcome, in order to form a league of friendship with him to whom victory came. For this reason Clovis was angry, and went out against him. He entrapped and captured him and his son also, and kept them in prison, and gave them the tonsure; he gave orders to ordain

Chararic priest and his son deacon. And when Chararic complained of his degradation and wept, it is said that his son remarked: "It was on green wood," said he, "that these twigs were cut, and they are not altogether withered. They will shoot out quickly, and be able to grow; may he perish as swiftly who has done this." This utterance was reported to the ears of Clovis, namely, that they were threatening to let their hair grow, and kill him. And he ordered them both to be put to death. When they were dead, he took their kingdom with the treasures and people.

42.

Ragnachar was then king at Cambrai, a man so unrestrained in his wantonness that he scarcely had mercy for his own near relatives. He had a counselor Farro, who defiled himself with a like vileness. And it was said that when food, or a gift, or anything whatever was brought to the king, he was wont to say that: it was enough for him and his Farro. And at this thing the Franks were in a great rage. And so it happened that Clovis gave golden armlets and belts, but all only made to resemble gold-for it was bronze gilded so as to deceive-these he gave to Ragnachar's *leudes* to be invited to attack him. Moreover, when Clovis had set his army in motion against him, and Ragnachar was continually sending spies to get information, on the return of his messengers, he used to ask how strong the force was. And they would answer: is a great sufficiency for you and your Farro." Clovis came and made war on him, and he saw that his army was beaten and prepared to slip away in flight, but was seized by his army, and with his hands tied behind his back, he was taken with Ricchar his brother before Clovis. And Clovis said to him: "Why have you humiliated our family in permitting yourself to be bound? It would have been better for you to die." And raising his ax he dashed it against his head, and he turned to his brother and said: "If you had aided your brother, he would not have been bound" And in the same way he smote him with his ax and killed him. After their death their betrayers perceived that the gold which they had received from the king was false. When they told the king of this, it is said that he answered: " Rightly," said he, " does he receive this kind of gold, who of his own will brings his own master to death;" it ought to suffice them that they were alive and were not put to death, to mourn amid torments the wicked betrayal of their masters. When they heard this, they prayed for mercy, saying it was enough for them if they were allowed to live The kings named above were kinsmen of Clovis, and their brother Rignomer by name, was slain by Clovis' order at the city of Mans. When they were dead Clovis received all their kingdom and treasures And having killed many other kings and his nearest relatives, of whom he was jealous lest they take the kingdom from him, he extended his rule over all the Gauls. However he gathered his people together at one time, it is said, and spoke of the kinsmen whom he had himself destroyed. "Woe to me, who have remained as a stranger among foreigners, and have none of my kinsmen to give me aid if adversity comes." But he said this not because of grief at their death but by way of a ruse, if perchance he should be able to find some one still to kill.

43.

After all this he died at Paris, and was buried in the church of the holy apostles, which he himself had built together with his queen Clotilda. He passed away in the fifth year after the battle; of Vouillé, and all the days of his reign were thirty years, and his age was forty-five. From the death of St. Martin to the death of king Clovis, which happened in the eleventh year of the episcopate of Licinius, bishop of Tours, one hundred and twelve years are reckoned. Queen Clotilda came to Tours after the death of her husband and served there in the church of St. Martin, and dwelt in the place with the greatest chastity and kindness all the days of her life, rarely visiting Paris.

HERE ENDS THE SECOND BOOK

BOOK III

HERE BEGIN THE CHAPTERS OF THE THIRD BOOK

1. The sons of Clovis.

2. Episcopates of Dinifius, Apollinaris and Quintian.

3 The Danes make an attack on the Gauls.

4 The kings of the Thuringi.

5. Sigimand kills his own son.

6. Death of Chlodomer.

7. War with the Thuringi.

8. Hermenfied's death.

9. Childebert visits Auvergne.

10. Amalaric's death.

11. Childebert and Clothar go to the Burgundies.

12. Devastation of Auvergne.

13. Lovolautrum and ChastelMarlhac.

14. Munderic's death.

15. Captivity of Attalus.

16. Sigivald.

17. The bishops of Tours.

18. Death of Chlodomer's sons.

19. The holy Gregory and the site of Dijon.

20. Theodobert is betrothed to Visigard.

21. Theodobert departs for Provence.

22. He later marries Deoteria.

23. Sigivald's death.

HERE ENDS THE LIST OF CHAPTERS

IN CHRIST'S NAME HERE BEGINS THE THIRD BOOK

I wish, if it is agreeable, to make a brief comparison of the successes that have come to Christians who confess the blessed Trinity and the ruin which has come to heretics who have tried to destroy the same. And let us omit how Abraham worshipped the Trinity at the oak, [*note:* ' ad ilicem'. *Not in the Vulgate. Gregory probably used in part a rude popular version of the Scriptures. See Bonnet, p. 66.*] and Jacob preached it in his blessing, and Moses recognized it in the bush, and the people followed it in the cloud and dreaded the same in the mountain, and how Aaron carried it on his breastplate, or how David made it known in the Psalms, praying to be made new by a right spirit and that the holy spirit should not be taken from him and that he be comforted by the chief spirit. And, for my part, I consider this a great mystery, namely that the voice of the prophet proclaimed as the chief spirit that which the heretics assert to be the lesser. But passing over these, as we have said, let us return to our times. For Arius, who was the first wicked inventor of this wicked sect, was subjected to infernal fires after he had lost his entrails in a privy. But Hilarius, the blessed defender of the undivided Trinity, though sent into exile for its sake, was restored both to his native land and to Paradise. King Clovis confessed it, and crushed the heretics by its aid and extended his kingdom over all the Gauls; Alaric, on the other hand, who denied it, was deprived of kingdom and people, and what is more, of eternal life itself. And to true believers, even if through the plots of the enemy they lose something, the Lord restores it a hundred fold, but heretics do not gain any advantage, but what they seem to have is taken from them. This is proved by the deaths of Godegisel, Gundobad, and Godomar, who at the same time lost their country and their souls. But we confess one God, invisible, [*note: 2 Reading* invisibilem *for* indivisibilem] infinite, incomprehensible, glorious, always the same, and everlasting, one in Trinity in respect to the number of persons, that is, the Father, the Son and the Holy Spirit; we confess him also triple in unity in respect to equality of substance deity, omnipotence or power, the one greatest omnipotent God ruling for eternal centuries.

1.

Now on the death of king Clovis, his four sons, namely, Theodoric, Chlodomer, Childebert and Chlothar, received his kingdom and divided it among them in equal parts. Theodoric had already at that time a handsome and valiant son named Theodobert. And since they were very brave and had abundant strength in their army, Amalaric, son of Alaric, king of Spain, asked for their sister in marriage, and they kindly granted his request, and sent her into the Spanish country with a great quantity of beautiful things.

[**2.** Quintianus, exbishop of Rodez, is rewarded for his faithfulness to the Franks by being made bishop of Clermont. **3.** The Danes plunder the coast of Theodoric's kingdom. **4.** Hermenfred becomes sole king of the Thuringi by Theodoric's help.]

5.

Now on Gundobad's death his son Sygismund held his kingdom, and he built with great skill the monastery of St. Maurice, with its dwellings and churches. And losing his first wife, the daughter of Theodoric, king of Italy, he married another, and she began to malign his son bitterly and make charges against him as is the custom of stepmothers. From this it came about that on a day of ceremonial when the boy recognized his mother's dress on her, he was filled with anger, and said to her: " You are not worthy to have on your back those garments which are known to have belonged to your mistress, that is, my mother." And she was set on fire with rage and she stirred her husband up with crafty words, saying: "The wicked boy wishes to possess your kingdom, and he plans when you are killed to extend it as far as Italy, forsooth, that he may possess the kingdom which his grandfather Theodoric held in Italy. For he knows that while you live he cannot accomplish this; and unless you fall he will not rise." Sygismund was aroused by these words, and taking the advice of his wicked wife he became a wicked parricide. For when his son had been made drowsy by wine he bade him sleep in the afternoon; and while he slept a napkin was placed under his neck and tied under his chin, and he was strangled by two servants who drew in opposite directions. When it was done the father repented too late, and falling on the lifeless corpse began to weep most bitterly. And a certain old man is reported to have spoken to him in these words: " Henceforth wail for yourself," said he, "that you have become a most cruel parricide through base counsel. For there is no need to wail for this innocent boy who has been strangled." Nevertheless he went off to the holy Saint Maurice and spending many days in weeping and fasting he prayed for pardon. After establishing there a perpetual service of song he returned to Lyons, the divine vengeance attending on his footsteps. King Theodoric had married his daughter.

6.

Queen Clotilda spoke to Chlodomer and her other sons, saying: "Let me not repent, dearest sons, that I have nursed you lovingly; be angry, I beg you, at the insult to me, and avenge with a wise zeal the death of my father and mother." They heeded this; and they hastened to the Burgundies and marched against Sygismund and his brother Godomar. Their army was completely routed and Godomar fled. But Sygismund was taken by Chlodomer when he was endeavoring to make his escape to the holy St. Maurice, and led away captive with his wife and sons, and was placed under guard and kept prisoner in the territory of the city of Orleans. When the kings `departed Godomar recovered his courage and gathered the Burgundians and gained his kingdom back. And Chlodomer was making preparations to march against him a second time and determined to kill Sygismund. And the blessed abbot Avitus, a great priest of that time, said to him: "If," said he, "you would look to God and amend your counsel so as not to allow these men to be killed, God will be with you and you shall go and win the victory; but if you kill them you shall : be surrendered yourself into the hands of your enemies and shall perish in the same way. And what you do to Sygismund and his wife and children shall be done to you and your wife and sons." But he despised listening to this counsel, and said: "I think it is foolish advice to leave enemies at home and march against the rest, and when the former rise up in the rear and the latter in front I shall fall between two armies. The victory will be won better and more easily if one is separated from the other; if one is slain it will be possible to doom the others to death easily." He gave orders to slay Sygismund at once, with his wife and children, by casting them into a well in the village Columna, of the city Orleans, and hastened to the Burgundies, summoning to his aid king Theodoric. And the latter promised to go, not caring to avenge the wrong done to his fatherinlaw. And when they met near Visorontia, a place of the city of Vienne, they fought with Godomar And when Godomar had fled with his army and Chlodomer was pursuing and was separated a considerable distance from his men, the others, imitating his rallying cry, called to him saying: "This way, come this way, we are your men." And he believed it and went, and fell in the midst of his enemies cutting off his head and setting it on a pike they raised it aloft. The Franks saw this and perceived that Chlodomer was dead, and rallying, they put Godomar to flight and crushed the Burgundians and reduced their country to subjection, and Clothar immediately married his brother's wife, Guntheuca by name. And queen Clotilda, after the period of mourning was past, took his sons and kept them; and one of these was called Theodoald, a second, Gunther, a third, Chlodovald. Godomar recovered his kingdom a second time.

7.

Afterward Theodoric, remembering the wrongs done by Hermenfred, king of the Thuringi, called his brother Clothar to his aid and prepared to march against him, promising that a share of the plunder should be given to king Clothar, if by God's help the gift of victory should come to them. So he called the Franks together and said to them.: "Be angry, I beg of you, both because of my wrong and because of the death of your kinsmen, and recollect that the Thuringi once made a violent attack upon our kinsmen and inflicted much harm on them. And they gave hostages and were willing to conclude peace with them, but the Thuringi slew the hostages with various tortures, and made an attack upon our kinsmen, took away all their property, and hung youths by the sinews of their thighs to trees, and cruelly killed more than two hundred maidens, tying them by their arms to the necks of horses, which were then headed in opposite directions, and being started by a very sharp goad tore the maidens to pieces. And others were stretched out upon the city streets and stakes were planted in the ground, and they caused loaded wagons to pass over them, and having broken their bones they gave them to dogs [and birds for food. And now Hermenfred has deceived me in what he promised, and refuses to perform it at all. Behold, we have a plain word. Let us go with God's aid against them." They heard this and were angry at such a wrong, and with heart and mind they attacked Thuringia. And Theodoric took his brother Clothar and his son Theodobert to help him and went with his army. And the Thuringi prepared stratagems against the coming of the Franks. For they dug pits in the plain where the fight was to take place, and covering the openings with thick turf they made it seem a level plain. So when they began to fight, many of the Frankish horsemen fell into these pits and it was a great obstacle to them, but when this stratagem was perceived they began to be on their guard. When finally the Thuringi saw that they were being fiercely cut to pieces and when their king Hermenfred had taken to flight, they turned their backs and came to the stream Unstrut. And there such a slaughter of the Thuringi took place that the bed of the stream was filled with heaps of corpses, and the Franks crossed upon them as if on a bridge to the further shore. The victory being won they took possession of that country and brought it under their control. And Clothar went back, taking with him as a captive Radegunda, daughter of king Berthar, and hè married her, and her brother he afterwards killed unjustly by the hands of wicked men. She also turned to God, changing her garments, and built a monastery for herself in the city of Poitiers. And being remarkable for prayer, fasting and charity, she attained such fame that she was considered great by the people. And when the kings who have been mentioned were still in Thuringia, Theodoric wished to kill his own brother Clothar, and preparing armed men secretly, he summoned him on the pretext that he wished to consult him privately. And stretching a tentcloth in one part of the house from one wall to the other, he ordered the armed men to stand behind it. And since the cloth was somewhat short the feet of the armed men were in full sight. Clothar learned of this, and came into the house with his men armed also. And Theodoric perceived that he had learned of these things and he made a pretence, and talked of one thing after another. Finally, not knowing how to put a good appearance on his stratagem, he gave him as a favor a great silver dish. And Clothar said goodby and thanked him for the gift and returned to his place of encampment. But Theodoric complained to his people that he had lost his dish for no evident reason, and he said to his son Theodobert; "Go to your uncle and ask him to give you of his own free will the gift I gave him." He went, and got what he asked for. In such stratagems Theodoric was very skilful.

8.

He returned to his own country and urged Hermenfred to come to him boldly, pledging his faith, and he enriched him with honorable gifts. It happened, however, when they were talking one day on the walls of the city of Tolbiac that Hermenfred was pushed by some one or other, and fell from the height of the wall to the ground and there died. But we do not know who cast him down from there; many however assert that a stratagem of Theodoric was plainly revealed in this.

[9. King Childebert takes possession of Auvergne on a false report of Theodoric's death. 10. He leaves Auvergne and makes an expedition into Spain to avenge the ill-treatment of his sister Chlotchild by her husband Amalaric. 11-13. King Theodoric takes vengeance on the people of Auvergne for receiving Childebert.]

14.

Now Munderic, who asserted that he was a kinsman of the king, was puffed up with pride and said: "What have I to do with king Theodoric. For the throne of the kingdom is as much my due as his. I shall go out and gather my people, and exact an oath from them, that Theodoric may know that I am king just as much as he." And he went out, and began to lead the people astray, saying: "I am a chief, follow me, and it will be well with you." A multitude of country people followed him, as one might expect from the frailty of mankind, taking the oath of fidelity and honoring him as a king. And when Theodoric found this out he sent a command to him, saying: " Come to see me, and if any share of my kingdom is due you, take it." Now Theodoric said this deceitfully, thinking that he would kill him when he came. But the other was unwilling and said: " Go, bear back word to your king that I am king just as he is." Then the king gave orders to set his army in motion, in order to crush him by force and punish him. And he learned this, and not being strong enough to defend himself, he hastened to the walls of the stronghold of Vitry, and strove to fortify himself in it with all his property, gathering together those whom he had led astray. Now the army got underway, and surrounded the stronghold, and besieged it for seven days. And Munderic resisted with his people, saying: "Let us make a brave stand, and fight together even to death, and not submit to the enemy." And when the army kept hurling javelins against them on every side, and accomplished nothing, they reported this to the king. And he sent for a certain one of his people, named Aregyselus, and said to him: "You see," said he, "what this traitor is able to do in his arrogance. Go and swear an oath to him that he shall go forth safe. And when he has come forth, kill him, and blot out his memory from our kingdom." He went away and did as he had been ordered. He had however first given a sign to the people, saying: "When I speak words thus and so, rush upon him immediately and kill him." Now Aregyselus went in and said to Munderic: "How long will you sit here like one without sense? You will not be able to resist the king long, will you? Behold, your food has been cut off. When hunger overcomes you, you will come forth whether or no, and surrender yourself into the hands of the enemy, and you will die like a dog. Listen rather to my advice, and submit to the king,` that you may be able to live, you and your sons." Then the other, disheartened by these words, said: "If I go out, I shall be seized by the king and slain, both I and my sons and all my friends who are gathered with me." And Aregyselus said to him: "Do not be afraid, but if you decide to go forth, receive my oath as to your crime, and stand securely before the king. Do not be afraid. You shall be o n the same terms with him as you were before." To this Munderic answered: " I wish I were sure I should not be killed." Then Aregyselus put his hands on the holy altar, and swore to him that he should go out safely. So when the oath had been taken, Munderic went out from the gate of the stronghold, holding Aregyselus' hand, and the people gazed at him from a distance. Then as a sign Aregyselus said: "Why do you gaze so intently, O people? Did you never see Munderic before?" And at once the people rushed upon him. But he understood and said: " I see very plainly that by these words you gave a sign to the people to kill me, but I tell you who have deceived me by perjury, no one shall ever see you alive again. And he drove his lance into his back, and thrust it through him and he fell and died. Then Munderic unsheathed his sword, and with his followers made great slaughter of the people, and until he died did not shrink back from any one he could reach. And after he had been slain his property was added to the treasury.

15.

Theodoric and Childebert made a treaty, and swearing to each other that neither would attack the other, they took hostages from each other, in order that their agreement might be more secure. Many sons of senators were given as hostages on that occasion, but a quarrel arose later between the kings, and they were given over to servitude and those who had taken them to guard now made slaves of them. Many of them however escaped by flight, and returned to their native place, but a good many were kept in slavery. Among these was Attalus, nephew of the blessed Gregory, bishop of Langres, who became a slave and was appointed keeper of horses. He was in servitude to a certain barbarian in the territory of Trèves. Now the blessed Gregory sent servants to inquire for him, who found him, and offered presents to the man, but he rejected them contemptuously, saying: "This fellow, belonging to such a family, ought to be ransomed with ten pounds of gold." And when they had returned, a certain Leo belonging to the kitchen of his master, said: "I wish you would give me permission, and perhaps I might be able to bring him back from captivity." His master was glad of the offer, and he went straight to the place, and desired to carry the youth away secretly, but could not. Then bargaining with a certain man he said: "Come with me, and sell me in the house of that barbarian, and take the profit of my price, only let me have a freer opportunity of doing what I have decided." After taking an oath, the man went and sold him for twelve gold pieces, and departed. The purchaser asked the new slave what work he could do, and he answered "I am very skilled in preparing all the things that ought to be eaten at the tables of masters, and I am not afraid that my equal in skill can be found. For I tell you that even if you desire to make ready a feast for the king, I can prepare kingly viands, and no one better than I." And he said; "The day of the sun is near,"- for thus the Lord's day is usually named in the barbarian fashion "on this day my neighbors and kinsmen shall be invited to my house. I ask you to make me such a feast as to make them wonder and say 'we have not seen better in the king's palace.'" And the other said: "Let my master order a great number of fowls, and I will do what you command." Accordingly the preparations which the slave had asked for were made, and the Lord's day dawned and he made a great feast full of delicacies. And when all had feasted and praised the viands, the master's kinsmen went away. The master thanked this slave, and gave him authority over the food that he had ready for use, and he loved him greatly, and the slave used to serve food to all who were with his master. After the space of a year, when his master was now certain of him, Leo went out into a meadow which was near the house, with the slave Attalus, the keeper of the horses, and lying on the ground with him a long distance off, with their backs turned so they would not be recognized as together, he said to the youth: "It is time that we ought to be thinking of our native place. Therefore I advise you not to allow yourself to go to sleep tonight when you bring the horses to be shut in, but as soon as I call you, come, and let us undertake the journey." Now the barbarian had invited many of his kinsmen to a feast, and among them was his soninlaw, who had married his daughter. And at midnight they rose from g the banquet and retired to rest, and Leo attended his master's soninlaw to the place assigned and offered him drink. The man said to him: "Tell me, if you can, trusted servant of my father-in-law, when will you decide to take his horses and go to your own country " He said this in a joking way. In the same way the other jokingly gave the truthful answer: "Tonight, I think, if it is God's will." And he said: "I hope my attendants will be on the watch that you take nothing of mine." They parted laughingly And when all were asleep, Leo called Attalus, and when the horses were saddled, he asked him if he had a sword. He answered: "I do not need one, I have only a small lance." But the other went into his master's house, and took his shield and spear. And when he asked who it was, and what he wanted, he answered: "I am Leo, your slave. and I am waking Attalus. So that he may rise quickly and take the horses to pasture; for he is sleeping as soundly as if he were drunk." And he said: "Do as you please. And saying this he fell asleep. The other went out of doors and armed the youth, and found unbarred, by divine help, the gates of the yard, which at nightfall he had barred with wedges driven by a hammer, to keep the horses safe; thankingr God they took the remaining horses and went off, taking also a roll of garments. They came to the river Moselle in order to cross it, and being detained by certain persons they left their horses and clothes and swam over the river, supported on a shield and climbing the further bank they hid themselves in the woods amid the darkness of the night. The third night was come since they had been on their way without tasting food. Then by God's will they found a tree full of the fruit which is commonly called plums, and ate and were strengthened somewhat, and began the journey through Champagne. And as they hastened, they heard the tramping of horses going at a rapid gait, and they said: "Let us throw ourselves down on the ground, so as not to be seen by the men who are coming." And behold they suddenly came upon a great bramble bush, and they passed behind and threw themselves on the ground with their swords unsheathed, in order to defend themselves quickly from wicked men if they should be noticed. And when the others had come to the thornbush they stopped; and one of them said, while their horses were making water: "Woe is me that these accursed wretches are escaped and cannot be found; but by my salvation, if they are found I command one to be condemned to the gallows, and the other to be cut to fragments by strokes of the sword." Now the barbarian who said this was their master who was coming from the city of Rheims seeking for them, and he would certainly have found them on the way if night had not prevented. Then starting their horses, they went off. The fugitives reached the city on this very night, and going in, they found a man of whom they made inquiries, and he told them where the house of the priest Paulellus was. And while they were passing through the square, the bell was rung for matins -for it was the Lord's day-and knocking at the priest's door, they went in, and Leo told about his master. And the priest said to him: "It was a true vision I had. For last night I saw two doves fly toward me and settle on my hand, and one of them was white, and the other black." And Leo said to the priest: "May the Lord be kind as the day is holy. For we ask you to give us some food; for the fourth day is dawning since we have tasted bread and meat." He hid the slaves, and gave them bread soaked in wine, and went away to matins. The barbarian followed them, asking for the boys a second time, but he was deceived by the priest, and he went back. For the priest had an old friendship with the blessed Gregory. Then the youths, after refreshing their strength with food, and remaining two days in the home of the priest, departed, and thus they came to the holy Gregory. The bishop rejoiced at seeing them, and wept on the neck of Attalus his nephew; he set Leo free from the yoke of slavery with all his family, and gave him land of his own, on which he lived a free man with his wife and children all the days of his life.

[**16.** Sigivald, duke of Auvergne is miraculously punished for taking church property. **17.** ~n~ successive bishops of Tours are mentioned, one of them, Leo, being "a man of energy and skill in the building of wooden structures."]

18.

While queen Clotilda was staying at Paris, Childebert saw that his mother loved with especial affection the sons of Chlodomer, whom we have mentioned above, and being envious and fearful that they would have a share in the kingdom through the favor of the queen, he sent secretly to his brother king Clothar, saying: "Our mother keeps our brother's sons with her, and wishes them to be kings. You must come swiftly to Paris, where we will take counsel together and discuss what ought to be done about them, whether their hair shall be cut and they be treated like the rest of the common people, or whether we shall kill them and divide our brother's kingdom between ourselves equally." And Clothar was very glad at these words, and came to Paris. Now Childebert had spread the report among the people that the kings were meeting for the purpose of raising the little ones to the throne. And when they met, they sent to the queen, who was then dwelling in the city, saying: "Send the little ones to us, that they may be raised to the throne." And she rejoiced, not knowing their treachery, and giving the boys food and drink, she sent them saying: " I shall not think that I have lost my son, if I see you occupy his place in the kingdom." And they went, and were seized at once, and were separated from their servants and tutors, and they were guarded separately, in one place the servants, in another these little ones. Then Childebert and Clothar sent Arcadius, whom we have mentioned before, to the queen, with a pair of scissors and a naked sword. And coming he showed both to the queen, and said: "Most glorious queen, your sons, our masters, ask your decision as to what you think ought to be done with the boys, whether you give command for them to live with shorn hair, or for both to be put to death." She was terrified by the news and at the same time enraged, especially when she saw the naked sword and the scissors, and being overcome with bitterness, and not knowing in her grief what she was saying, she said imprudently: " It is better for me to see them dead rather than shorn, if they are not raised to the kingship." But he wondered little at her grief, and did not think what she would say later in less haste, but went swiftly, taking the news and saying: "Finish the task you have begun with the queen's favor; for she wishes your design to be accomplished." There was no delay. Clothar seized the older boy by the arm, and dashed him to the earth, and plunging his hunting knife into his side, he killed him pitilessly. And while the child was screaming, his brother threw himself at Childebert's feet and seized his knees and said: "Help me, kind father, lest I perish like my brother." Then Childebert, his face covered with tears, said: "Dearest brother, I ask you to grant his life to me in your generosity, and let me pay for his life what you wish, only let him not be killed." But the other attacked him with abuse, and said: " Cast him from you, or you shall surely die in his place. It is you," said he, " that are the guilty instigator [*note: 1 Reading for* incestotor, instecator. *Bonnet*, Le Latin de Gregoire de Tours, *p. 454-5.*] of this matter. Do you so easily break faith?" Childebert heeded this and cast the boy away from him to the other, who seized him and plunged his knife into his side and slew him as he had his brother before: then they killed the servants and the tutors. When they were killed Clothar mounted his horse and went off, making a small matter of the killing of his nephews. And Childebert retired to the outskirts of the city. And the queen placed their little bodies on a bier and followed them to the church of St. Peter with loud; singing and unbounded grief, and buried them side by side. One ; was ten years old, the other seven. But the third, Clodoald, they were unable to seize, since he was freed by the aid of brave men. . He gave up his earthly kingdom and passed to the Lord's service, and cutting his hair with his own hand he became a clerk, busied with good works, and as a priest passed from this life. The two kings divided equally between them the kingdom of Chlodomer. And queen Clotilda showed herself such that she was honored by all; she was always diligent in alms, able to endure the whole : night in watching, unstained in chastity and uprightness; with a generous and ready goodwill she bestowed estates on churches, monasteries, and holy places wherever she saw there was need, so that she was believed to serve God diligently, not as a queen but as his own handmaid, and neither her royal sons, nor worldly ambition, nor wealth, raised her up for destruction, but her humility exalted her to grace.

19.

There lived at that time in the city of Langres the blessed Gregory, a great bishop of God, renowned for his signs and miracles. And since we have spoken of this bishop, I think it not unpleasing to insert in this place an account of the site of Dijon, where he was especially active. It is a stronghold with very solid walls, built in the midst of a plain, a very pleasant place, the lands rich and fruitful, so that when the fields are ploughed once the seed is sown and a great wealth of produce comes in due season. On the south it has the Ouche, a river very rich in fish, and from the north comes another little stream, which runs in at the gate and flows under a bridge and again passes out by another gate, flowing around the whole fortified place with its quiet waters, and turning with wonderful speed the mills before the gate. The four gates face the four regions of the universe, and thirty-three towers adorn the whole structure, and the wall is thirty feet high and fifteen feet thick, built of squared stones up to twenty feet, and above of small stone. And why it is not called a city I do know. It has all around it abundant springs, and on the west are hills, very fertile and full of vineyards, which produce for the inhabitants such a noble Falernian that they disdain wine of Ascalon. The ancients say this place was built by the emperor Aurelian.

[**20.** Betrothal of Theodoric's son Theodobert to Visigard. **21.** The Franks retake some of the cities taken by Clovis from the Goths. **22.** Theodobert falls in love with Deoteria.]

23.

In those days Theodoric killed his kinsman Sigivald with the sword, sending secretly to Theodobert that he should slay Sigivald's son Sigivald whom he had with him. But he was unwilling to destroy him, because he had taken him from the sacred font. But he gave him the letter to read which his father had sent, saying: "Flee from here, because I have received my father's command to kill you; and if he dies and you hear that I am reigning, then return to me safely." On hearing this Sigivald thanked him, said goodby, and departed. Now at that time the Goths had taken possession of the city of Arles, from which Theodobert still had hostages. To it Sigivald fled. But he saw that he was not safe there, and went to Latium, and remained hidden there. While this was going on, word was brought to Theodobert that his father was seriously ill, and that if he did not hasten swiftly to him so as to find him alive, he would be excluded by his uncles, and would never be allowed to return. And he postponed everything on hearing this, and hastened thither, leaving Deoteria with her daughter at Clermont. And not many days after he had gone, Theodoric died, in the twenty-third year of his reign. And Childebert and Clothar rose against Theodobert and wished to take the kingdom from him, but he was defended by his *leudes,* after they had received gifts from him, and was established in his kingdom. He sent later to Clermont and summoned Deoteria thence, and married her.

24.

Childebert saw that he was not able to prevail, and sent an embassy to him, and bade him come to him, saying: "I have no sons, I wish to treat you as a son." And when he came he bestowed such rich gifts upon him that all wondered. For he presented him with three pairs of all the articles of armor, vestments, and other equipments that it becomes a king to have, and likewise with horses and chains. Sigivald heard this, namely, that Theodobert had received his father's kingdom, and returned to him from Italy. And Theodobert rejoiced, and kissed him, and bestowed upon him a third part of the gifts which he had received from his uncle, and he gave orders that all that his father had seized of the property of Sigivald's father, should be returned to him.

25.

And he was established in his kingdom, and showed himself great, and distinguished by every goodness. For he ruled his kingdom with justice, respecting this bishops, making gifts to the churches, relieving the poor, and doing kindnesses to many persons with a pious and generous heart. He kindly remitted all the tribute which was payable to his treasury from the churches situated in Auvergne.

26.

Now Deoteria saw that her daughter was quite grown up, and was afraid that the king would desire and take her. She placed her in a litter to which wild oxen were yoked, and sent her headlong over a bridge; and she lost her life in the river. This happened in the city of Verdun.

27.

As it was now the seventh year since Theodobert and Visigard had been betrothed, and he was unwilling to take her on account of Deoteria, the Franks, when they met, were greatly scandalized at him because he had abandoned his betrothed. Then he was alarmed, and abandoning Deoteria, by whom he had a little son named Theodobald, he married Visigard. And when she died not long after, he took another wife. But he did not have Deoteria after that.

[28. Childerbert and Theodobert against Chlothar but are turned back by a miraculous hailstorm. Sent by St. Martin.]

29.

Later king Childebert set out for Spain. And entering the country with Clothar, they surrounded the city of Saragossa with their army, and besieged it. But the besieged turned to

God in `such humility that they put on haircloth, abstained from food and drink, and made the round of the walls of the city with psalm-singing, carrying the tunic of the blessed Vincent, the martyr; the women, too, followed wailing, clothed in black robes, with their hair hanging loose and ashes upon it, so that one would think they were attending the funerals of their husbands. And to such a degree did that city place its whole hope in God's mercy that it was said they were celebrating the fast of the Ninevites there, and there was no idea of any other possibility than that the divine mercy might be won by prayers. But the besiegers did not know what was going on, and when they saw them go around the wall in such a way they supposed they were engaged in some sorcery. Then seizing one of the common people of the place, they asked him what it was they were doing. And he said: " They are carrying the blessed Vincent's tunic, and at the same time they are praying the Lord to pity them." And they were afraid at this, t and went away from that city. However, they acquired a very large part of Spain, and returned to the Gauls with great spoils.

30.

After Amalaric, Theoda was ordained king in the Spains. But when he was slain they raised Theodegisil to the throne. When he was dining with his friends and was very cheerful, suddenly the lights were put out in the dining hall and he was slain by his enemies, being thrust through with a sword. After him Agila became king. For the Goths had formed the detestable habit of attacking with the sword any one of their kings who did not please them, and they would appoint as king any one that took their fancy.

31.

Theodoric of Italy having married a sister of king Clovis, died, and left his wife and a little daughter. When this girl was grown, because of her fickle temper she refused the counsel of her mother, who was looking out for a king's son for her, and took her slave named Traguilanis, and fled with him to a city where she hoped to defend herself. And when her mother raged at her furiously, and begged her not to disgrace further a noble family and said it was her duty to send the slave off and take one of equal rank with herself from a royal family, whom her mother had provided, she was by no means willing to agree to it. Then her mother, still raging at her, set an army in motion. And they came upon them, and killed Traguilanis with the sword, chastised the girl herself, and took her to her mother's house. Now they belonged to the Arian sect, and as it is their custom that of those going to the altar the kings receive one cup and the lesser people another, she put poison in the cup from which her mother was going to , receive the communion. And she drank it and died forthwith. There is no doubt that such harm is from the devil. What shall the wretched heretics answer to this charge that the enemy dwells in their holy place? But as for us who confess the Trinity in one similar equality and omnipotence, even if we should drink a deadly draught in the name of the Father, Son and holy Spirit, the true and incorruptible God, it would not do us any harm. The Italians were indignant this woman, and they invited Theodad, king of Tuscia, and made him king over them. When he learned what the harlot had been guilty of, how she had slain her mother on account of a slave whom she had taken, he gave orders that a bath be raised to a great heat, and that she be shut in the same with one maid. And when she entered the hot vapors she fell at once on the pavement, and died, and was consumed. And when the kings Childebert and Chlothar, her cousins, as well as Theodobert, learned this, namely, that she had been put to death in so shameful a manner, they sent an embassy to Theodad, blaming him for her death, and saying: "If you do not make an arrangement with us for what you have done, we will take your kingdom from you, and condemn you to a like punishment." Then he was afraid, and sent to them fifty thousand gold pieces. And Childebert, being envious of king Clothar, and deceitful, joined with Theodobert his nephew, and they divided the gold between them, and refused to give any of it to king Clothar. But he made an attack upon the treasures of Chlodomer, and took much more from them than that of which they had defrauded him.

32.

Theodobert went to Italy, and there made great gains. But as those places according to report are full of diseases, his army was attacked by various fevers, and many of them died there. Seeing this, Theodobert returned from the country and brought much spoil, himself and his men. It is related at that time he went as far as the city of Pavia to which he again sent Buccelenus. And he captured lesser Italy and brought it under the sway of the king who has been mentioned, and attacked greater Italy; here he fought against Belsuarius many times and won the victory. And when the emperor saw that Belsuarius was being beaten more frequently he removed him, and put Narses in his place, and, as a humiliation, he made Belsuarius count of the stable, a place he had held before. But Buccelenus fought great battles against Narses: capturing all Italy he extended his boundaries to the sea, and he sent great treasures from Italy to Theodobert. When Narses made this known to the emperor, the emperor hired nations and sent aid to Narses, and in the battle later he was defeated. Then Buccelenus seized Sicily and exacting tribute from it he sent it to the king. He enjoyed great prosperity in these matters.

[33. Feud between Asteriolus and Secundinus, advisers of King Theodobert]

34.

Desideratus, bishop of Verdun, to whom king Theodoric had done many wrongs, was restored to liberty at the Lord's command, after many losses and reverses and griefs, and received the office of bishop, as we have said, at the city of Verdun, and seeing its inhabitants very poor and destitute he grieved for them, and since he was left without his own property because of Theodoric, and had nothing of his own with which to relieve them, knowing the goodness and kindness to all of king Theodobert, he sent an embassy to him saying: " The fame of your goodness is spread over all the earth, since your generosity is such that you give aid even to those who do not seek it. I beg of your kindness if you have any money, that you lend it to us that we may be able to relieve our fellowcitizens; and when those in charge of business secure a return in our city such as the rest have, we will repay your money with lawful interest." Then Theodobert was stirred with pity and furnished seven thousand gold pieces, which the bishop received and paid out among his fellowcitizens. And they who were engaged in business were made rich through this and are considered great to the present day. And when the bishop who has been just mentioned offered the money which was due to the king, the king answered: "I have no need to take this; it is enough for me if the poor men who were suffering want have been relieved by your care because of your suggestion and my generosity." And he whom we have mentioned made the citizens rich without demanding anything.

[35. Syagrius avenges wrongs done to his father by killing Syrivald.]

36.

After this king Theodobert began to be sick. And the physicians gave him much care; but he did not get well because the Lord was already bidding him be summoned. And so after a very long illness he died of his infirmity. And as the Franks hated Parthenius intensely, because he had subjected them to tribute in the time of the king just mentioned, they began to attack him. He saw that he was in danger, and fled from the city, and humbly begged two bishops to conduct him to the city of Trèves, and check the sedition of the frenzied people by their preaching. While they were on their way he was lying on his bed at night, and suddenly he made a loud cry in his sleep, saaing: "Ho ! Ho ! Help, you who are here, and assist one who is perishing." By this shouting those who were there were awakened, and they asked him what the matter was. He answered: "Ausanius, my friend, and my wife Papianella, whom I slew long ago, were summoning me to judgment, saying: 'Come to defend yourself, since you are going to plead with us in the presence of the Lord." Now he had slain his innocent wife and his friend some years before, under the influence of jealousy. Accordingly, the bishops approached the city just mentioned, and since they could not calm the sedition among the rebellious people, they wished to hide him in the church, placing him in a chest, and strewing above him vestments which were used in the church. The people came in, and after searching every corner of the church, went out in a rage when they found nothing. Then one said suspiciously: "Behold a chest in which our enemy has not been sought for." And when the guards said that there was nothing in it except that it contained furniture of the church, they demanded the key, saying: "Unless you quickly unlock it we will break it open ourselves." Finally the chestwas unlocked, the linen cloths were removed, and they found him and dragged him out, rejoicing and saying: " God has delivered our enemy into our hands." Then they struck him with their fists, and spat on him, and tying his hands behind his back, they stoned him to death beside a column. He was very voracious in eating, and what he ate he digested speedily, taking aloes in order to be made hungry soon again.... And so he perished, meeting this kind of end.

37.

In that year the winter was a grievous one and more severe than usual, so that the streams were held in the chains of frost and furnished a path for the people like dry ground. Birds, too, were affected by the cold and hunger, and were caught in the hand without any snare when the snow was deep.

Now from the death of Clovis to the death of Theodobert there are reckoned thirty-seven years. When Theodobert died in the fourteenth year of his reign, Theodoald his son reigned in his stead.

HERE ENDS THE THIRD BOOK

BOOK IV

HERE END THE CHAPTERS

HERE BEGINS THE FOURTH BOOK WITH HAPPY AUSPICES

[**1.** Queen Clotilda dies at Tours and is buried at Paris.]

2.

King Clothar had ordered all the churches of his kingdom to pay into his treasury a third of their revenues. But when all the other bishops, though grudgingly, had agreed to this and signed their names, the blessed Injuriosus scorned the command and manfully refused to sign, saying, "If you attempt to take the things of God, the Lord will take away your kingdom speedily because it is wrong for your storehouses to be filled with the contributions of the poor whom you yourself ought to feed." He was irritated with the king and left his presence without saying farewell. Then the king was alarmed and being afraid of the power of the blessed Martin he sent after him with the gifts, praying for pardon and admitting the wrongfulness of what he had done, and asking also that the bishop avert from him by prayer the power of the blessed Martin.

3.

The king had seven sons by several wives; namely, by Ingunda, Gunthar, Childeric, Charibert, Gunthram, Sigibert, and a daughter Chlotsinda; by Aregunda, sister of Ingunda, Chilperic; and by Chunsina he had Chramnus. I will tell you why it was he married his wife's sister. When he was already married to t d: her alone, he received a hint from her saying: "My Lord has done with his handmaid what he pleased and has taken me to his couch. Now let my lord the king hear what his servant would suggest to make his favor complete. I beg that you consent to find a husband for my sister, a man who will be of advantage to your servant and possess wealth, so that I shall not be humiliated but rather exalted and shall be able to serve you more faithfully. To this request he gave heed and being of a wanton nature he fell in love with Aregunda and went to the estate on which she was living and married her himself. Having do this he returned to Ingunda and said: "I have tried to do the favor which your sweet self asked of me. I sought for a man of riches a wisdom to unite to your sister but I found no one better than myself. And so allow me to tell you that I have married her, which I think will not displease you." And she replied; "Let my Lord do what seems good in his eyes; only let his handmaid live i favor with the king."

Now Gunthar, Chramnus and Childeric died in their father's lifetime. Of the death of Chramnus I shall write later. And Albin, king of the Lombards, married Chlotsinda, his daughter Injuriosus, bishop of Tours, died in the seventeenth year of his episcopate and Baudinus, a former official of king Clothar, succeeded him, the sixteenth after the death of the blessed Martin.

4.

Chanao, count of the Bretons, killed three of his brothers He wished to kill Macliavus also, and seized him and kept him in prison loaded with chains. But he was freed from death by Felix, bishop of Nantes. After this he swore he would be faithful to his brother, but from some reason or other he became inclined to break his oath. Chanao was aware of this and began to attack him again and when Macliavus saw that he could not escape, he fled to another count of that district, Chonomor by name. When Chonomor learned that Macliavus' pursuers were near at hand, he hid him in a box underground and heaped a mound over it in the regular way leaving a small airhole so that he could breathe And when his pursuers came, they said: " Behold here lies Macliavus dead and buried." On hearing this they were glad and drank on his tomb and reported to his brother that he was dead And his brother took the whole of his kingdom. For since Clovis's death the Bretons have always been under the dominion of the Franks and [their rulers have been called counts, not kings Macliavus rose from underground and went to the city of Vannes and there received the tonsure and was ordained bishop. But when Chanao died he left the priesthood, let his hair grow long, and took back not only his brother's kingdom but also the wife whom he had abandoned when he became a priest. However he was excommunicated by the bishops. What his end was I shall describe later. Now bishop Baudinus died in the sixth year of his episco pate, and the abbot Gunthar was appointed in his place, the seventeenth after the passing of the blessed Martin.

[5. How St. Gall, bishop of Clermont, averted the plague from his people.]

And when Saint Gall had departed from this world and his body had been washed and carried to the church, Cato the priest immediately received the congratulations of the clergy on becoming bishop. And as if he were already bishop he took under his control all the church property, removed the superintendents and cast the lesser officials out and regulated everything himself.

6.

The bishops who came to St. Gall's funeral said to Cato the priest after the funeral: "We see that you are the choice of by far the largest part of the people ; come then, join us, and we will bless and ordain you as bishop. The king is very young and if any fault is found with you, we will take you under our protection and deal with the leading men of Theodovald's kingdom so that no wrong shall be done you. Trust us faithfully, since we promise that even if some loss shall come to you, we will make it all good from our own properties." But he was puffed up with the pride of vainglory and said: "You know from widespread report that from the beginning of my life I have always lived religiously, that I have fasted, delighted in almsgiving, often kept watch without ceasing and have frequently continued the singing of psalms without a break the whole night through. The Lord God to whom I have paid such service will not allow me to be deprived of this office. For I attained all the grades of the clergy as directed in the canons. I was reader ten years, I performed the duties of subdeacon five years, I have been priest now for twenty years. What more is left or me except to receive the office of bishop which my faithful service deserves. You then return to your cities and busy yourselves with whatever tends to your advantage. For I intend to gain this office in the manner prescribed by the canons." The bishops heard this and departed cursing his empty boasting.

7.

He was accordingly designated to be bishop by the choice of the clergy, and when he had taken charge of everything though he was not yet ordained, he began to make various threats against the archdeacon Cautinus, saying: "I will cast you out, I will degrade you, I will cause many sorts of violent death to threaten you." And he answered: "I wish to have your favor, pious master and if I win it, there is one kindness I can do. Without any trouble on your part and without any deceit I will go to the king and obtain the office of bishop for you, asking no reward except to win your favor. But the other was suspicious that he meant to make a mock of him and rejected the offer with great disdain And when Cautinus perceived that he was in disgrace and was the object of ill report he pretended sickness, and left the city by night going to king Theodovald and reporting the death of Saint Gall. And when he and his court were informed of it they assembled the bishops at the city of Metz, and Cautinus the archdeacon was ordained bishop. And on the arrival of the messengers of the priest Cato he was already bishop. Then by the king's order these clerks were delivered over to him and all that they had brought from the property of the church, and bishops and officials of the treasury were appointed to accompany him, and they sent him on his way to Clermont. And he was gladly received by the clergy and citizens and was thus made bishop of Clermont But later enmity arose between him and Cato the priest because no one was ever able to influence Cato to submit to his bishop. A division of the clergy appeared and some followed the bishop Cautinus and others the priest Cato. This was a great drawback to them. And Cautinus saw that Cato could not be forced in any way to submit to him and took all church property from him and his friends and whoever took his part, and left them weak and empty. But whoever of them returned to him, again received what he had lost.

[**8.** King Agila of Spain loses cities to the emperor which his successor Athanagild recovers.]

9.

When Theodovald had grown up he married Vuldetrada. This Theodovald, they say, had a bad disposition so that when he was angry with anyone whom he suspected of taking his property he would make up a fable, saying: "A snake found a jar full of wine. He went in by its neck and greedily drained what was inside. But being puffed out by the wine he could not go out by the opening by which he had entered. And the owner of the wine came, and when the snake tried to get out but could not, he said to him: 'First vomit out what you have swallowed and then you will be able to go free.'" This fable made him greatly feared and hated. Under him Buccelenus after bringing all Italy under the rule of the Franks was slain by Narses, and Italy was taken by the emperor's party and there was no one to recover it later. In his time we saw grapes grow on the tree we call *saucum* [eldertree] without having any vine on it, and the blossoms of the same trees, which as you know usually produce black reeds, yielded the seeds of grapes. At that time a star coming from the opposite direction was seen to enter the disk of the fifth moon. I suppose these signs announced the death of the king. He became very sick and could not move from the waist down. He gradually grew worse and died in the seventh year of his reign, and king Clothar took his kingdom, taking Vuldetrada his wife to his bed. But being rebuked by the bishops he left her, giving her to duke Garivald and sending his son Chramnus to Clermont.

[**10.** King Clothar destroys the greater part of the rebellious Saxons and lays Thuringia waste.]

11.

Bishop Gunthar died at Tours, and at a suggestion, it is said, of bishop Cautinus the priest Cato was requested to undertake the government of the church at Tours. And the clergy accompanied by Leubastes, keeper of the relics and abbot, went in great state to Clermont. And when they had declared the king's will to Cato he would not answer them for a few days. But they wished to return and said: "Declare your will to us so that we may know what we ought to do; otherwise we will return home. For it was not of our own will that we came to you but at the command of the king." And Cato in his greed for vainglory got together a crowd of poor men and instructed them to shout as follows: " Good father, why do you abandon us your children, whom you taught until now? Who will strengthen us with food and drink if you go away? We beg you not to leave us whom you are wont to support." Then he turned to the clergy of Tours and said: "You see now, beloved brothers, how this multitude of the poor loves me; I cannot leave them to go with you." They received this answer and returned to Tours. Now Cato had made friends with Chramnus and got a promise from him that if king Clothar should die at that time, Cautinus was to be cast out at once from the bishop's office and Cato was to be given control of the church. But he who despised the chair of the blessed Martin did not get what he desired, and in this was fulfilled that which David sang, saying: "He refused the blessing and it shall be kept far from him." He was puffed up f with vanity thinking that noone was superior to him in holiness. Once he hired a woman to cry aloud in the church as if possessed and say that he was holy and great and beloved y God, but Cautinus the bishop was guilty of every crime and unworthy to hold the office of bishop.

12.

Now Cautinus on taking up the duties of bishop became greatly addicted to wine, and proved to be of such a character that he was loathed by all. He was often so befuddled by drink that four men could hardly take him away after dinner. Because of this habit he became an epileptic later on-a disease which frequently showed itself in public. He was also so avaricious that if he could not get some part of the possessions of those whose boundaries touched him he thought it was ruin for him. He took from the stronger with quarrels and abuse, and violently plundered the weaker. And as our Sollius [*note: Sidonius Apollinarius*] says, he would not pay the price because he despised doing so, and would not accept deeds because he thought them useless.

There was at that time a priest Anastasius, of free birth, who held some property secured by deeds of queen Clotilda of glorious memory. Usually when he met him the bishop would entreat him to give him the deeds of the queen mentioned above, and place the property under his charge. And when Anastasius postponed complying with the will of his bishop, the latter would try now to coax him with kind words and now to terrify him with threats. When he continued unwilling to the end, he ordered him to be brought to the city and there shamelessly detained, and unless he surrendered the deeds, he was to be loaded with insults and starved to death. But the other made a spirited resistance and never surrendered the deeds, saying it was better for him to waste away with hunger for a time than to leave his children in misery. Then by the bishop's command he was given over to the guards with instructions to starve him to death if he did not surrender these documents. Now there was in the church of St. Cassius the martyr a very old and remote crypt, in which was a great tomb of Parian mable wherein it seems the body of a certain man of long ago had been placed. In this tomb upon the dead body the living priest was placed and the tomb was covered with the stone with which had been covered before, and guards were placed at the entrance. But the faithful guards seeing that he was shut in by a stone as it was winter lit a fire and under the influence of hot wine fell asleep. But the priest like a new Jonah prayed insistently to the Lord to pity him from the interior of the tomb as from the belly of hell, and the tomb being large, as we have said, he was able to extend his hands freely wherever he wished although he could not turn his whole body. There came from the bones of the dead, as he used to relate, a killing stench, which made him shudder not only outwardly but in his inward parts as well. While he held his robe tightly against his nose and could hold his breath his feelings were not the worst, but when he thought that he was suffocating and held the robe a little away from his face he drank in the deadly smell not merely through mouth and nose but even, so to speak, through his very ears. Why make so long a story! When he had suffered, as I suppose, like the Divine Nature, he stretched out his right hand to the side of the sarcophagus and found a crowbar which had been left between the cover and the edge of the tomb when the cover sank into place. Moving this by degrees he found that with God's help the stone could be moved, and when it had been moved so far that the priest could get his head out he made a larger opening with greater ease and so came out bodily. Meanwhile the darkness of night was overspreading the day though it had not spread everywhere as yet. So he hastened to another entrance to the crypt. This was closed with the strongest bars and bolts, but was not so smoothly fitted that a man could not see between the planks. The priest placed his head close to this entrance and saw a man go by. He called to him in a low voice. The other heard, and having an ax in his hand he at once cut the wooden pieces by which the bars were held and opened the way for the priest. And he went off in the darkness and hastened home after vigorously urging the man to say nothing of the matter to any one. He entered his home and finding the deeds which the queen mentioned before had given him took them to king Clothar, informing him at the same time how he had been committed to a living burial by his own bishop. All were amazed and said that never had Nero or Herod done such a deed as to place a live man in the grave Then bishop Cautinus appeared before king Clothar but upon the priest's accusation he retreated in defeat and confusion. The priest according to directions received from the king maintained his property as he pleased and kept possession of it and left it to his children. In Cautinus there was no holiness, no quality to be esteemed. He was absolutely without knowledge of letters both ecclesiastical and secular. He was a great friend of the Jews and subservient to them, not for their salvation, as ought to be the anxious care of a shepherd, but in order to purchase their wares which they sold to him at a higher price than they were worth, since he tried to please them and they very plainly flattered him.

13.

At this time Chramnus lived at Clermont. He did many things contrary to reason and for this his departure from the world was hastened; and he was bitterly reviled by the people. He made friends with no one from whom he could get good and useful counsel, but he gathered together young men of low character and no stability and made friends of them only, listening to their advice and at their suggestion he even directed them to carry off daughters of senators by force. He offered serious insults to Firmin and drove him out of his office as count of the city, and placed Salust son of Euvodius in his place. Firmin with his motherinlaw took refuge in the church. It was Lent and bishop Cautinus had made preparations to go in procession singing psalms to the parish of Brioude, according to the custom established by St. Gall as we described above. And so the bishop went forth from the city with loud weeping, afraid that he would meet some danger on the way. For king Chramnus had been uttering threats against him. And while he was on the way the king sent Innachar and Scaphthar his chief adherents, saying: "Go and drag Firmin and Cæsaria his motherinlaw away from the church by force." So when the bishop had departed with psalm singing, as I have said before, the men sent by Chramnus entered the church and strove to calm the suspicions of Firmin and Cæsaria with many deceitful words. And when they had talked over one thing after another for a long time, walking to and fro in the church, and the fugitives had their attention fixed on what was being said, they drew near to the doors of the sacred temple which were then open. Then Innachar seized Firmin in his arms and Scaphthar Cæsaria, and cast them out from the church, where their slaves were ready to lay hold of them. And they sent them into exile at once. But on the second day their guards were overcome with sleep and they saw that they were free and hastened to the church of the blessed Julian, and so escaped from exile. However their property was confiscated. Now Cautinus had suspected that he himself would be subjected to outrage, and as he walked along on the journey I have told of, he t kept near by a saddled horse, and looking back he saw men coming on horseback to overtake him and he cried: "Woe is me, for here are the men sent by Chramnus to seize me." And he mounted his horse and gave up his psalm singing and plying his steed with both heels arrived all alone and half-dead at the entrance of Saint Julian's church. As I tell this tale I am reminded of Sallust's saying which he uttered with reference to the critics of historians. He says: "It is difficult to write history; first because deeds must be exactly represented in words and second because most men think that the condemnation of wrong doing is due to ill will and envy." However. Let us continue.

14.

Now when Clothar after Theodovald's death had received the kingdom of Francia and was making a progress through it, he heard from his people that the Saxons were engaged in a second mad outburst and were rebelling against him and contemptuously refusing to pay the tribute which they had been accustomed to pay every year. Aroused by the reports he hastened toward their country, and when he was near their boundary the Saxons sent legates to him saying: "We are not treating you contemptuously, and we do not refuse to pay what we have usually paid to your brothers and nephews, and we will grant even more if you ask for it. We ask for only one thing, that there be peace so that your army and our people shall not come into conflict." King Clothar heard this and said to his followers: "These men speak well. Let : us not go against them for fear that we sin against God." But .they said: "We know that they are deceitful and will not do at all what they have promised. Let us go against them." Again the Saxons offered half of their property in their desire for peace. And Clothar said to his men: "Give over, I beg you, from these men, lest the anger of God be kindled against us." But they wotld not agree to it. Again the Saxons brought garments, cattle and every kind of property, saying: "Take all this together with half of our land, only let our wives and little ones remain free and let war not arise between us." But the Franks were unwilling to agree even to this. And king Clothar said to them: "Give over, I beseech you, give over from this purpose; for we have not the right word; do not go to war in which we may be destroyed. If you decide to go of your own will I will not follow." Then they were enraged at king Clothar and rushed upon him and tore his tent in pieces and overwhelmed him with abuse and dragged him about violently and wished to kill him if he would not go with them. Upon this Clothar went with them though unwillingly. And they began the battle and were slaughtered in great numbers by their adversaries and so great a multitude from both armies perished that it was impossible to estimate or count them. Then Clothar in great confusion asked for peace, saying that it was not of his own will that he had come against them. And having obtained peace he returned home.

15.

The people of Tours heard that the king had returned from the battle with the Saxons and making choice of the priest Eufronius they hastened to him. When their suggestion had been made the king replied: "I had given directions for Cato the priest to be ordained there; why has my command been slighted ? " They answered "We invited him but he refused to come." And while they were speaking Cato the priest suddenly appeared to request the king to expel Cautinus and command that he himself be appointed in Clermont. When the king laughed at him he made a second request, that he should be ordained at Tours which he had contemptuously refused before. And the king said to him: "I at first gave directions that they should ordain you bishop of Tours, but as I hear, you looked down on that church; therefore you shall be kept from becoming master of it." And so he went off in confusion. When the king asked about the holy Eufronius they told him that he was grandson of the blessed Gregory, whom I have mentioned before. The king answered: " It is a great and leading family Let the will of God and the blessed Martin be done; let the choice be confirmed." And according to his command the holy Eufronius was ordained bishop, the eighteenth after the blessed Martin.

[16. Chramnus, king Clothar's son, opposes bishop Cautinus at Clermont. He goes to Poitiers and enters into an agreement with his uncle Childebert against Clothar. He assumes authority over part of Clothar's realm and Clothar sends two other sons, Charibert and Gunthram, against him. When they are ready to fight Chramnus causes a report of Clothar's death to be circulated and Charibert and Gunthram hasten off; Chramnus marches to Dijon where he consults the Bible as to his future. King Clothar u meanwhile fights the Saxons. 17. Chramnus joins Childebert in ;t Paris. Childebert ravages Clothar's territory as far as Rheims. 18. Duke Austrapius takes refuge in St. Martin's church in fear of Chramnus. Chramnus orders him to be starved in the church. But he obtains drink miraculously and is saved. He later become a priest. 19. Medard bishop of Soissons dies.]

20.

King Childebert fell ill and after being bedridden for a long time died at Paris. He was buried in the church of the blessed Vincent which he had built. King Clothar took his kingdom and : treasures and sent into exile Vulthrogotha and her two daughters. Chramnus presented himself before his father, but later he proved disloyal. And when he saw he could not escape punishment he fled to Brittany and there with his wife and daughters lived in concealment with Chonoober count of the Bretons. And Wilichar, his fatherinlaw, fled to the church of Saint Martin. Then because of Wilichar and his wife the holy church was burned for the sins of the people and the mockeries which occurred in it. This we relate not without a heavy sigh. Moreover the city of Tours had been burned the year before and all the churches built in it were deserted. Then by order of king Clothar the church of the blessed Martin was roofed with tin and restored in its former beauty. Then two hosts of locusts appeared which passed through Auvergne and Limousin and, they say, came to the plain of Romagnac where a battle took place between them and there was great destruction. Now king Clothar was raging against Chramnus and marched with army into Brittany against him. Nor was Chramnus afraid to come out against his father. And when both armies were gathered and encamped on the same plain and Chramnus with the Bretons had marshaled his line against his father, night fell and they refrained from fighting. During the night Chonoober, count of the Bretons, said to Chramnus: "I think it wrong for you to fight against your father; allow me tonight to rush upon him and destroy him with all his army." But Chramnus would not allow this to be done, being held back I think by the power of God. When morning came they set their armies in motion and hastened to the conflict. And king Clothar was marching like a new David to fight against Absalom his son crying aloud and saying: "Look down Lord, from heaven and judge my cause since I suffer wicked outrage from my son; look down, Lord, and judge justly, and give that judgment that thou once gavest between Absalom and his father. ' When they were fighting on equal terms the count of the Bretons fled and was slain. Then Chramnus started in flight, having ships in readiness at the shore; but in his wish to take his wife and daughters he was overwhelmed by his father's soldiers and was captured and bound fast. This news was taken to king Clothar and he gave orders to burn Chramnus with fire together with his wife and daughters. They were shut up in a hut belonging to a poor man and Chramnus was stretched on a bench and strangled with a towel; and later the hut was burned over them and he perished with his wife and daughters.

21.

In the fifty-first year of his reign king Clothar set out for the door of the blessed Martin with many gifts and coming to the tomb of the bishop just mentioned at Tours, and repeating all the deeds he had perhaps done heedlessly, and praying with loud groaning that the blessed confessor of God would obtain God's forgiveness for his faults and by his intercession blot out what he had done contrary to reason, he then returned, and in the fifty-first year of his reign, while hunting in the forest of Cuise, he was seized with a fever and returned thence to a villa in Compiègne There he was painfully harassed by the fever and said: "Alas! What do you think the king of heaven is like when he kills such great kings in this way? " Laboring under this pain he breathed his last, and his four sons carried him with great honor to Soissons and buried him in the church of St. Medard. He died the next day in the revolving year after Chramnus had been slain.

[**22.** The four sons of Clothar make "a lawful division" of his kingdom To Charibert is assigned Paris for his capital, to Gunthram, Orleans, to Chilperic, Soissons, to Sigibert, Rheims. **23.** The Huns attack Sigibert and Chilperic takes the opportunity to seize some of his cities. Sigibert recovers them.]

24.

When king Gunthram had taken his part of the realm like his brothers, he removed the patrician Agricola and gave the office of patrician to Celsus, a man of tall stature, strong shoulders, strong arms and boastful words, ready in retort and skilled in the law. And then such a greed for possessing came upon him that he often took the property of the churches and made it his own. Once when he heard a passage from the prophet Isaiah being read in the church, which says: "Woe to those who join house to house and unite field to field even to the boundaries of the place," he is said to have exclaimed: " It is out of place to say; woe to me and my sons." But he left a son who died without children and left the greater part of his property to the churches which his father had plundered.

25.

The good king Gunthram first took a concubine Veneranda, a slave belonging to one of his people, by whom he had a son Gundobad. Later he married Marcatrude, daughter of Magnar, and sent his son Gundobad to Orleans. But after she had a son Marcatrude was jealous, and proceeded to bring about Gundobad's death. She sent poison, they say, and poisoned his drink. And upon his death, by God's judgment she lost the son she had and incurred the hate of the king, was dismissed by him, and died not long after. After her he took Austerchild, also named Bobilla. : He had by her two sons, of whom the older was called Clothar and the younger Chlodomer.

26.

Moreover king Charibert married Ingoberga, by whom he had a daughter who afterwards married a husband in Kent and was taken there. At that time Ingoberga had in her service two daughters of a certain poor man, of whom the first was called Marcovefa, who wore the robe of a nun, and the other was Merofled. The king was very much in love with them. They were, as I have said, the daughters of a worker in wool. Ingoberga was jealous that they were loved by the king and secretly gave the father work to do, thinking that when the king saw this he would dislike his daughters. While he was working she called the king. He expected to see something strange, but only saw this man at a distance weaving the king's wool. Upon this he was angry and left Ingoberba and married Merofled. He also had another, a daughter of a shepherd, named Theodogild, by whom he is said to have had a son who when he came from the womb was carried at once to the grave. In this king's time Leontius gathered the bishops of his province at the city of Saintes and deposed Emeri from the bishopric, saying that this honor had not been given him in accordance with the canons. For he had had a decree of king Clothar that he should be ordained without the consent of the metropolitan who was not present. When he had been expelled from his office they made choice of Heraclius, then a priest of the church of Bordeaux, and they sent word of these doings in their own handwriting by the priest just named to king Charibert. He came to Tours and related to the blessed Eufronius what had been done, begging him to consent to subscribe to this choice. But the man of God flatly refused to do so. Now after the priest had come to the gates of the city of Paris and approached the king's presence he said: "Hail, glorious king. The apostolic see sends to your eminence the most abundant greetings." But the king replied: " You haven't been at Rome, have you, to bring us the greeting of the pope?" "It is your father Leontius" the priest went on, "who, together with the bishops of his province, sends you greeting and informs you that Cymulus-this was what they used to call Emeri as a child-has been expelled from the episcopate because he neglected the sacred authority of the canons and sought actively for the office of bishop in the city of Saintes. And so they have sent you their choice in order that his place may be filled, so that when men who violate the canons are condemned according to rule, the authority of your kingdom will be extended into distant ages." When he said this the king gnashed his teeth and ordered him to be dragged from his sight, and placed on a wagon covered with thorns and thrust off into exile, saying: "Do you think that there is no one left of the sons of king Clothar to uphold his father's acts, since these men have cast out without our consent the bisho whom he chose ? " And he at once sent men of religion and restored the bishop to his place, sending also certain of his officers of the treasury who exacted from bishop Leontius 1000 gold pieces and fined the other bishops up to the limit of their power of payment And so the insult to the prince was avenged. After this he married Marcovefa, sister of Merofled. For which reason they were both excommunicated by the holy bishop Germanus. But since the king did not wish to leave her, she was struck by a judgment of God and died. Not long after the king himself died. And after his death, Theodogild, one of his queens, sent messengers to king Gunthram offering herself in marriage to him. To which the king sent back this answer: "Let her not be slow to come to me with her treasures. For I will take her and make her great among the people, so that she will surely have greater honor with me than with my brother who has just died." And she was glad and gathered all together and set out to him. And the king seeing this said: " It is better for these treasures to be in my control than in the hands of this woman who has unworthily gone to my brother's bed." Then he took away much and left little, and sent her to a convent at Arles. But she took it very hard to be subject to fasts and watches, and made proposals to a Goth by secret messengers, .promising that if he would take her to Spain and marry her she would leave the monastery with her treasures and follow him willingly. This promise he made without hesitation, but when she had got her things together and packed and was ready to go from the convent, the diligence of the abbess frustrated her purpose, and the wicked project was detected and orders were given to beat t her severely and put her under guard. And she continued in confinement to the end of her life on earth, consumed with no slight passions.

27.

Now when king Sigibert saw that his brothers were taking wives unworthy of them, and to their disgrace were actually marrying slave women, he sent an embassy into Spain and with many gifts asked for Brunhilda, daughter of king Athanagild. She was a maiden beautiful in her person, lovely to look at, virtuous and wellbehaved, with good sense and a pleasant address. Her father did not refuse, but sent her to the king I have named with great treasures. And the king collected his chief men, made ready a feast, and took her as his wife amid great joy and mirth. And though she was a follower of the Arian law she was converted by the preaching of the bishops and the admonition of the king him self, and she confessed the blessed Trinity in unity, and believed and was baptized. And she still remains catholic in Christ's name.

28.

When Chilperic saw this, although he had already too many wives, he asked for her sister Galsuenda, promising through his ambassadors that he would abandon the others if he could only obtain a wife worthy of himself and the daughter of a king. Her father accepted these promises and sent his daughter with much wealth, as he had done before. Now Galsuenda was older than Brunhilda. And coming to king Chilperic she was received with great honor, and united to him in marriage, and she was also greatly loved by him. For she had brought great treasures. But because of his love of Fredegunda whom he had had before, there arose a great scandal which divided them. Galsuenda had already been converted to the catholic law and baptized. And complaining to the king that she was continually enduring outrages and had no honor with him, she asked to leave the treasures which she had brought with her and be permitted to go free to her native land. But he made ingenious pretenses and calmed her with gentle words. At length he ordered her to be strangled by a slave and found her dead on the bed. After he death God caused a great miracle to appear. For the lighted lamp which hung by a rope in front of her tomb broke the rope without being touched by anyone and dashed on the pavement and the hard pavement yielded under it and it went down as if into some soft substance and was buried to the middle but not at all damaged. Which seemed a great miracle to all who saw it. But when the king had mourned her death a few days, he married Fredegunda again. After this action his brothers thought that the queen mentioned above had been killed at his command, and they tried to expel him from the kingdom. Chilperic at that time had three sons by his former wife Audovera, namely Theodobert, whom we have mentioned above, Merovech and Clovis. But let us return to our task.

29.

The Huns were again endeavoring to make an entrance into the Gauls. Sigibert marched against them with his army, leading a great number of brave men. And when they were about to fight, the Huns, who were versed in magic arts, caused false appearances of various sorts to come before them and defeated them decisively. Sigibert's army fled, but he himself was taken by the Huns and would have remained a prisoner if he had not overcome by his skill in making presents the men whom he could not conquer in battle. He was a man of fine appearance and good address He gave gifts and entered into an agreement with their king that all the days of their lives they should fight no battles with one another. And this incident is rightly believed to be more to his credit than otherwise. The king of the Huns also gave many gifts to king Sigibert. He was called Gaganus. All the kings of that people are called by this name.

[30. King Sigibert attempts to take Arles from his brother Gunthram but fails.]

31.

Now a great prodigy appeared in the Gauls at the town of Tauredunum, situated on the river Rhone. After a sort of rumbling had continued for more than sixty days, the mountain was finally torn away and separated from another mountain near it, together with men, churches, property and houses, and fell into the river, and the banks of the river were blocked and the water flowed back. For that place was shut in on either side by mountains and the torrent flowed in a narrow way. It overflowed above and engulfed and destroyed all that was on the bank. Then the gathered water burst its way downstream and took men by surprise, as it had above, and caused a loss of life, overturned houses, destroyed beasts of burden, and overwhelmed with a sudden and violent flood all that was on the banks as far as the city of Geneva. It is told by many that the mass of water was so great that it went over the walls into the city mentioned. And there is no doubt of this tale because as we have said the Rhone flows in that region between mountains that hem it in closely, and being so closely shut in, it has no place to turn aside. It carried away the fragments of the mountain that had fallen and thus caused it to disappear wholly. And after this thirty monks came to the place where the town fell in ruins and began to dig in the ground which remained when the mountain had fallen, trying to find bronze and iron. And while engaged in this they heard a rumbling of the mountain like the former one. And while they were kept there by their greed the part of the mountain which had not yet fallen on them and covered and destroyed them and none of them was found. In like manner too before the plague at Clermont great prodigies terrified that region. For three or four great shining places frequently appeared about the sun and the rustics used to call them suns, saying: "Behold, three or four suns in the sky." Once on the first of October the sun was so darkened that not a quarter of it continued bright, but it looked hideous and discolored, about like a sack. Moreover a star which certain call a comet, with a ray like a sword, appeared over that country through a whole year, and the sky seemed to be on fire and many other signs were seen. In the church at Clermont while the morning watches were being observed at a certain festival, a bird of the kind we call lark entered, flapping its wings above the lights, and so swiftly extinguished them all that one would think they had been taken by the hand of a single man and plunged into water. The bird passed under the veil into the sanctuary and attempted to put out the light there but it was prevented from doing so by the doorkeepers and killed. In the church of the blessed Andrew another bird did the same with the lighted lamps. And presently the plague came, and such a carnage of the people took place through the whole district that the legions that fell could not be counted. For when sepulchers and gravestones failed, ten or more would be buried in a single trench. Three hundred dead bodies were counted one Sunday in the church of the blessed Peter alone. Death was sudden. A wound the shape of a serpent would appear on groin or armpit and the man would be so overcome by the poison as to die on the second or third day. Moreover the power of the poison rendered the victim insensible. At that time Cato the priest died. For when many had fled from the plague he never left the place, but remained courageously burying the people and celebrating mass. He was a priest of great kindliness and a warm friend of the poor. And if he had some pride, thus virtue I think counterbalanced it. But the bishop Cautinus, after running from place to place in fear of this plague, returned to the city, caught it and died on the day before Passion Sunday. At that very hour too, Tetradius his cousin died. At that time Lyons, Bourges, Cahors, and Dijon were seriously depopulated from this plague.

[32. The remarkable virtue of the priest Julian. 33. The good abbot and the warning he received to be more severe with his monks]

34. I will relate what happened at that time in a certain monastery, but I do not wish to give the name of the monk, who is still alive, for fear that when this account comes to him he may become vainglorious and lose merit. A young man came to the monastery and presented himself to the abbot with the proposal to pass his life in God's service. The abbot made many objections, explaining that the service there was hard, and he could never accomplish what was required of him. But he promised that he would call on the Lord's name and accomplish it all. And so he was admitted by the abbot. After a few days during which he proved to all that he was humble and holy, it happened that the monks threw out of the granary about three *chori* of grain and left it to dry in the sun and appointed this monk to guard it. And while the others were taking refreshment and he was left to guard the grain, the sky suddenly became overcast, and a heavy rain with roaring wind came swiftly in the direction of the heap of grain. Upon seeing it the monk knew not how to act or what to do. He thought however that even if he called the rest considering the great quantity of grain they would not be able to store it in the granary before the rain, and so giving up everything else he devoted himself to prayer, beseeching the Lord not to allow a drop of the rain to fall on the wheat. And when he threw himself on the ground and prayed the cloud was divided, and although there was a heavy downpour all arond, if it is right to say so, it did not dampen a single grain of the wheat. And when the other monks and the abbot became aware of the coming storm they came quickly to

take the grain within, and saw this miracle, and looking for the man in charge of the grain they found him close by stretched out on the sand praying The abbot on seeing this prostrated himself close to him, and when the rain had passed and the prayer was finished he called to him to arise, and gave orders to seize him and punish him with stripes, saying: "My son, you must grow in the fear and service of God with humility, and not be puffed up with prodigies and miracles." He ordered him to remain shut up in his cell seven days, and to fast as if he were at fault, in order to keep vainglory from forming an obstacle before him. At the present time, as we learn from men of the faith, the same monk is so abstemious that he eats no bread in the forty days of Lent and drinks only a cup of barley-water every third day. And may the Lord with your prayers deign to keep him as is pleasing to himself until his life is ended.

[**35.** The priest Eufrasius and the archdeacon Avitus are candidates for the bishopric of Auvergne. The former Gregory describes in these words: "He was indeed a man of refined manners, but his acts were not virtuous and he often made the barbarians drunk and rarely helped the needy." **36.** Nicetius succeeds Sacerdos as bishop of Lyons. He is succeeded in turn by the wicked Priscus. **37.** Death of the holy Friard. **38.** Leuva and Leuvield, kings of Spain. The latter slew "all who had been accustomed to kill the kings." **39.** Palladius and Parthenius, respectively count and bishop of Gévaudan, quarrel. Palladius accuses the bishop of unnatural crime; he is removed and Romanus becomes count.]

39.

... It happened that one day Palladius and Romanus met in Clermont, and in their dispute about the office of count Palladius was told that he was going to be put to death by king Sigibert. However the story was false, and was ascertained to have been put in circulation principally by Romanus. Then Palladius was terrified and reduced to such despair that he threatened to kill himself with his own hand. And although he was carefully watched by his mother and his kinsmen, to prevent the deed which he had conceived in the bitterness of his heart, he escaped from his mother's sight for a short time and went into his chamber where he could be alone, unsheathed his sword, and putting his feet on the crosshilt of the sword he put its point at his breast and pushed on the sword from above, and it entered at one of his breasts and came out at the shoulderblade, and raising himself up a second time he thrust himself in like manner in the other breast and fell dead. I regard this deed with astonishment since it could not have been done without the help of the devil. For the first wound would have killed him if the devil had not supported him so that he could accomplish his wicked purpose. His mother rushed in half dead with alarm, and fell in a faint on the body of the son she had lost, and the whole household uttered cries of lamentation. Nevertheless he was carried to the monastery of Cournon and buried there, but without being placed near the bodies of Christians or receiving the solemn service of the mass. And this evidently happened to him for nothing else than his insult to the bishop.

[**40.** Justin, a man of many vices, succeeds the emperor Justinian. He associates with himself Tiberius "who was just, charitable, a discerner of the right and winner of victories and - a feature that surpasses all other excellences - a most orthodox Christian.]

41.

Albin, king of the Lombards, who had married Chlotsinda, daughter of king Clothar, abandoned his country and set out for t Italy with all the Lombard people. They put their army in motion and went with their wives and children, purposing to remain t there. They entered the country and spent seven years chiefly in wandering through it, despoiling the churches, killing the bishops, and bringing the land under their control. When his wife Chlotsinda died,

Albin married another wife whose father he had killed :. a short time before. For this reason the woman always hated her husband and awaited an opportunity to avenge the wrong done her father, and so it happened that she fell in love with one of the household slaves and poisoned her husband. When he died she went off with the slave but they were overtaken and put to death together. Then the Lombards chose another king over them.

42.

Eunius, who was also named Mummulus, was made patrician by king Gunthram. I think that certain details should be given as to the beginning of his military service. He was a son of Peonius and native of the city of Auxerre. Peonius governed this town as count. And when he had sent gifts to the king by his son to secure reappointment, the son gave his father's presents and asked for his father's office, and took his place when he should have helped him. From this start he gradually rose and attained a greater prominence. And upon the invasion of the Gauls by the Lombards the patrician Amatus, who had lately succeeded Celsus, went against them and engaged in battle, but was defeated and slain. And it is said that the slaughter of the Burgundians by the Lombards was so great on that occasion that the slain could not be counted. And the Lombards loaded with plunder departed again for Italy. And upon their departure Eunius, also named Murmmulus, was summoned by the king and raised to the high office of patrician. When the Lombards made a second inroad into the Gauls and came as far as *Mustiœ Calmes* near the city of Embrun, Mummulus set his army in motion and came to that place with the Burgundians. He surrounded the Lombards with his army and made an abattis and attacked them in pathless woods, and killing many took a number of captives whom he sent to the king. The king ordered them to be kept under guard in various places through the country, but a few in one way or another escaped and took the news to their native land. There were present in this battle Salonius and Sagittarius, brothers and.bishops, who armed themselves-not 'with the cross of heaven but with the worldly helmet and what is worse, are reported to have killed many with their own hands. This was Mummulus' first victory. Then the Saxons, who had entered Italy with the Lombards, made a second expedition into the Gauls, and pitched camp in the territory of Riez, that is, near the village of Estoublon, scattering from there among the villages belonging to neighboring cities, taking booty, leading off captives and laying all waste. When Mummulus learned of this he set his army in motion and attacked them, killing many thousands, and he did not cease to cut them down until evening when night made an end. For he had taken them off their guard when they expected nothing of what happened. In the morning the Saxons marshaled their army and made ready for battle, but messengers passed from one army to the other and they made peace. They gave presents to Mummolus, and surrendered all the plunder of the region with the captives, and departed after taking oath that they would return to the Gauls in obedience to the kings and as allies to the Franks. And so the Saxons returned to Italy, and taking their wives and little ones and all their possessions undertook the return journey into the Gauls with the intention of presenting themselves to king Sigibert and establishing themselves again in the district which they had left. They formed two wedges *[cunios]* as they call them; and one came by way of Nice and the other by Embrun, keeping in fact to the road they had come the previous year, and the two divisions united the territory of Avignon. It was then harvest time, and that country had its crops chiefly in the open fields and the inhabitants had not stored any of them. When the Saxons came they divided the crops among them and gathered and threshed the grain and used it, leaving nothing to those who had done the work. But after the harvest had been used up and they came to the shore of the river Rhone in order to cross the torrent and present themselves in the kingdom of king Sigibrt, Mummolus met them and said: "You shall not cross this torrent. Behold, you have devastated the land of my lord the king, you have gathered the crops, plundered the herds, burned the houses, cut down the olive groves and vineyards. You shall not go up unless you first satisfy those whom you have left in want;

otherwise you shall not escape my hands, but I shall draw my sword against you and your wives and little ones and avenge the wrong done to my lord king Gunthram." Then they were very much afraid and gave many thousand pieces of coined gold as a ransom, and were allowed to cross, and thus they came to Clermont. It was then springtime. They brought there pieces of bronze engraved like gold, and any one seeing them would have no doubt that it was gold tested and weighed for it was colored by some device or other. And a good many were deceived by the false appearance and gave gold and received bronze and became poor. And they went on to king Sigibert and ere settled in the land they had left.

[**43**. Albinus, governor of Provence, seizes archdeacon Virgilius on Christmas day in the church for failing to punish his men; Albinus is fined. **44**. Three Lombard chiefs invade Gaul but are defeated and driven back into Italy by Mummolus. **45**. Mummolus recovers Tours and Poitiers for Sigibert from Chilperic.]

46.

As I am about to speak of the death of Andarchius, it seems best to tell first of his birth and native place. He was a slave of the senator Felix as they say, and being assigned to attend is young master he entered with him upon the study of letters and became distinguished for his learning. For he was fully instructed in the works of Virgil, the books of the Theodosian law, and the art of calculation. Being puffed up with such knowledge he began to hold his masters in contempt, and devoted himself to the service of duke Lupus when he went to the city of Marseille by order of king Sigibert. When Lupus left Marseilles he told Andarchius to go with him and secured for him the favor of king Sigibert and put him at his service. And Sigibert sent him to various places and gave him an opportunity for military service Being held in a sort of honor because of this he came to Clermont and there entered into friendship with Ursus, a citizen of the city Then being of an ambitious temper he wished to be betrothed to Ursus' daughter, and concealed a coat of mail, as they tell, in a chest in which documents used to be kept, and said to Ursus' wife: "I give in your care a multitude of gold pieces, more than sixteen thousand, which I have placed in this chest, and it shall be yours if you will cause your daughter to be betrothed to me." "To what do you not drive the hearts of men, accursed greed for gold? The woman believed him without reserve and in her husband's absence agreed to betroth the girl to him. He went back to the king and brought an order to the judge of the place commanding him to marry this girl, saying: "I paid the earnest money at the betrothal." But Ursus denied it saying: "I do not know who you are and I have none of your property." When the quarrel continued and grew hotter Andarchius had Ursus summoned to the presence of the king. And coming to the village of Braine he found another man named Ursus whom he caused to be taken secretly to the altar and to swear and say: "By this holy place and the relics of the blessed martyrs I will not delay in paying you the sixteen thousand *solidi*, since I am not to give my daughter in marriage to you." Now witnesses were standing in the sanctuary listening secretly to what was said but not seeing the person who spoke. Then Andarchius soothed Ursus with gentle words and caused him to return to his native place without seeing the king After this he made an oath and when Ursus went away he produced before the king a document containing the oath and said: "Such and such is the writing I have from Ursus, and therefore I request an order from your glory that he give his daughter to me in marriage. Otherwise let me have authority to take his possessions until I receive sixteen thousand *solidi* and am satisfied in this case " Then he received the order and returned to Clermont and showed the judge the king's order. Ursus retired into the territory of Velay. And when his property was turned over to Andarchius he also went to Velay, and going into one of Ursus' houses he bade them prepare supper for him and heat water for bathing. And when the slaves of the household did not obey their new master, he beat some with clubs, others with switches, and struck some on head, drawing blood. The whole household was in confusion but the supper was prepared; he bathed in hot water, became drunk with wine and stretched himself on his couch. He had only seven slaves with him. And when they were sound asleep, weighed down by drowsiness not less than by wine, the household was gathered together, and Ursus closed the doors of the house which were made of wooden boards. He took the keys and tore down the stacks of grain near by and heaped piles of the grain which was then in the sheaf around and above the house until it was seen that the house was entirely covered. Then he set fire to in different places and when the burning timbers of the building were falling on the luckless ones they awoke and began to shout but there was no one to listen to them and the whole house was burned and the fire consumed all alike. Ursus fled in fear to the church of St. Julian, and after making presents to the king he received again a good title to his property.

[**47.** Civil war between Chilperic and Sigibert " There was at that time a worse outcry among the churches than in the time of Diocletian's persecution." **48.** The wickedness of the people of Gaul as compared to earlier times; the plundering of the monastery of Latta **49.** The civil war is continued. Sigibert forces Chilperic to restore his cities. **50.** Chilperic shuts himself up in Tournai.]

51.

In that year lightning was seen to traverse the sky as once we saw before the death of Clothar. Now Sigibert took the cities this side of Paris and marched as far as Rouen, wishing to destroy these same cities with his army. But he was prevented from doing so by his own people. He returned thence and entered Paris. And there Brunhilda came to him with her children. Then the Franks who had once looked to the older Childebert, sent an embassy to Sigibert that if he would come to them they would abandon Chilperic and make him king over them. On hearing this he sent men to besiege his brother in the city mentioned above, and he himself purposed to hasten thither. And, the holy bishop Germanus said to him, "If you go and do not purpose to kill your brother you shall return alive and victorious; but if you have another purpose in mind you shall die. For thus said the Lord through Solomon: 'You who prepare a pit for your brother shall fall into it.' But because of his wickedness he failed to pay heed. And when he came to the village named Vitry, all the army was gathered about him, and they placed him on a shield and made him king over them. Then two slaves who had been placed under a charm by Queen Fredegunda, carrying strong knives with poisoned blades - of the sort commonly called *scramasaxi* - approached him on some pretext and stabbed him one on each side. He cried aloud and fell and died in a short time. At the same time Charigysel, his chamberlain, was slain and Sigila who came from the land of the Goths was seriously wounded. He was afterwards seized by King Chilperic and met a cruel death, every joint being burned with white-hot irons and his limbs being torn one from the other. Charigysel was both fickle and avaricious. He had risen from a lowly place and become great with the king by flattery. He was a man who grasped other men's property, and was a breaker of wills, and the end of his life was such that he did not succeed in making his own will when death threatened, he who had so often destroyed the wills of others.

Chilperic was in suspense and did not know whether he should escape or perish, when messengers came to him to tell of his brother's death. Then he left Tournai with his wife and children and clothed Sigibert and buried him in the village of Lambres. Whence he was later transferred to Soissons to the church of the holy Medard which he had built, and was buried there by the side of his father Clothar. He died in the fourteenth year of his reign, the fortieth of his life. From the death of Theodobert the elder to that of Sigibert twenty-nine years are included, and there were eighteen days between his death and that of his nephew Theodobert. Upon the death of Sigibert, Childebert his son reigned in his place.

From the beginning to the flood there were 2242 years; from the flood to Abraham 942 years; from Abraham to the going out of the children of Israel from Egypt 462 years; from the going of the children of Israel from Egypt to the building of the temple of Solomon 480 years; from the building of the temple to its desolation and the migration to Babylon 390 years; from the migration to passion of the Lord 668 years; from the passion of the Lord to the death of St. Martin 412 yers; from the death of St. Martin to the death of King Clovis 112 years; from the death of King Clovis to the death of Theodobert 37 years; from the death of Theodobert to the death of Sigibert 29 years. Which make a total of 5774 years. [*note: =590AD*]

HERE ENDS THE FOURTH BOOK.

BOOK V

HERE BEGIN THE CHAPTERS OF THE FIFTH BOOK

50. Prediction of the blessed Salvius about Chilperic.

HERE END THE CHAPTERS

HERE BEGINS THE FIFTH BOOK WITH HAPPY AUSPICES. AMEN

I am weary of relating the details of the civil wars that mightily plague the nation and kingdom of the Franks; and the worst of it is that we see in them the beginning of that time of woe which the Lord foretold: "Father shall rise against son, son against father, brother against brother, kinsman against kinsman." They should have been deterred by the examples of former kings who slain by their enemies as soon as they were divided. How often has the very city of cities, the great capital of the whole earth, been laid low by civil war and again, when it ceased, has risen as if from the ground! Would that you too, O kings, were engaged in battles like those in which your fathers struggled, that the heathen terrified by your union might be crushed by your strength ! Remember how Clovis won your great victories, how he slew opposing kings, crushed wicked peoples and subdued their lands, and left to you complete and unchallenged dominion over them! And when he did this he had neither silver nor gold such as you now have in your treasuries. What is your object ? What do you seek after?' What have you not in plenty? In your homes there are luxuries in abundance, in your storehouses wine, grain and oil abound, gold and silver are piled up in your treasuries. One thing you lack: without peace you have not the grace of God. Why does one take from another? Why does one desire what another has? I beg of you, beware of this saying of the apostle: "But if ye bite and devour one another, take heed that ye be not consumed one of another." ~ Examine carefully the books of the ancients and you will see what civil wars beget. Read what Orosius writes of the Carthaginians, who says that after seven hundred years their city and country were ruined and adds: "What preserved this city so long? Union. What destroyed it after such a period? Disunion." Beware of disunion, beware of civil wars which destroy you and your people. What else is to be expected but that your army will fall and that you will be left without strength and be crushed and ruined by hostile peoples. And, king, if civil war gives you pleasure, govern that impulse which the apostle says is urgent within man, let the spirit struggle against the flesh and the vices fall before the virtues; and be free and serve your chief who is Christ, you who were once a fettered slave of the root of evil.

[1. Sigibert's son, Childebert, not yet five years old, is made king. Chilperic seizes Brunhilda and keeps her in exile at Rouen.]

2.

Chilperic sent his son Merovech to Poitiers with an army. But he disobeyed his father's orders and came to Tours and spent there the holy days of Easter. His army did great damage to that district. Merovech himself in pretense that he wanted to go to see his mother went to Rouen and there met queen Brunhilda and married her. Upon news of this Chilperic became very bitter because Merovech had married his uncle's widow contrary to divine law and the canons, and quicker than speech he hastened to the above mentioned city. But when they learned that he was determined to separate them they took refuge in the church of St. Martin that is built of boards upon the wall of the city. But when the king on his arrival strove to entice them thence by many artifices and they refused to trust him, thinking that he was acting treacherously, he took oath to them, saying: "If it was the will of God, he himself would not attempt to separate them." They accepted this oath and came out of the church and Chilperic kissed them and gave them a fitting welcome and feasted with them. But after a few days he returned to Soissons, taking Merovech with him.

[3. Godin makes an attack on Chilperic's territory but is defeated. Chilperic suspects Merovech of being involved in the attack. Godin's wife after his death marries a notorious character, Rauching.]

3. Godins's wife married Rauching, a man full of every vanity, swollen with haughtiness, wanton pride, who treated those under him in such a way that one could not perceive that he had any human feeling in him, and he vented his rage on his own people beyond the limits of human wickedness and folly and committed unspeakable wrongs. For whenever a slave held a candle for him at dinner, as the custom is, he would make him bare his legs and hold the candle against them until it went out; when it was lighted he would do the same thing again until the legs of the slave who held the candle were burned all over. And if he uttered a cry or tried to move from that place to another a naked sword at once threatened him, and when he wept Rauching could scarcely contain himself for delight. Certain ones tell the story that two of his slaves at that time loved one another, namely, a man and a maid - a thing that often happens. And when this love had lasted a space of two years or more, they were united together and took refuge in the church. When Rauching found it out he went to the bishop of the place and demanded that his slaves be returned to him at once, and said they would not be punished. Then the bishop said to him: "You know what respect should I be paid to the churches of God; you cannot take them unless you give a pledge of their permanent union, and likewise proclaim that they shall remain free from every bodily punishment." When he had continued silent for a long time in doubtful thought, he finally turned to the bishop and placed his hands on the altar and swore, saying: "They shall never be parted by me but I will rather cause them to continue in this union permanently, because although it is annoying to me that this was done without my consent, still I welcome this feature of it, that he has not married a maid belonging to another nor she another's slave." The bishop in a simplehearted say believed the crafty fellow's promise and restored the slaves under the promise that they would not be punished. Rauching took them and thanking the bishop went home. He at once directed a tree to be cut down and the trunk cut off close to the ranches and split with wedges and hollowed out. He ordered the earth to be dug to a depth of three or four feet and half the trunk put in the trench. Then he placed the maid there as if she were dead and ordered them to throw the man in on top. And he put the covering on and filled the trench and buried them alive, saying: "I have not broken my oath that they should never be separated." When this was reported to the bishop he ran swiftly, and fiercely rebuking the man he finally succeeded in having them uncovered. However it was only the man who was alive when dragged out; he found the girl suffocated. In such actions Rauching showed himself very wicked, having no other aptitude except in loud laughter and trickery and every perversity. Therefore he justly met a I fitting death since he so behaved himself when he enjoyed this y life; but I shall tell of this later.

4.

In these days Roccolenus being sent by Chilperic came to Tours with great boasting and pitching camp beyond the Loire he sent messengers to us that we ought to drag from the holy church Gunthram, who was at that time wanted for the death of Theodobert; if we would not do it he would give orders to burn the city with fire and all its suburbs. On hearing this we sent messengers to him saying that what he asked to have done had not been done from ancient time; moreover the holy church could not now be violated; if it should be, it would not be well for him or for the king who had given this command; let him rather stand in awe of the holiness of the bishop whose power only the day before had given strength to paralytic limbs. But he had no fear of such words and while he was dwelling in a house belonging to the church beyond the river Loire he tore down the house itself which had been built with nails. The people of Mans who had come on that occasion with him carried the nails off, filling their bags, and they destroyed the grain and laid everything waste. But while Roccolenus was engaged on this he was struck by God, and becoming saffron color from the royal disease he sent harsh commands saying: "Unless you cast duke Gunthram out of the church today I will destroy every green thing around the city so that the country will be ready for the plow. [*note: Cf.* ad aratrum reducere, *to ravage thoroughly.*] Meantime the sacred day of Epiphany came and he began to be in greater and greater torture. Then after taking counsel with his people he crossed the river and approached the city. And when [the clergy] were hastening from the cathedral to the holy church singing psalms, he rode on horseback behind the cross, preceded by his standards. But when he entered the holy church his rage and threats cooled and going back to the cathedral he could take no food on that day. Then being very short of breath he departed for Poitiers. Now these were the days of I holy Lent during which he often ate young rabbits. And after setting for the first of March the actions by which he meant to ruin and fine the citizens of Poitiers, he rendered up his life on the preceding day; and so his pride and insolence ceased.

5.

At that time Felix bishop of Nantes wrote me a letter full of insults writing also that my brother had been slain because he had killed a bishop, being himself greedy for the bishopric. But the reason Felix wrote this was because he wanted an estate belonging to the church. And when I would not give it he was full of rage and vented on me, as I have said, a thousand insults. I finally replied to him: "Remember the words of the prophet 'Woe unto them that join house to house, that lay field to field! They are not going to inhabit the earth alone, are they? ' I wish you had been bishop of Marseilles ! For ships would never have brought oil or other goods there, but only paper that you might have greater opportunity for writing to defame honest men. It is the scarcity of paper that sets a limit to your wordiness." He was a man of unlimited greed and boastfulness. Now I shall pass over these matters, not to appear like him, and merely tell how my brother passed from the light of day and how swift a vengeance the Lord visited upon his assassin. The blessed Tetricus [*note: Great uncle to Gregory on his mother's side*], bishop of the church of Langres, who was already growing old, expelled the deacon Lampadio from his place as procurator, and my brother in his desire to aid the poor men whom Lampadio had wickedly despoiled, joined in bringing about his humiliation and thus incurred his hatred. Meantime the blessed Tetricus had an apoplectic stroke. And when the poultices of the doctors did him no good, au the clergy were disquieted, and seeing they were bereft of their shepherd they asked for Monderic. The king granted their request and he was given the tonsure and ordained bishop with the understanding that while the blessed Tetricus lived he should govern the town of Tonnerre as archpriest and dwell there, and when his predecessor died he should succeed him. But while he lived in the town he incurred the king's anger. For it was charged against him that he had furnished supplies and made gifts to king Sigibert when he was marching against his brother Gunthram. And so he was dragged from the town and thrust off into exile on the bank of the Rhone in a certain tower that was very small and had lost its roof. Here he lived for nearly two years to his great hurt, and then through the intercession of the blessed bishop Nicetius he returned to Lyons and dwelt with him for two months. But since he could not prevail on the king to restore him to the place from which he had been expelled he fled in the night and passed over to Sigibert's kingdom and was made bishop of the village of Arisitum with fifteen parishes more or less under him. These the Goths had held at first, and now Dalmatius, bishop of Rodez, judges them. When he went away the people of Langres again requested as bishop, Silvester, a kinsman of ours and of the blessed Tetricus. Now they asked for him at the instigation of my brother Meantime the blessed Tetricus passed away and Silvester received the tonsure and was ordained priest and took the whole authority over the property of the church. And he made preparations to go and receive the blessing of the bishops at Lyons. While this was going on he was stricken by an attack of epilepsy, having been long a victim of the disease, and being more cruelly bereft of his senses than before he kept continually uttering a moaning cry for two days and on the third day breathed his last. After this Lampadius who had lost his position and his means as is described above, united with Silvester's son in hatred of Peter the deacon, plotting and asserting that his father had been killed by Peter's evil arts. Now the son being young and light-minded was aroused against him, accusing him in public of murder. Upon hearing this Peter carried his case before the holy bishop Nicetius, my mother's uncle, and went to Lyons and there in the presence of bishop Siagrius and many other bishops as well as secular princes he cleared himself by oath of ever having had any part in Silvester's death. But two years later, being urged to it again by Lampadius, Silvester's son followed Peter the deacon on the road and killed him with a lance wound. When the deed was done Peter was taken from that place and carried to the town of Dijon and buried beside the holy Gregory, our greatgrandfather. But Silvester's son fled and passed over to king Chilperic, leaving his property to the treasury of king Gunthram. And when he was wandering through distant parts because of the crime he had committed, and there was no safe place for him to dwell in, at length, I suppose, innocent blood called upon the divine power against him and when he was traveling in a certain place he drew his sword and slew a man who had done him no harm. And the man's kinsmen, filled with grief at the death of their relative, roused the people, and drawing their swords they cut him in pieces and scattered him limb by limb. Such a fate did the wretch meet by God's just judgment, so that he who slew the innocent kinsman should not himself liv longer in guilt. Now this happened to him in the third year.

After Silvester's death the people of Langres again demanded a bishop, and received Pappolus who had once been archdeacon at Autun. According to report he did many wicked deeds, which are omitted by us that we should not seem to be disparagers of our brethren. However, I shall not fail to mention what this end was. In the eighth year of his episcopate, while he was making the round of the parishes and domains of the church, one night as he slept the blessed Tetricus appeared to him with threatening face and said:: "What are you doing here, Pappolus? Why do you pollute my .see? Why do you invade my church? Why do you so scatter the flock that was put in my charge? Yield your place, leave the see, go far from this territory." And so speaking he struck the rod he had in his hand sharply against Pappolus' breast. Upon this Pappolus woke up and while he was thinking what this meant a sharp pang darted in that place and he was tortured with the keenest pain. He loathed food and drink and awaited the approach of death. Why more? He died on the third day with a rush of blood from the mouth. Then he was carried forth and buried at Langres. In his place the abbot Mummolus, called also Bonus, was made bishop. To him many give great praise: that he is chaste, sober, moderate, very ready for every goodness, a friend of justice and a zealous lover of charity. When he took the bishopric he perceived that Lampadius had taken much of the church property by fraud, and by spoiling the poor had gathered lands, vineyards and slaves, and he ordered him to be stripped of all and driven out from his presence. He now lives in the greatest want and gets his living by his own hands. Let this be enough on these.

6.

In the same year as that mentioned above, that is, the year in which Sigibert died and Childebert his son began to reign, many miracles were done at the tomb of the blessed Martin which I have described in the books I have attempted to compose about these miracles. And though my speech is unpolished I have still not allowed the things that I saw with my own eyes or learned from trustworthy persons to pass unknown. Here I shall relate merely what happens to the heedless who after a miracle from heaven have sought for earthly cures, because his power is shown in the punishment of fools just as much as in the gracious working of cures. Leonastis, archdeacon of Bourges, lost his sight through cataracts that grew over his eyes. And when he altogether failed to recover it by going around among many physicians, he came to the church of St. Martin and remaining here for two or three months and fasting continuously he prayed to recover his sight. And when the festival came his eyes brightened and he began to see. He returned home and summoned a certain Jew and applied cupping glasses to his shoulders by the help of which he was to increase his eyesight. But as the blood flowed his blindness revived again. When this happened he again returned to the holy temple. And remaining there again a long time he did not succeed in recovering t his sight. Which I think was refused because of his sin, according to the words of the Lord: "For whosoever hath, to him shall be given, and he shall have abundance; but whosoever hath not, from him shall be taken away even that which he hath." "Behold thou art made whole; sin no more lest a worse thing befall thee." For he would have continued in health if he had not brought in the Jew in addition to the divine miracle. For such is the warning and reproof of the apostle saying: "Be not yoked with unbelievers. For what fellowship have righteousness and iniquity? Or what communion hath light with darkness? And what concord hath Christ with Belial? Or what portion hath a believer with an unbeliever? And what agreement hath a temple of God with idols ? For you are a temple of the living God. Therefore come ye out from among them and be ye separate, saith the Lord." Therefore let this case teach every Christian that when he has merit to receive heavenly medicine he should not seek after earthly help

[7. Death of the priest Senoch, one "of the tribe of Theifali." 8. Germanus, bishop of Paris, dies. As he is taken to be buried his body bears heavily down on the street when the prisoners raise a cry and when they are released it is easily taken up again." 9. The recluse Caluppa dies. 10. The recluse Patroclus dies. He was very abstemious and "always wore a hair shirt next his body." "His eyes never grew dim."]

11.

And since our God always deigns to give glory to his bishops, I shall relate what happened to the Jews in Clermont this year. Although the blessed bishop Avitus often urged them to put aside the veil of the Mosaic law and interpret the Scriptures in their spiritual sense, and with pure hearts contemplate in the sacred writings Christ, son of the living God, promised on the authority of prophets and kings, there remained in their hearts, I will not now call it the veil which dimmed the light for Moses face, but a wall. The bishop prayed also that they should be converted to the Lord and that the veil of the letter should be torn from them, and one of them asked to be baptized on holy Easter, and being born again in God by the sacrament of baptism, in his white garments he joined the whiteclad procession with the others. When the people were going in through the gate of the city one of the Jews, urged to it by the devil, poured stinking oil on the head of the converted Jew. And when all the people, horrified at this, wished to stone him, the bishop would not allow it. But on the blessed day on which the Lord ascends to heaven in glory after the redemption of man, when the bishop was walking in procession from the cathedral to the church singing psalms, a multitude of those who followed rushed upon the synagogue of the Jews and destroying it from the foundations they leveled it to the ground. On another day the bishop sent messengers to them saying: "I do not compel you by force to confess the Son of God, but nevertheless I preach him and I offer to your hearts the salt of wisdom. I am the shepherd put in charge of the Lord's sheep, and as regards you, the true Shepherd who suffered for us said that he had other sheep which are not in his sheepfold but which should be brought in, so that there may be one flock and one shepherd. And therefore if you are willing to believe as I, be one flock with me as your guardian; but if not, depart from the place." Now they continued a long time in turmoil and doubt and on the third day because of the prayers of the bishop, as I suppose, they met together and sent word to him saying; "We believe in Jesus, son of the living God, promised to us by the words of the prophets, and therefore we ask that we be purified by baptism and remain no longer in this guilt." The bishop was rejoiced at the news and keeping watch through the night of holy pentecost went out to the baptistery beyond the walls and there the whole multitude prostrated themselves before I him and begged for baptism. And he wept for joy, and cleansing all with water he anointed them with ointment and gathered them in i: the bosom of the mother church. Candles were lit, lamps burned brightly, the whole city was whitened with the white throng and the joy was as great as once Jerusalem saw when the holy spirit ! descended on the apostles. The baptized were more than five hundred. But those who refused baptism left that city and returned I turned to Marseilles.¶

[12. The abbot Brachio, a Thuringian and formerly a hunter dies. 13. Great battle between Chilperic's duke, Desiderius, and Gunthram's patrician, Mummolus. Desiderius is defeated.]¶

14.

After this Merovech, who was kept in custody by his father received the tonsure, and changing his garments for those which it is customary for the clergy to wear he was ordained priest and sent to the monastery at Mans called Anninsola [Saint-Calais] to be instructed in the duties of priests. Hearing this Gunthram Boso who was then living in the church of St. Martin, as we have stated sent the subdeacon Rigulf to advise him secretly to take refuge in the church of St. Martin. And when Merovech was on his way, Galen his slave went to meet him from the other side. And since his escort was not a strong one he was rescued by Galen on the way, and covering his head and putting on secular clothes he took refuge in the temple of the blessed Martin. We were celebrating mass in the holy church when he entered, finding the door open. After the mass he asked us to give him the consecrated bread. Now there was with us at that time Ragnemodus, bishop of the see of Paris, who had succeeded the holy Germanus; and when we refused, Merovech began to raise a disturbance and to say that we did not rightly suspend him from the communion without the assent of our brethren. When he said this we examined the case in the light of canon law, and with the consent of the brother who was present he received the consecrated bread from us. I was afraid that if I suspended one from communion I would become a slayer of many. For he threatened to kill some of our people if he did not receive the communion from us. The country of ours has sustained many disasters on this account. In these days Nicetius, my niece's husband, went with our deacon to king Chilperic on business of his own, and he told the king of Merovech's flight On seeing them queen Fredegunda said: "They are spies and have come to learn what the king is doing, in order to know what to report to Merovech." And she at once ordered them to be spoiled and thrust off into exile, from which they were released in the seventh month. Now Chilperic sent messengers to us saying: "Cast that apostate out of the church. If you don't I will burn that whole country with fire." And when we wrote back that it was impossible that what had not happened in the time of the heretics should now happen in Christian times, he set his army in motion and sent it toward this country.

In the second year of king Childebert, when Merovech saw that his father was set in this purpose, he proposed to take with him duke Gunthram and go to Brunhilda, saying: "Far be it from me that the church of the master Martin should submit to outrage on my account, or his country be put into captivity for me." And going into the church and keeping watch he offered the things he had with him on the tomb of the blessed Martin, praying to the saint to help him and to grant him his favor so that he could take the kingdom. At that time count Leudast after setting many traps for him out of love for Fredegunda, at last craftily entrapped his slaves who had gone out into the country and slew them with the sword, and he desired to slay Merovech himself if he could find him in a suitable place. But Merovech followed Gunthram's advice and, desiring to avenge himself, he ordered Marileif the chief physician to be seized as he was returning from the king's presence, and after beating him most cruelly he took away the gold and silver and other valuables which he had with him and left him naked, and would have killed him if he had not escaped from the hands of those who were beating him and taken refuge in the church. And later we clothed him and having obtained his life sent him back to Poitiers. Now Merovech charged many crimes to his father and stepmother. But although they were partly true it was not acceptable to God I suppose that they should be made known through a son. This I learned to be so later on. For one day I was invited to dine with him and when we were sitting together he begged urgently that something be read for the instruction of his soul. So I opened the book of Solomon and took the first verse that came which contained the following: " The eye of him who looketh at his father askance, the ravens of the valleys shall pick it out." Although he did not understand it, I believed that this verse had been given by the Lord. Then Gunthram sent a slave to a certain woman known to him from the time of king Charibert, who had a familiar spirit, in order that she should relate what was to happen. He asserted besides that she had foretold to him the time, not only the year but also the day and hour, at which king Charibert was to die. And she sent back this answer by the slaves: " King Chilperic will die this year and king Merovech will exclude his brothers and take the whole kingdom. And you shall hold the office of duke over all his kingdom for five years. But in the sixth year you shall win the honor of the bishop's office, with the consent of the people, in a city which lies on the river Loire on its right bank, and you shall pass from this world old and full of days. " And when the slaves had come back and reported this to their master he was at once filled with vanity as if he were already sitting In the chair of the church of Tours, and he reported the words to me. But I laughed at his folly and said: "It is from God that this should be sought; what the devil promises is not to be believed. He went off in confusion and I had a hearty laugh at the man who thought such things credible. At length one night when the watch was being kept in the church of the holy bishop and I had lain down and fallen asleep on my bed, I saw an angel flying through the air. And when he passed the holy church he cried in a loud voice: "Alas. Alas. God has stricken Chilperic and all his sons and there shall remain no one of those who came forth from his loins to rule his kingdom forever." He had at this time four sons by different wives, not to speak of daughters. And when this was fulfilled later on, then I saw clearly that what the soothsayers promised was false. Now while these men were staying in the church of St. Martin, queen Fredegunda who already favored Gunthram Boso secretly for the death of Theodobert, sent to him saying: "If you can cast Merovech forth from the church so that he will be killed you shall receive a great gift from me." And he thought the assassins were close at hand and said to Merovech: "Why are we so spiritless and timid as to sit here and hide sluggishly around the church? Let our horses be brought and let us take hawks and hunt with dogs and enjoy the hunting and the open views." He was acting cunningly to get Merovech from away the holy church. Now Gunthram otherwise was a very good man but he was too ready for perjury, and he never took an oath to any of his friends but that he broke it forthwith. They went out, as we have said, from the church and went as far as the house of Jocundiacus near the city; but Merovech was harmed by no one. And as Gunthram was at that time wanted for the killing of Theodobert, as we have said, king Chilperic sent a letter all written out to the tomb of St. Martin which contained the request that the blessed Martin would write back to him whether it was permissible to drag Gunthram from his church or not. And the deacon Baudegisih who brought the letter, sent to the holy tomb a clean sheet of paper along with the one he had brought. And after waiting three days and getting no answer he returned to Chilperic. And he sent others to exact an oath of Gunthram not to leave the church without his knowledge. Gunthram took the oath eagerly and gave an altarcloth as pledge that he would never go thence without the king's command. Now Merovech did not believe the sorcerers but placed three books on the saint's tomb, namely,

Psalms, Kings and the Gospels, and keeping watch the whole night he prayed the blessed confessor to reveal to him what was coming and whether he could be king or not, in order that he might know by evidence from the Lord. After this he continued three days in fasting, watching and prayer, and going to the blessed grave a second time he opened the book of Kings.

And the first verse on the page which he opened was this: "Because you have forsaken the Lord your God and have gone after other gods and have not done right in his sight, therefore the Lord your God has betrayed you into the hands of your enemies." And this verse was found in the Psalms: " But thou hast brought evils upon them because of their deceitfulness; thou hast hurled them down when they were lifted up. How have they been brought to desolation? They have suddenly failed and perished because of their iniquities." And in the Gospels this was 'found: "Ye know that after two days the passover cometh and the Son of man is delivered up to be crucified."

At these answers he was troubled and wept long at the tomb of the blessed bishop, and then taking duke Gunthram with him he went off with five hundred men or more. He left the holy church and while marching through the territory of Auxerre he was captured by Erpo, king Gunthram's duke. And while he was being held by him he escaped by some chance and entered the church of the holy Germanus. On hearing this king Gunthram was angry and fined Erpo seven hundred gold pieces and removed him from office, saying: "You held prisoner one who my brother says is his enemy. Now if you intended to do this, you should first have brought him to me; otherwise you should not have touched him whom you pretended to hold prisoner."

King Chilperic's army came as far as Tours and plundered this region and burned it and laid it waste, and did not spare St. Martin's property, but whatever he got his hands on he took without regard for God or any fear. Merovech remained nearly two months in the church I have mentioned and then fled and went to queen Brunhilda, but he was not received by the Austrasians. And his father set his army in motion against the people of Champagne, believing that he was hiding there. He did no injury, but he could not find Merovech.

15.

Inasmuch as Clothar and Sigibert had settled the Suevi and other tribes on their land when Albin had gone to Italy, they who returned in the time of Sigibert, namely the men who had been with Albin, rose against them, wishing to thrust them out from that country and destroy them. But they offered the Saxons a third of the land, saying: "We can live together without interfering with one another." But the Saxons were angry at them because they had themselves held this land before and they were by no means willing to be pacified. Then the Suevi made them a second offer of a half and then of twothirds, leaving onethird for themselves. And when the Saxons refused this, they offered all their flocks and herds with the land, provided only they would refrain from attacking them. But they would not agree even to this and demanded battle. And before the battle, thinking that they had the Suevi already as good as slain, they discussed among themselves how they should divide their wives and what each should receive after their defeat. But God's mercy which does justice turned their thoughts another way. For when they fought there were 26,000 Saxons of whom 20,000 fell and of the Suevi 6000 of whom 480 only were laid low; and the remainder won the victory. The Saxons who were left took oath that they would cut neither beard nor hair until they had taken vengeance on their adversaries. But when they fought again they were defeated with greater loss and so the war was ended.

18.

After this Chilperic heard that Prætextatus, bishop of Rouen, was giving presents to the people to his disadvantage, and ordered him to appear before him. When he was examined he was found to have property intrusted to him by queen Brunhilda. This was taken away and he was ordered to be kept in exile until should be heard by the bishops. The council met and he was brought before it. The bishops, who went to Paris, were in the church of the holy apostle Peter. And the king said to him; " Why did you decide, bishop, to unite in marriage my enemy Merovech who ought to be my son, and his aunt, that is, his uncle's wife. Did you not know what the canons have ordained for such a case? And not only is it proven that you went too far in this matter but you actually gave gifts and urged him to kill me. You have made a son an enemy of his father, you have seduced the people with money so that no one of them would keep faith with me and you shed to give my kingdom over into the hands of another." When he said this a multitude of Franks raised an angry shout and wished to break through the church doors as if to drag the bishop out and stone him; but the king prevented them. And when the bishop Praetextatus denied that he had done what the king charged him with, false witnesses came who showed some articles of value saying: "These and these you gave on condition that we would plight faith with Merovech." Upon this he made answer; "You Speak the truth in saying you have often received gifts from me, but it was not for the purpose of driving the king from the kingdom. For when you furnished me with excellent horses and other things what else could I do but repay you with equal value?" The king returned to his lodging, and we being gathered together sat in the consistory of the church of the blessed Peter. And while we were talking together Ætius, archdeacon of the church of Paris, came suddenly and greeting us said: "Hear me, bishops of God who are gathered together; at this time you shall either exalt your name and shine with the grace of good report or else no one will treat you hereafter as bishops of God if you do not wisely assert yourselves or if you allow your brother to perish." When he said this no one of the bishops made him any answer. For they feared the fury of the queen at whose instance this was being done. As they continued thoughtful with finger on lip, I said: "Most holy bishops, give your attention, I beg, to my words, and especially you who seem to be on friendly terms with the king; give him holy and priestly counsel not to burst out in fury at God's servant and perish by his anger and lose kingdom and fame." When I said this all were silent. And in this silence I added: " Remember, my lord bishops, the word of the prophet when he says: ' If the watchman sees the iniquity of a man and does not declare it, he shall be guilty for a lost soul.' Therefore do not be silent but speak and place the king's sins before his eyes, lest perchance some evil may befall him and you be guilty for his soul. Do you not know what happened lately? How Chlodomer seized Sigismund and thrust him into prison, and Avitus, God's priest, said to him: 'Do not lay violent hands on him and when you go to Burgundy you shall win the victory.' But he disregarded what was said to him by the priest and went and killed him with his wife and sons. And then he marched to Burgundy and was there defeated by the army and slain. What of the emperor Maximus ? When he forced the blessed Martin to give communion to a certain bishop who was a homicide and Martin yielded to the wicked king in order the more easily to free the condemned from death, the judgment of the eternal King pursued him and Maximus was driven from the imperial throne and condemned to the worst death." When I said this no one made any answer but all stared in amazement. Still two flatterers from among them - it is painful to say it of bishops - carried the report to the king, saying that he had no greater foe to his purposes than I. At once one of the attendants at court was sent inall haste to bring me before him. When I came the king stood beside a bower made of branches and on his right bishop Bertram stood and on his left Ragnemod - and there was before them a bench covered with bread and different dishes. On seeing me the king said: "Bishop, you are bound to give justice freely to all; and I behold I do not obtain justice from you; but, as I see, you consent to iniquity and in you the proverb is fulfilled that crow does not tear out the eye of crow." To this I replied: "If any of us, O king, desires to leave the path of justice, he can be corrected by you; but if you leave it, who shall rebuke you ? We speak to you; but you listen only if you wish; and if you refuse to listen who will condemn you except him who asserts that he is justice? " To this he answered, being inflamed against me by his flatterers: "With all I have found justice and with you only I cannot find it. But I know what I shall do that you may be disgraced before the people and that it may be evident to all that you are unjust. I will call together the people of Tours and say to them 'Cry against Gregory, for he is unjust and renders justice to no man.' And when they cry this out I will reply: 'I who am king cannot find justice with him and shall you who are less than I find it.'" At this I said: "You do not know that I am unjust. But my conscience knows, to which the secrets of the heart are revealed. And if the people cry aloud with false cries when you attack me, it is nothing, because all know that this comes from you. And therefore it is not I but rather you that shall be disgraced in the outcries. But why speak further? You have the law and the canons; you ought to search them diligently; and then you will know that the judgment of God overhangs you if you do not observe their commands." But he tried to calm me, thinking that I did not understand that he was acting craftily, and pointing to the broth which was set in front of him he said: "It was for you I had this broth prepared; there is nothing else in it but fowl and a few peas." But I saw his flattery and said to him: " Our food ought to be to do the will of God and not to delight in these luxuries, in order by no means to neglect what he commands. Now do you who find fault with others for injustice promise first that you will not neglect the law and the canons; and then we will believe that you follow justice." Then he stretched out his right hand and swore by all-powerful God that he would in no way neglect the teaching of the law and the canons. Then I took bread and drank wine and departed. But that night when the hymns for the night had been sung I heard the door of my lodging struck with heavy blows, and sending a slave I learned that messengers from queen Fredegunda stood there. They were brought in and I received greetings from the queen. Then the slaves entreated me not to take a stand opposed to her. And at the same time they promised two hundred pounds of silver if I would attack Prætextatus and bring about his ruin. For they said: "We have already the promise of all the bishops; only don't you go against us." But I answered: "If you give me a thousand pounds of silver and gold what else can I do except what the Lord instructs me to do? I promise only one thing, that I will follow the decision that the rest arrive at in accordance with the canons." They did not understand what I meant but thanked me and went away. In the morning some of the bishops came to me with a similar message; to which I gave a similar answer.

We met in the morning in St. Peter's church and the king was present and said: "The authority of the canons declares that a bishop detected in theft should be cast from the office of bishop." When I asked who was the bishop against whom the charge of theft was made the king answered: " You saw the articles of value which he stole from us." The king had showed us three days before two cases full of costly articles and ornaments of different sorts which were valued at more than three thousand *solidi;* moreover a bag heavy with coined gold, holding about two thousand pieces. The king said this had been stolen from him by the bishop. And the bishop answered: "I suppose you remember that when queen Brunhilda left Rouen I went to you and said that I had her property in keeping, to wit, five parcels, and that her slaves came to me frequently to take them back but I was unwilling to give them without your advice. And you said to me, O king: ' Rid yourself of these things and let the woman have her property back, lest enmity rise over this matter between me and Childebert my nephew.' I went back to the city and gave one case to the slaves for they could not carry more. They returned a second time and asked for the others. I again took counsel with your greatness. And you gave me directions saying 'Get rid of these things, bishop, get rid of them for fear that the matter may cause a scandal.' I again gave them two cases and two more remained with me. But why do you calumniate me now and accuse me, when this case should not be put in the class of theft but of safekeeping." Then the king said: " If you had this property deposited in your possession for safekeeping, why did you open one of them and cut in pieces a girdle woven of gold threads and give to men to drive me from the kingdom." Bishop Prætextatus answered: "I told you before that I had received their gifts and as I had nothing at hand to give I therefore took this and gave it in return for their gifts. I regarded as belonging to me what belonged to my son Merovech whom I received from the font of regeneration." King Chilperic saw that he could not overcome him by false charges, and being greatly astonished and thrown into confusion by his conscience, he withdrew from us and called certain of his flatterers and said: "I confess that I've been beaten by the bishop's replies and I know that what he says is true. What am I to do now, that the queen's will may be done on him ? " And he said: " Go and approach him and speak as if giving your own advice; ' You know that king Chilperic is pious and merciful and is quickly moved to compassion; humble yourself before him and say that you are guilty of the charges he has made. Then we will all throw ourselves at his feet and prevail on him to pardon you.'" Bishop Prætextatus was deceived and promised he would do this. In the morning we met at the usual place and the king came and said to the bishop: "If you gave gifts to these men in return for gifts, why did you ask for an oath that they would keep faith with Merovech?" The bishop replied: "I confess I did ask their friendship for him; and I would have asked not men alone but, if it were right to say so, I would have called an angel from heaven to be his helper; for he was my spiritual son from the baptismal font, as I have often said." And when the dispute grew warmer, bishop Prætextatus threw himself on the ground and said: " I have sinned against heaven and before thee, most merciful king: I am a wicked homicide; I wished to kill you and raise your son to the throne. "When he said this the king threw himself down at the feet of the bishops and said: "Hear, most holy bishops, the accused confesses his awful crime." And when we had raised the king from the ground with tears, he ordered Prætextatus to leave the church He went himself to his lodging, and sent the book of canons to which a new quaternion had been added containing the canons called apostolic and having the following: *Let a bishop detected in homicide, adultery or perjury be cast out from his office.* This was read and while Prætextatus stood in a daze, bishop Bertram spoke: "Hear, brother and fellowbishop; you have not the king's favor and therefore you cannot enjoy our mercy before you win the indulgence of the king." After this the king demanded that his robe should be torn from him and the hundred and eighth psalm which contains the curses against Iscariot be read over his head and at the least, that the judgment be entered against him to be excommunicated forever. Which proposals I resisted according to the king's promise that nothing be done outside the canons Then Prætextatus was taken from our sight and placed in custody. And attempting to flee in the night he was grievously beaten and was thrust off into exile in an island of the sea that lies near the city of Coutances.

After this the report was that Merovech was a second time trying to take refuge in the church of St. Martin. But Chilperic gave orders to watch the church and close all entrances. And leaving one door by which a few of the clergy were to go in for the services guards kept all the rest closed. Which caused great inconvenience to the people. When we were staying in Paris signs appeared in the sky, namely, twenty rays in the northern part which rose in the east and sped to the west; and one of them was more extended and overtopped the rest and when it had risen to a great height it soon passed away, and likewise the remainder which followed disappeared. I suppose they announced Merovech's death. Now when Merovech was kurking in Champagne near Rheims and did not trust himself to the Austrasians openly, he was entrapped by the people of Therouanne, who said that they would abandon his father Chilperic and serve him if he came to them And he took his bravest men and went to them swiftly. Then they revealed the stratagem they had prepared and shut him up at a certain village and surrounded him with armed men and sent messengers to his father. And he listened to them and purposed to hasten thither. But while Merovech was detained in a certain inn he began to fear that he would pay many penalties to satisfy the vengeance of his enemies, and called to him Galen his slave and said: "Up to the present we have had one mind and purpose. I ask you not to allow me to fall into the hands of my enemies, but to take your sword and rush upon me." And Galen did not hesitate but stabbed him with his dagger. The king came and found him dead. There were some at the time who said that Merovech's words, which we have just reported, were an invention of the queen, and that Merovech had been secretly killed at her command. Galen was seized and his hands, feet, ears, and the end of his nose were cut off, and he was subjected to many other tortures and met a cruel death. Grindio they fastened to a wheel and raised aloft, and Ciucilo, once count of king Sigibert's palace, they executed by beheading. Moreover they cruelly butchered by various forms of death many others who had come with Merovech. Men said at that time that bishop Egidius and Gunthram Boso were the leaders in the betrayal, because Gunthram enjoyed the secret friendship of Fredegunda for the killing of Theodobert, and Egidius had been her friend for a long time.

[19. Tiberius Caesar, his alms to the poor, and the treasures miraculously discovered by him.]

20.

An uproar arose against the bishops Salunius and Sagittarius. They had been trained by the holy Nicetius, [*note: Gregory's great-uncle*] bishop of Lyons, and had attained the office of deacon; and in his time Salunius was made bishop of Embrun and Sagittarius of Gap. Having reached the office of bishop they became their own masters and in a mad way began to seize property, wound, kill, commit adultery, and various other crimes, and at one time when Victor, bishop of SaintPaul TroisChâteaux was celebrating his birthday, they sent a band of men to attack him with swords and arrows. They went and tore his robes, wounded his servants, and carried off the dishes and everything used at the dinner, leaving the bishop overwhelmed by abuse. When king Gunthram learned of it he ordered a synod to meet in Lyons. The bishops assembled with the patriarch, blessed Nicetius, and after examining the case found that they were absolutely convicted of the crimes charged to them, and they ordered that men guilty of such acts should be removed from the office of bishop. But since Salunius and Sagittarius knew, that the king was still favorable to them they went to him complaining that they were unjustly removed and asking for permission to go to the pope of the city of Rome. The king listened to their prayers and gave them letters and let them go. They went to John the pope and told that they had been removed without any good reason. And he sent letters to the king in which he directed that they should be restored to their places. This the king did without delay, first rebuking them at length. But, what is worse, no improvement followed. However they did ask pardon of bishop Victor and surrendered the men whom they had sent at the time of the disturbance. But he remembered the Lord's teaching that evil should not be repaid one's enemies for evil and did them no harm but allowed them to go free. For this he was afterward suspended from the communion, because after making a public accusation he had secretly pardoned his enemies without the advice of the brethren to whom he had made the charge. But by the king's favor he was again restored to communion. But these men daily engaged in greater crimes and, as we have stated before, they armed themselves like laymen, and killed many with their own hands in the battles which Mummolus fought with the Lombards. And among their fellowcitizens they were carried away by animosity and beat a number with clubs and let their fury carry them as far as the shedding of blood. Because of this the outcry of the people again reached the king. The king ordered them to be summoned. On their arrival he refused to let them come into his presence, thinking that their hearing should be held first and that if they were found good men they would deserve an audience with the king. But

Sagittarius was transported with rage, taking the matter hard, and being light and vain and ready with thoughtless speech, he began to make many loud declarations about the king and to say that his sons cannot inherit the kingdom because their mother had been taken to the king's bed from among the slaves of Magnachar; not knowing that the families of the wives are now disregarded and they are called the sons of a king who have been begotten by a king. On hearing this the king was greatly aroused and took away from them horses, slaves and whatever they had, and ordered them to be taken and shut up in distant monasteries to do penance there, leaving not more than a single clerk to each, and giving terrible warnings to the judges of the places to guard them with armed men and leave no opportunity open for any one to visit them. Now the king's sons were living at this time, and the older of them began to be sick. And the king's friends went to him and said: "If the king would deign to hear favorably the words of his servants they would speak in his ears." .And he said; "Speak whatever you wish." And they said: "Beware lest perhaps these bishops be condemned to exile though innocent, and the king's sin be increased somewhat, and because of it the son of our master perish." And the king said; "Go with all speed and release them and beg them to pray for our little ones." They departed and the bishops were released and leaving the monasteries they met and kissed each other because they had not seen each other for a long time, and returned to their cities and were so penitent that they apparently never ceased from psalmsinging, fasting, almsgiving, reading the book of the songs of David through the day and spending the night in singing hymns and meditating on the readings. But this absolute piety did not last long and they fell a second time and generally spent the nights in feasting and drinking, so that when the clergy were singing the matins in the church these were calling for cups and drinking wine. There was no mention at all of God, no services were observed. When morning came they arose from dinner and covered themselves with soft coverings and buried in drunken sleep they would lie till the third hour of the day. And there were women with whom they polluted themselves. And then they would rise and bathe and lie down to eat; in the evening they arose and later they devoted themselves greedily to dinner until the dawn, as we have mentioned above. So they did every day until God's anger fell upon them, which we will tell of later.

[**21.** Winnoc the Breton is made a priest. The miracle of the holy water from the tomb of St. Martin. **22.** Death of Chilperic's young son. **23.** List of prodigies. **24.** Chilperic takes Poitiers from Childebert. **25.** Duke Dracolen captures the deserter Dacco and takes him to Chilperic. He commits suicide. Dracolen then meets Gunthram Boso, fights him on horseback and is killed. Violent end of Gunthram's fatherinlaw. **26.** Chilperic sends an army including " the people of Tours " against the Bretons. Later he orders fines to be paid by the poor and the younger clergy of the church because they had not served in the army" although there was no custom for these to perform any state service." **27.** Salunius and Sagiitarius the bishops are degraded.]

28.

King Chilperic ordered new and heavy impositions to be made in all his kingdom. For this reason many left these cities and abandoned their properties and fled to other kingdoms, think ing it better to be in exile elsewhere than to be subject to such danger. For it had been decreed that each landowner should pay a measure of wine per acre *[aripennis]*. Moreover many other taxes were imposed both on the remaining lands and on the slaves which could not be paid. When the people of Limoges saw that they were weighed down by such burdens they assembled on the first of March and wished to kill Marcus the referendary who had been ordered to collect these dues, and they would have done so had not bishop Ferreolus freed him from the threatening danger. The assembled multitude seized the tax books and burned them At this the king was greatly disturbed and sent officials from his court and fined the people huge sums and frightened them with tortures and put them to death. They say, too, that at that time abbots and priests were stretched on crosses and subjected to various tortures, the royal messengers accusing them falsely of having been accomplices in the burning of the books at the rising of the people. And henceforth they imposed more grievous taxes.

[29. Fighting between Bretons and Franks goes on. 30. Tiberius succeeds Justin as emperor. 31. The Bretons pillage the country about Nantes and Rennes.]

32.

At Paris a certain woman fell under reproach, many charging that she had left her husband and was intimate with another. Then her husband's kinsmen went to her father saying: "Either make your daughter behave properly or she shall surely die, lest her wantonness lay a disgrace on our family." "I know," said the father, " that my daughter is wellbehaved and the word is not true that evil men speak of her. Still, to keep the reproach from going further, I will make her innocent by my oath." And they replied "If she is without guilt declare it on upon the tomb here of the blessed Denis the martyr." "I will do so," said the father. Then having made the agreement they met at the church of the holy martyr and the father raised his hands above the altar and Swore that his daughter was not guilty. On the other hand, others the part of the husband declared that he had committed perjury. They entered into a dispute, drew their swords and rushed on one ,another, and killed one another before the very altar. Now they were men advanced in years and leaders with king Chilperic. Many received sword wounds, the holy church was spattered with human blood, the doors were pierced with darts and swords and godless missiles raged as far as the very tomb. When the struggle had with difficulty been stopped, the church was put under an interdict until the whole matter should come under the king's notice. They hastened to the presence of the prince but were not received with favor. They were sent back to the bishop of the place and the order was given that if they were not found guilty of this crime they might rightly be admitted to communion. Then they atoned for their evil conduct and were taken back to the communion of the church by Ragnemod, bishop of Paris. Not many days later the woman on being summoned to trial hanged herself.

[33. A long list of prodigies]

34.

A very grievous plague followed these prodigies For while the kings were quarreling and again preparing for civil war, dysentery seized upon nearly the whole of the Gauls. The sufferers had a high feverh with vomiting and excessive pain in the kidneys; the head and neck were heavy. Their expectorations were of a saffron color or at least green. It was asserted by many that it was a secret poison. The common people called it internal pimples and this is not incredible, seeing that when cupping glasses were placed on the shoulders or legs mattery places formed and broke and the corrupted blood ran out and many were cured. Moreover herbs that are used to cure poisons were drunk and helped a good many. This sickness began in the month of August and seized upon the little ones and laid them on their beds. We lost dear sweet children whom we nursed on our knees or carried in our arms and nourished with attentive care, feeding them with our own hand. But wiping away our tears we say with the blessed Job: "The Lord has given; the Lord has taken away; the Lord's will has been done. Blessed be his name through the ages."

In these days king Chilperic was very sick. When he got well his younger son, who was not yet reborn of water and the Holy Spirit, fell ill, and when they saw he was in danger they baptized him. He was doing a little better when his older brother named Clodobert was attacked by the same disease. Their mother Fredegunda saw they were in danger of death and she repented too late, and said to the king: "The divine goodness has long borne with our bad actions; it has often rebuked us with fevers and other evils but repentance did not follow and now we are losing our sons. It is the tears of the poor, the outcries of widows and the sighs of orphans that are destroying them. We have no hope left now in gathering wealth. We get riches and we do not know for whom. Our treasures will be left without an owner, full of violence and curses. Our storehouses are full of wine and our barns of grain, and our treasuries are full of gold, silver, precious stones, necklaces, and all the wealth of rulers. But we are losing what we held more dear. Come, please, let us burn all the wicked tax lists and let what sufficed for your father king Clothar, suffice for your treasury." So the queen spoke, beating her breast with her fists, and she ordered the books to be brought out that had been brought from her cities by Marcus, and when she had thrown them in the fire she said to the king: "Why do you delay; do what you see me do, so that if we have lost our dear children we may at least escape eternal punishment." Then the king repented and burned all the tax books and when they were burned he sent men to stop future taxes. After this the younger child wasted away in great pain and died. They carried him with great grief from Braine to Paris and buried him in the church of St. Denis. Clodobert they placed on a litter and took him to St. Medard's church in Soissons, and threw themselves down at the holy tomb and made vows for him, but being already breathless and weak he died at midnight. They buried him in the holy church of the martyrs Crispin and Crispinian. There was much lamenting among all the people; for men and women followed this funeral sadly wearing the mourning clothes that are customary when a husband or wife dies. After this king Chilperic was generous to cathedrals and churches and the poor.

35. In these days Austrechild, wife of prince Gunthram, succumbed to this disease, but before she breathed out her worthless life, seeing she could not escape, she drew deep sighs and wished to have partners in her death, intending that at her funeral there should be mourning for others. It is said that she made a request of the king in Herodian fashion saying: "I would still have had hopes of life if I had not fallen into the hands of wicked physicians; for the draughts they gave me have taken my life away perforce and have caused me swiftly to lose the light of day. And therefore I beg you let my death not go unavenged, and I conjure you with an oath to have them slain by the sword as soon as I depart from the light; so that, just as I cannot live longer, so they too shall not boast after my death, and the grief of our friends and of theirs shall be one and the same." So speaking she gave up her unhappy soul. And the king after the customary period of public mourning fulfilled her wicked order, forced by the oath to his cruel wife. He ordered the two physicians who had attended her to be slain with the sword, and the wisdom of many believes that this was not done without sin.

[36. Nanthinus, count of Angoulême, dies of the plague. He had been a bitter enemy of the bishops. 37. Death of Martin, bishop of Galicia. 38. The Arian queen of Spain, Gaisuenta, is enraged at her Catholic daughterinlaw. "She seizes the girl by the hair of her head, dashes her on the ground, kicks her for a longtime and covers her with blood and orders her to be stripped and ducked in the fishpond." The girl however converts her husband but he is sent into exile. 39. Fredegunda brings about the death of Clovis, Chilperic's son. 40. Elafius, bishop of Châlons, and Eonius, exiled bishop of Vannes, die. 41. Chilperlc seizes legates sent by the king of Galicia to king Gunthram. List of prodigies including a destructive wind of which Gregory says; "Its space was about seven acres in width but one could not estimate its lengtht"]

42. Maurilio, bishop of the city of Cahorss was seriously ill of gout, but in addition to the pain which the humor caused, he subjected himself to added tortures. For he often put whitehot iron against his feet and legs in order to make his pain greater. While many were candidates for his office he himself preferred Ursicinus who had once been referendary to queen Vulthrogotha

and he begged that Ursicinus be ordained before his death, and then passed away from the world. He was a very liberal almsgiver, very learned in the church writings, so much so that he often repeated from memory the succession of generations given in the books of the Old Testament which many find it difficult to remember. He was also just in judgments, and he defended the poor of his church from the hand of the wicked according to the judgment of Job: "I delivered the poor from the hand of the mighty and I helped the needy which had no helper. The mouth of the widow blessed me, for I was an eye to the blind, a foot to the lame, and a father to the weak."

[**43.** Debate over the Trinity between Gregory and the Spanish Legate]

44. At the same time king Chilperic wrote a little treatise to the effect that the holy Trinity should not be so called with reference to distinct persons but should merely have the meaning of Gaod, saying that it was unseemly that god should be called a person like a man of flesh; affirming also that the Father is the same as Son and that the Holy Spirit also is the same as the Father and the Son. "Such," said he, "was the view of the prophets and patriarchs and such is the teaching the law itself has given." When he had had this read to me he said: "I want you and the other teachers of the church to hold this view." But I answered him: "Good king, abandon this belief; it is your duty to follow the doctrine which the other teachers of the church left to us after the time of the apostles, the teachings of Hilarius and Eusebius which you professed at baptism." Then the king was angry and said: "It is plain that in this case Hilarius and Eusebius are my bitter enemies." And I answered him: " It is better for you to be careful and not make enemies either of God or his saints. Now let me tell you that as persons the Father, the Son and the Holy Spirit are distinct. It was not the Father who took on flesh, nor the Holy Spirit, but the Son, so that he who was Son of God became the son of a virgin also for the redemption of man. It was not the Father who suffered, nor the Holy Spirit, but the Son, so that he who had taken on flesh in the world, was himself offered for the world. And what you say about persons must be understood not in a material but in a spiritual sense. In these three persons, then, there is one glory, one eternity, one power." But he became excited and said: "I will explain these matters to wiser men than you and they will agree with me." I replied: "No wise man will he be but a fool, who will consent to follow your proposals." At this he ground his teeth and said no more. A few days later bishop Salvius of Albi visited him and he had this treatise read to him, begging him to accept his views. But upon hearing them Salvius was so revolted that if he could have laid hands on the paper containing the writing he would have torn it into bits. And so the king gave up the project. The king wrote also other books in verse following Sedulius as a model. But those poor verses have no relation of any sort with meter. He also added letters to our alphabet, namely [omega] as the Greeks have it, ae, *the, [upsilon, upsilon iota],* which are written by the following characters: [omega] as [theta], a/e as [psi], the as [Zeta], *[upsilon, upsilon iota] as [delta].* And he wrote to all the cities of his kingdom that boys should be taught these letters and that books written in previous times should be erased with pumice and rewritten.

[**45.** Agriicola, bishop of ChalonsurSâone, dies. "He constructed many buildings in that city, erecting houses, and building a church which he supported with columns and adorned with vari-colored marbles and mosaics."]

46. At that time also Dalmatius shiop of Rodez passed away, a man distinguished for every kind of holiness, an abstainer from food and the desires of the flesh, a great almsgiver and kind to all, steadfast enough in prayer and watching. He built a church, but frequently tore it down to build it better and left it unfinished. After his death, as usual there were many candidates for his office. And the priest Transobad, who at one time had been his archdeacon, was making a great effort for it, relying on the fact that he had put his son in care of Gogo who was then tutor to the king. Now the bishop had made a will in which he indicated to the king who was to receive this office after his death, adjuring him with terrible oaths not to appoint a stranger in that church, nor a greedy man, nor one entangled by marriage, but that one free from all these drawbacks should be put in his place, who would spend his days in the praise of the Lord and nothing else. Now the priest Transobad prepared a feast for the clergy in the city. And while they were seated one of the priests began to abuse shamelessly the bishop mentioned above, and he went so far as to call him a mad: man and a fool. While he was speaking the butler came to offer him a cup. He took it, but as he was raising it to his mouth he h began to tremble and the cup dropped from his hand and he leaned his head on the man next him and gave up the ghost. He was carried from the feast to the grave and covered with earth. After this the bishop's will was read in the presence of king Childebert and his chief men, and Theodosius who was then archdeacon in that city was ordained bishop.

47.

Now Chilperic heard of all the harm Leudast was doing to the churches of Tours and to all the people and he sent Ansoald thither. He came at the festival of St. Martin and, giving us and t e people a choice, raised Eunomius to the office of count. Then Leudast perceived that he had lost his place and went to Chilperic saying: "Most pious king, up to now I have guarded the city of Tours; but now that I have been removed see how it will be guarded. For let me tell you that bishop Gregory purposes to surrender it to Sigibert's son." Upon hearing this the king said: "By no means, but you make this charge only for the reason that you have been removed. " But he answered: " There is more that the bishop says about you; for he says that the queen committed adultery with bishop Bertram." Then the king was enraged and struck and kicked him and ordered him to be loaded with chains and thrust into prison.

48.

Now as this book should soon be finished I wish to tell something of his actions; and first it seems best to describe in order his family, his native place, and his character. There is an island of Poitou called Gracina in which he was born to a slave (named Leuchadius) belonging to a vinedresser of the fisc. Thence he was sent to service and assigned to the royal kitchen. But as his eyes were bleared when he was young and the bitter smoke hurt them, he was removed from the pestle and promoted to the basket, but he only pretended to be happy among the fermented dough, and soon ran away and left his service. And when he had been brought back twice or three times and could not be prevented from running away, he was punished by having one ear cut off. Then as he was not able by any power to conceal the mark of disgrace on him, he fled to queen Marcovefa, whom king Charibert loved greatly and had married in her sister's place. She received him gladly and appointed him keeper of her best horses. Then he was filled with vanity and given over to pride and began to intrigue for the office of count of the stables. Getting this, he despised and disregarded all; he was puffed up with vanity, softened with wantonness, inflamed with greed and he hastened hither and thither in the service of his patroness. After her death, being now with plunder, he made gifts to king Charibert and began to hold a place with him. Then the sins of the people increased and he was sent as count to Tours, and here he was more uplifted by the pride of his high office and here he showed himself to be a greed plunderer, a loudmouthed disputer and a foul adulterer. .And here by sowing discord and bringing false charges he acquired no small treasure. After Charibert's death, when the city had fallen to Sigibert's share he went over to Chilperic and all that he had wickedly accumulated was taken by the adherents of the king I have named. Then king Chilperic took possession of Tours through his son Theodbert, I having by this time come to Tours, and he was strongly recommended to me by Theodobert to hold the office of count which he had held before. He showed himself very humble and submissive to us, swearing often by the tomb of the holy bishop that he would never go against reason and that he would be loyal to me in his own causes as well as in all needs of the church. For he was afraid that, as later happened, king Sigibert would bring the city again under his rule. When Sigibert died Chilperic succeeded him and Leudast again became count. But when Merovech came to Tours he plundered all Leudast's property. Now during the two years that Sigibert held Tours, . Leudast lay hid among the Bretons. And when he took the office of count, as we have said, he was so foolish as to enter the bishop's house with breastplate and coat of mail, girt with a quiver and carrying a lance in his hand, and with a helmet on his head, being secure with no-one because he was an enemy to all. And if he sat a at trial with the chief men of the clergy and laity and saw anyone seeking justice, he would at once be transported into a rage and would pour out abuse on the citizens; he would order priests to be dragged away in fetters and soldiers beaten with clubs, and he showed such cruelty as can scarcely be described. And when Merovech, who had plundered his property, went away, Leudast began to accuse me falsely, asserting that Merovech had followed my advice in taking his property. But after doing me damage he again repeated his oath and gave a cloth from the tomb of the blessed Martin as security that he would never oppose me.

49.

But as it is a tedious thing to relate in order his perjuries and other crimes, let us come to the story of how he wished by vile and wicked calumnies to oust me from my place, and how the divine vengeance fell upon him, so that the saying was fulfilled "Every supplanter shall be supplanted," and again; "Whoso diggeth a pit shall fall therein." After the many wrongs he did to me and mine, after many plunderings of the Church property, he united to himself the priest Riculf, as perverse and wicked as himself, and went so far as to say that I had made a charge against queen Fredegunda, asserting that if my archdeacon Plato or my friend Galien should be subjected to torture they would certainly convict me of such words. It was then that the king was angry, as I have stated above, and after beating and kicking him ordered him to be loaded with chains and thrust into prison. Now he said that he had Riculf, a cleric, on whose authority he said this. But this Riculfus was a subdeacon, as unstable as Leudast, who a year before had entered into this design with Leudast, and had looked for causes of offense in order, forsooth, to go over to Leudast because I was angry, and he found them and went to him, and for four months they prepared all their tricks and laid their traps, and then he came back to me with Leudast and begged me to pardon and take him back. I did it, I confess, and publicly received a secret enemy into my household. And when Leudast went away, Riculf threw himself at my feet and said: " Unless you come quickly to my help I shall perish. Behold, at Leudast's urging I have said what I should not have. Now send me to another kingdom; if you do not I shall be seized by the king's men and suffer the punishment of death." And I said to him: "If you have said anything out of the way your words shall be on your own head; for I will not send you to another kingdom, lest I be held in suspicion by the king." After this Leudast became his accuser, saying that he had the words already mentioned from Riculf, the subdeacon. And he was bound and put under guard and Leudast was released. And Riculf said that Galien and the archdeacon Plato were present on the same day when the bishop said this. But the priest Riculf, who by this time had the promise of the bishop's office from Leudast, was so elated that he more than equaled Simon in his pride. And he who had sworn to me three times or more on the tomb of St. Martin, on the sixth day of Easter week made at me so furiously with abuse and spittings that he all but laid hands on me, confident, of course, in the trap he had prepared. On the next day, that is, the day before Easter Sunday, Leudast came to the city of Tours and pretending to have other business, seized Plato the archdeacon and Galien, and bound them and ordered them led to the queen, loaded with chains and without their robes. I heard of this while I sat in the bishop's house, and in sadness and worry I went into the oratory and took the book of David's song, that when opened a verse might give some consolation.

And this is what I found: "He led them in hope and they did not fear, and the sea covered their enemies." Meantime they embarked on the river above the bridge which was supported by two boats, and the boat which carried Leudast sank, and if he had not escaped by swimming he would perhaps have perished with his comrades. And the other boat which was in tow of this one and carried the prisoners, was kept above water by God's help. So the prisoners were taken to the king and were immediately accused in such terms that their punishment would be death. But the king thought it over and freed them from chains and kept them unharmed in free custody. Now at the city of Tours duke Berulf and count Eunomius concocted a story that king Gunthram wished to take the city of Tours and " therefore, " said they, " the city ought to be guarded so that there would be no carelessness." They craftily set guards at the gates who pretended they were guarding the city but were really watching me. They also sent persons to advise me to take the valuables of the church and flee secretly to Clermont. But I did not take the advice. Then the king summoned the bishops of his kingdom and ordered the case carefully gone into. And when the clerk Riculf was talking secretly as he often did, and was telling many lies against me and my friends, Modestus, a carpenter, said to him, " Illfated man, who talk so insubordinately against your bishop. It would be better for you to be silent and to beg pardon from the bishop and obtain his favor." At this Riculf began to cry with a loud voice and say: "Behold the man who orders me to be silent that I may not make the truth public. Behold the queen's enemy who does not permit the charge against her to be looked into." This was at once reported to the queen. Modestus was seized, tortured whipped, put in chains, and kept under guard. And though he was between two guards and held by chains to a pillar, the guards fell asleep and at midnight he prayed to the Lord that his power should deign to visit a wretched man and that an innocent prisoner should be freed by the visitation of the bishops Martin and Medard Then the chains were broken, the pillar was shattered, the door opened, and he came to the church of St. Medard where I was keeping watch by night.

The bishops assembled at Braine and were ordered to meet in a house. Then the king came, and after greeting all and receiving their blessing, he took his seat. Then Bertram, bishop of Bordeaux, against whom and the queen this charge had been brought, explained the case and questioned me, saying that the charge had been brought against him and the queen by me. I denied in truth that I had said these things, saying others might have heard them but I had not invented them. Now outside the doors there was a great shouting among the people, who said: " Why are these charges made against a bishop of God ? Why does the king prosecute such charges? The bishop could not have said such things even about a slave. Alas, Alas ! Lord God help thy servant." But the king said: " The charge against my wife is an insult to me. If therefore it is your will that witnesses be heard against the bishop behold here they are. But if it is your decision that this should not be done, and the matter be left to the honor of the bishop, speak. I will gladly hear your command." All wondered both at the king's wisdom and his patience. Then all said: "An inferior cannot be believed against a bishop," and the case came to this, that masses were said at three altars and I cleared myself of these words by oath. And though it was contrary to the canons, still it was done for the king's sake. Moreover I cannot pass over the fact that queen Riguntha sympathized with my grief and fasted with all her household until the slave reported that I had done all as was arranged. Then the bishops returned to the king and said: "All that was required of the bishop has been done. What now remains for you, O king, except to be excommunicated together with Bertram, the accuser of his brother?" " O no," said he, " I only told what I had heard." When they asked who had told this, he answered that he had heard it from Leudast. But he had already fled, from the weakness either of his resolution or of his cause. Then all the bishops decided that the spreader of scandal, traducer of the queen, accuser of a bishop, should be kept out of all churches because he had withdrawn from their judgment. And they sent a letter with their signatures to the bishops who were not present. And so each returned to his own place. Leudast heard this and took refuge in the church of St. Peter in Paris. But when he heard the king's edict that he should be received by no one in his kingdom, and especially because his son whom he had left at home had died, he came to Tours secretly and carried his valuables to Bourges. And when the king's men pursued him he escaped by flight. But his wife was captured and sent into exile at a village of Tournai. But the clerk Riculf was sentenced to death. But I managed to secure his life, although I could not free him from torture. No material thing, no metal, could have endured such blows as this wretch. For from the third hour he hung suspended from a tree with his hands tied behind his back; at the ninth he was taken down, stretched on a wheel, beaten with clubs, rods, and doubled thongs, and not by one or two, but there were as many floggers as could reach his miserable limbs. When he was in danger, he disclosed the truth and made known the secret plot. He said that the charge had been made against the queen for this reason, that she might be driven from the kingdom and Clovis might kill his brothers and take the kingdom, and make Leudast a duke, and that the priest Riculf, who had been a friend of Clovis from the time of the blessed bishop Eufronius, might get the bishopric of Tours, while this clerk Riculf would get the archdeaconate. Returning to Tours by the grace of God we found the church thrown into confusion by the priest Riculf. Now this man had been raised from the poor under bishop Eufronius and made archdeacon. Later he was raised to the priesthood and returned to his own place. He was always lofty, inflated, and presumptuous While I was still with the king this man went shamelessly into the bishop's house as if already bishop, and made an inventory of the church silver and brought the rest of the property under his control. To the more important clergy he gave presents and distributed vineyards and meadows; the lesser he beat with clubs and many blows even with his own hand, saying: " Recognize your master, who has triumphed over his enemies and by his determination has cleared Tours of the people of Clermont." The wretch did not know that with the exception of five bishops all the other bishops of Tours are connected with my family stock. He used often to say to his friends that a wise man can be deceived only by perjuries. Now upon my return, when he continued to despise me and did not come to greet me as the other citizens did but rather threatened to kill me, by the advice of the provincials I had him removed to a monastery. And while he was closely watched there, messengers from bishop Felix who had been a supporter of the charge against me came; the abbot was deceived by perjuries and Riculf escaped and went to bishop Felix. He received him with respect though he should have cursed him. And Leudast hastened to Bourges and took with him all the treasures which he had got by spoiling the poor. Not long after, the people of Bourges with the judge of the place attacked him and carried off all his gold and silver and what he had brought with him, leaving nothing but what he had on him, and they would have taken life itself if he had not fled. Then he regained support and with some men of Tours attacked his plunderers, and killing one, he recovered some of his property and returned to the territory of Tours. Hearing this, duke Berulf sent his men well armed to seize him. He perceived that he would soon be taken and abandoned his property and fled to the church of St. Hilary in Poitiers. Duke Berulf sent the captured property to the king. Then Leudast left the church and attacked the houses of several and took plunder without concealment. Moreover he was often caught in adultery on the sacred porch itself. The queen was roused that a place consecrated to God should be so polluted, and ordered him to be cast from the holy church. And being cast out, he went a second time to his friends in Bourges asking to be concealed.

50.

Although I should have spoken before of my conversation with the blessed bishop Salvius, it slipped my mind, and I suppose is not wicked if it is written later. When I had said goodby to the king after the synod I mentioned, and was anxious to return home, I decided not to go before kissing this man and taking leave of him. And I found him in the entrance of the house of Braine. And I said to him that I was about to return home. Then we withdrew a little and speaking of this and that he said to me: "Do you see upon this roof what I see?" I replied:

"Why, I see the roof-covering which the king lately gave orders to place there". But he asked: "Don't you see anything else?" And I said: "Nothing else." For I suspected that he was making a joke. And I added: "Tell me what more you see." But he drew a deep sigh and said; "I see the sword of divine wrath unsheathed and threatening this house." The bishop's words were not wrong; for twenty days later there died the two sons of the king whose deaths I have described before.

HERE ENDS THE FIFTH BOOK.

BOOK VI

HERE BEGIN THE CHAPTERS OF THE SIXTH BOOK

HERE END THE CHAPTERS, THANKS BE TO GOD

HERE BEGINS THE SIXTH BOOK, STARTING WITH THE SIXTH YEAR OF KING CHILDEBERT

[**1.** Childebert allied himself with Chilperic instead of with Gunthram; a synod meets at Lyons.]

2.

Meantime King Chilperic's legates, who had gone three years before to the emperor Tiberius, returned, but not without i severe loss and danger. For as they did not dare to enter the harbor of Marseilles on account of the quarrels among the kings, they made for Agde [***note:*** *West of Marseille in Septmania*] which is situated in the Gothic kingdom. But before they could reach the shore the ship was driven by the wind and dashed on the land and broken to fragments. The legates and their men, seeing they were in danger, seized planks and with difficulty reached the shore, many of the men being lost:: but most escaped. The inhabitants took the articles that the waves carried ashore, but they recovered the more valuable of them and carried them to king Chilperic. The people of Agde nevertheless kept much. At that time I had gone to the villa of Nogent to see the king, and there he showed me a great basin of fifty pounds' weight which he had made of gold and gems and he said: "I made this to bring honor and glory to the Frankish people. And I shall make many more if I live." He showed me also gold coins each of a pound's weight sent by the emperor having on one side the likeness of the emperor and the inscription in a circle: *Tiberi Constantini Perpetui Augusti* and on the other a fourhorse chariot and charioteer with the inscription: *Gloria Romanorurn.* He showed me also many other beautiful things brought by the legates.

[**3.** The alliance between Chilperic and Childebert is confirmed and they agree to take Gunthram's kingdom away from him.]

4. Now Lupus, duke of Champagne, had long been continually: harassed and plundered by his enemies and especially by Ursio and Bertefred. And at length they made an agreement to kill him and they marched against him. But queen Brunhilda heard of it, and grieving at the unjust attacks on her loyal supporter she armed herself like a man and rushed into the midst of the opposing forces and cried: "Do not, O warriors, do not do this evil; do not attack the innocent; do not for one man engage in a battle which will destroy the welfare of the district." Ursio answered her: "Leave us, woman; let it suffice for you to have ruled under your husband; but now your son rules and his kingdom will be maintained not by your support but by ours. Leave us or our horses' hooves will trample you to the earth." When they had continued such talk as this a long time the queen's determination that they should not fight prevailed. However, on leaving that locality they burst into Lupus's houses, seized all his property and took it home, pretending they were going to place it in the king s treasury, and they threatened Lupus and said: " He will never escape alive from our hands." Lupus saw he was in danger and, placing his wife in safety within the walls of the city of Laon, he fled to king Gunthram, and being welcomed by him he remained in hiding, waiting till Childebert should come of age.

5.

While king Chilperic was still at the villa mentioned above he directed his baggage to be moved and made arrangements to go to Paris. And when I went to see him to say goodby, a certain Jew named Priscus came in who was on friendly terms with him and helped him buy costly articles. The king took him by the hair in a gentle way and said to me: "Come, bishop of God, and lay your hands on him." But he struggled and the king said to him: "O obstinate-minded and ever disbelieving race, which does not recognize the Son of God promised to it by the voices of its prophets and does not recognize the mysteries of the church prefigured in its own sacrifices." To these words the Jew replied: " God never married nor was blessed with offspring nor allowed any one to share his power, but he said by the mouth of Moses: 'See, see that I am the Lord and except me there is no God. I shall kill and I shall make alive; I shall wound and I shall heal.'… [*note: The argument is continued at length along this line between the Jew on the one hand and Chilperic and Gregory on the other.*]. Although I said this and more, the wretched man felt no remorse and refused to believe. Then when he was silent and the king saw that he was not conscience stricken because of my words, he turned to me and asked to receive my blessing that he might depart He said: "I will say to you, bishop, what Jacob said to the angel, for he said to him, ' I will not let you go until you bless me.'" So saying he ordered water brought for our hands. After washing them we prayed, and taking bread I thanked God and took it myself and offered it to the king, and after a draught of wine I said farewell and left. And the king mounted his horse and returned to Paris with his wife and daughter and all his household.

6.

There was at this time in the city of Nice a recluse Hospicius who was very abstemious. He wore iron chains next his body and over these a hair shirt and ate nothing but plain bread with a few dates. And during Lent he lived on the roots of Egyptian herbs such as the hermits use, which were brought to him by traders. First he would drink the soup in which they were cooked and eat the roots next day. The Lord did not disdain to work great miracles through him. For at one time the Holy Spirit revealed to him the coming of the Lombards into the Gauls and he foretold it as follows: "The Lombards," said he, "will come into the Gauls and will lay waste seven cities because their wickedness has grown in the sight of God, since no one understands, no one seeks God, no one does good to appease the anger of God. For all the people are unfaithful, given up to perjury, addicted to thievery, ready to kill, and from them comes no fruit of justice at all. Tithes are not paid, the poor are not fed, the naked are not clothed, strangers are not received with hospitality or satisfied with food. Therefore this affliction has come. And now I say to you: ' Gather all your substance within the inclosure of the walls that the Lombards may not take it, and fortify yourselves in the strongest places.'" At these words all stood gaping and they said goodby and returned home with great admiration. He also said to the monks: "You, too, depart from the place and take with you what you have. For behold the people I have named draw near. " But when they replied: "We will not leave you, most holy father," he said to them: " Don't fear for me; for they will offer me insults but they will not harm me unto death." The monks went away and that people came and laying waste all they found, they came to the place where the holy recluse of God was. And he showed himself to them at the window of the tower. They went all round the tower but could find no entrance by which they could come to him. Then two climbed up and pulled the roof off, and seeing him bound with chains and clad in a hair shirt they said: " Here is a malefactor who has killed a man and therefore is kept bound in these fetters." They called an interpreter and asked him what crime he had committed to be so confined in punishment. And he confessed that he was a homicide and guilty of all crime. Then one of them drew his sword to strike at his head, but his lifted right arm stiffened in the very act of striking and he could not draw it back to him. He let go the sword and let it fall on the ground. Seeing this, his comrades raised a shout to heaven begging the saint to declare to them kindly what they were to do. And he made the sign of salvation and restored the arm to health. The man was converted on the spot and received the tonsure and is now reckoned a most faithful monk. And two dukes who I listened to him returned safe to their native place but those who despised his command perished wretchedly in the province. Many of them were seized with demons and cried: " Why, holy and blessed one, do you so torture and burn us?" And he laid his I hand on them and cured them. After this there was a man of Angers who in a severe fever had lost both speech and hearing, and when he got better of the fever he continued deaf and dumb. Now a deacon was sent from that province to Rome to obtain relics of the blessed apostles and other saints who protect that city. And when he came to this infirm person's relatives they begged him to take him as a companion on the journey, believing that if he reached the tombs of the blessed apostles he would forthwith be cured. They went on their way and came to the place where the blessed Hospicius lived. After greeting and kissing him, the deacon told the purpose of his journey and said he was starting for Rome and asked the holy man to recommend him to ship captains who were friends of his. And while he was still staying there the blessed man felt that power was in him through the spirit of the Lord. And he said to the deacon: "I beg you to bring to my sight the infirm person who is the companion of your journey." The deacon made no delay but went swiftly to his lodging and found the infirm person full of fever, and he indicated by signs that there was a humming in his ears. The deacon seized him and led him to the saint of God. The holy man took hold of his hair and drew his head into the window, and taking oil that had been blessed, he took hold of his tongue with his left hand and poured the oil in his mouth and on the top of his head, saying: "In the name of my lord Jesus Christ let your ears be opened and let that power - which once drove a wicked demon from a deaf and dumb man open your lips." Having said this, he asked him his name, and he answered in a clear voice: "I am called soandso." When the deacon saw this he said: "I give thee endless thanks, Jesus Christ, who deignest to work such miracles by thy servant. I was seeking Peter, I was seeking Paul and Laurence and the others who made Rome glorious with their blood; here I have found them all, I have discovered every one." As he was saying this with loud weeping and great admiration the man of God, wholly intent on avoiding vanity, said: "Be silent, beloved brother, it is not I who do this, but he who created the universe out of nothing, who took on man for our sake, and gave sight to the blind, hearing to the deaf, speech to the dumb; who bestowed on lepers the skin they had before, on the dead life, and on all the infirm abundant healing." Then the deacon said farewell and departed rejoicing with his comrades. When they had gone a certain Dominic-this was the man's name-who had been blind from birth, came to prove his miraculous power, and when he had dwelt in the monastery two or three months praying and fasting, at length the man of God called him to him and said: "Do you wish to recover your sight?" And he replied: "I wish to know a thing unknown. For I do not know what the light is. Only one thing I know, that it is praised by men. But I have not deserved to see from the beginning of my life until now." Then he made the holy cross over his eyes with oil that had been blessed and said: "In the name of Jesus Christ our redeemer let your eyes be opened." And at once his eyes were opened and he wondered and contemplated the great works of God which he saw in this world. Then a certain woman who, as she herself asserted, had three demons, was brought to him. And he blessed her with a sacred touch and made the cross in holy oil on her forehead and the demons were driven out and she departed cleansed. Moreover he cured by his blessing a girl who was vexed with an unclean spirit. And when the day of his death was drawing nigh he summoned the prior of the monastery and said: " Bring iron tools to open the wall and send messengers to the bishop of the city to come and bury me: For on the third day I shall depart from this world and go to the appointed rest which the Lord has promised me." Upon this the prior sent messengers to the bishop of Nice to carry this word. After this one Crescens went to his window and seeing him bound with chains and full of worms he said: " O my master, how can you bear such tortures so bravely ? " And he replied: "He comforts me in whose name I suffer this. For I tell you that I am now freed from these bonds and am going to my rest." When the third day came he laid aside the chains by which he was bound and prostrated himself in prayer, and after he had prayed and wept a long time he lay down on a bench and stretched out his feet and raised his hands to heaven and thanked God and died. And immediately all the worms that were boring through his holy limbs disappeared. And bishop Austadius came and most carefully placed the blessed body in the grave. All these things I learned from the lips of the very deaf and dumb man who as I related above was healed by him. He told me many other miracles of his but I have been kept from describing them by the fact that I have been told that his life has been written by many persons.

[7. The bishops of Uzès.]

8.

Ebarchius died also, a recluse of Angoulême, a man of great holiness through whom God did many miracles, and leaving out most of them I will tell briefly of a few. He was a native of Perigueux, but after his conversion he entered the clergy and went to Angoulême and built a cell for himself. There gathered a few monks and prayed continually, and if any gold or silver was offered to him he would pay it out for the necessities of the poor or to ransom captives. No bread was baked in that cell while he lived but was brought in by the devout when it was needed. He ransomed a great number of people from the offerings of the devout. He often cured the poison of malignant pimples by the sign of the cross and by prayer drove demons out from the bodies that they posessed and with his charming manner often rather ordered than requested judges to spare the guilty. For he was so attractive in his address that they could not deny him when he asked a favor. On one occasion a prisoner who was vehemently accused by the inhabitants of many crimes, both thefts and homicides, was to be hanged for theft, and when this was reported to Ebarchius he sent his monk to entreat the judge to grant life to the guilty man. But since the throng insulted the judge and cried loudly that if he were let go it would be good neither for the country nor the judge, the prisoner could not be let go. Meanwhile he was stretched on the wheel, beaten with rods and clubs and condemned to the gallows And when the monk sadly brought the news to the abbot he said: "Go, wait at a distance, for, be assured, the Lord will grant us of his own gift what man has refused. When you see him fall, take him and bring him at once to the monastery." The monk went about his bidding and Ebarchius threw himself down in prayer and wept and poured forth prayers to God until, the bar and chains being broken, the hanged man should be placed on the ground. Then the monk took him and brought him safe and well to the abbot. And he thanked God and ordered the count summoned and said to him: " You were always used to hear me kindly, beloved son, and why did you harden yourself today and refuse to let the man go whose life I asked for ? " He replied: " I would willingly heed you, sacred priest, but the people rose and I could do nothing else for fear of a rebellion." The recluse answered: "You did not heed me, but God deigned to heed me, and he restored to life the one whom you gave to death. Behold," said he, "he stands alive before you." As he said this the man threw himself at the feet of the count who was astonished that he saw living one whom he left dead. This I heard from the lips of the count himself. Moreover he did many other miracles which I have thought tedious to relate. After fortyfour years as a recluse he contracted a fever and died. He was taken forth from his cell and buried. And a great assembly of those he had ransomed, as we have said, followed his funeral.

9.

Domnolos, bishop of Mans began to sicken. In the time of king Clothar he had been in charge of the monks at the church of St. Laurence in Paris. But as he had always been faithful to king Clothar while the older Childebert was still living and often concealed his messengers when sent to spy, the king was awaiting an opportunity to make him bishop. When the bishop of Avignon passed away he had purposed to appoint him there. But the blessed Domnolus heard of this and came to the church of St. Martin where king Clothar had then come for prayer, and after spending a whole night in watching, he sent a hint to the king through the leading men who were there not to remove him far from the king's sight like a captive and not to permit a man of his straightforward character to be worn out among sophistical senators and philosophizing judges, saying this was a place of humiliation for him rather than of honor. To this the king assented, and when Innocentius bishop of Mans died he appointed him as bishop of that church. When he had reached this honor he conducted himself so that he rose to the summit of holiness and restored the power of walking to a lame man and sight to one W]lo was blind. After twentytwo years in his episcopate he perceived that he was greatly worn out with the king's evil and gout and he selected the abbot Theodulf for his place. The king assented to his desire but not long after changed his mind, and the election was given to Batechisil the king's major domo. He received the tonsure, went through the grades of the clergy in forty days, and when the bishop passed away he succeeded him.

10.

In these days thieves broke into St. Martin's church. They placed a railing which was on the tomb of a dead man at a window of the apse and climbing up by it they broke the glass and entered; and taking a great quantity of gold and silver and silken cloths they went off, not fearing to set foot on the holy tomb where we ;í scarcely dare to touch our lips. But the saint's power made this foolhardy deed known by a terrible judgment. For after committing the crime they went to the city of Bordeaux and a quarrel arose and one killed the other, and thus their deed was found out and their theft was revealed, and the broken silver and the cloths were taken from their lodging. When this was reported to king Chilperic he ordered them to be bound and brought into his presence. Then I was afraid that men would die because of him who in his lifetime in the body often prayed for the lives of the lost, and sent the king a letter of entreaty not to put these men to death since we to whom prosecution belonged did not accuse them. And he received my request with kindness and restored them to life. And the valuable articles which had been scattered he collected very carefully and ordered them sent back to the holy place.

[11. Dinamius, governor of Provence, and Theodore, bishop of Marseilles, quarrel. Childebert supports Theodore and Gunthram Dinamius. 12. Chilperic takes advantage of the quarrel and seizes Perigueux, Agen, and a number of other cities belonging to Gunthram]

13.

Lupus, a citizen of Tours, having lost wife and children, desired to enter the clergy but was prevented by his brother Ambrose who was afraid that he would leave his property to the church of God if he were joined to it. Ambrose, persuading him to his harm, provided him with another wife and appointed the day to meet to give the betrothal gifts. Then they went together to the town of Chinon where they had a dwelling. But Ambrose's wife being an adulteress and loving another with the love of a lewd woman and hating her husband, made a plot for him. And when these brothers had feasted together and had drunk wine in the night until they were intoxicated, they lay down on the same bed. When the adulterer came in the night when all were sleeping heavily because of the wine and setting fire to the straw in order to see what he was doing, he drew his sword and struck Ambrose on the head so that the sword went in at his eyes and cut the pillow in two beneath his head. Lupus was aroused by the blow and finding himself wallowing in blood, he called in a loud voice saying: "Alas, Alas! Help; my brother is killed." But the adulterer who had committed the deed and was now going off, heard this and returned to the bed and attacked Lupus. Although he resisted he was wounded many times, and overwhelmed and given a mortal stroke and left half dead. But no one of the household knew of it. In the morning all were amazed at such a crime. Lupus however was found to be still alive and after telling the story as it occurred, he died. But the harlot did not take a long time to mourn. In a few days she joined her adulterer and departed.

14.

In king Childebert's seventh year, which was the twenty-first of Chilperic and Gunthram, in the month of January there were rains and heavy thunder and lightning; blossoms appeared on the trees. The star which I called above the comet, appeared in such a way that there was a great blackness all around it and it t was placed as it were in a hole and gleamed in the darkness, sparkling and scattering rays of light. And a ray of wonderful size extended from it which appeared like the smoke of a great fire a long way off. It appeared in the west in the first hour of the night. At Soissons on the day of holy Easter the heavens were seen to be on fire, and there appeared to be two fires, one greater and the other less. And after the space of two hours they united and formed a great flame and vanished. In the territory of Paris real blood fell from the clouds and dropped on the garments of many men and so defiled them with gore that they shuddered at their own clothes and put them away from them. This prodigy appeared in three places in the territory of that city. In the territory of Senlis a certain man's house when he rose in the morning appeared to have been sprinkled with blood from within. There was a great plague that year among the people. The sickness took various forms and was severe with pimples and tumors which brought death to many. Still many who were careful escaped. We heard that at Narbonne in that year the bubonic plague was very fatal, so that when a man was seized by it he ad no time to live.

15.

Felix. bishop of Nantes, was stricken by this plague and began to be seriously sick. Then he called the neighboring bishops to him and begged them to give the influence of their signatures to the choice which he had made of his nephew Burgundio. Then they sent him to me. At that time Burgundio was about twenty-five years old. He came and asked that I would consent to go to Nantes and give him the tonsure and consecrate him bishop in place of his uncle who was still living. This I refused to do since I knew it was not in accordance with the canons. Still I gave him advice saying: " We have it written in the canons, my son, that no one can rise to the office of bishop unless he first passes through the grades of the clergy in regular order. You then, dearly beloved. must return thither and request him who has made choice of you, to give you the tonsure; and when you reach the office of priest. be regular in attendance at church; and when God wills that he pass away, then you will readily attain to the office of bishop." He returned and pretended to take my advice, since the bishop Felix seemed to be recovering from his illness. But after the fever detparted his legs burst out in pimples from the humor. Then he put on too strong a poultice of cantharides and his legs putrefied and he died in the thirtythird year of his episcopate and in the seventieth of his life. And Nonnichius his cousin succeeded him by the king's order.

[16. Felix's niece had been married to Pappolenus but Felix brought about their separation. Pappolenus now recovered his wife from a nunnery.]

17.

King Chilperic ordered many Jews to be baptized that year and received a number of them from the sacred font. Some of them however were purified in body only, not in heart, and lying to God they returned to their former perfidy so that they could be seen to observe the Sabbath as well as honor the Lord's day. But Priscus could not be influenced in any way to recognize the truth. The king was angry at him and ordered him to be put into prison, in the idea that if he did not wish to believe of his own accord he would force him to hear and believe. But Priscus offered gifts and asked for time until his son should marry a Hebrew girl at Marseilles; he promised deceitfully that he would then do what the king required. Meantime a quarrel arose between him and Phatir, one of the Jewish converts who was now a godson to the king. And when on the Sabbath Priscus clad in an orary and carrying nothing of iron in his hand, was retiring to a secret place to fulfill the law of Moses, suddenly Phatir came upon him and slew him with the sword together with the companions who accompanied him. When they were slain Phatir fled with his men to the church of St. Julian, which was on a neighboring street. While they were there they heard that the king had granted to the master his life but ordered the men to be dragged like malefactors from the church and put to death. Then, their master being already gone, one of them drew his sword and killed his comrades and then left the church armed with his sword, but the people rushed upon him and he was cruelly killed. Phatir obtained permission and returned to Gunthram's ; kingdom whence he had come. But soon after he was killed by Priscus's kinsmen.

[**18.** Legates returning from Spain report that king Leuvigild admits that Christ is the equal of God but denies that the Holy Spirit is God at all. **19.** Gunthram's men cross the river Orge and do damage in Chilperic's territory.]

20.

In that year Chrodinus died, a man of magnificent goodness and piety, a great almsgiver and helper of the poor, a lavish enricher of churches and supporter of the clergy. For he often started at the beginning and cleared estates, laying out vineyards, building houses, making fields. And he would then invite bishops who were poor and give them a feast and generously distribute among them houses with fields and men to till them and silver and bedding and utensils and officers and slaves saying: "Let these properties be given to the church, that when poor men are supported upon them they may obtain pardon for me before God." I have heard many other good things of this man which it would take too long to tell. He died in his seventieth year.

[**21.** List of prodigies.]

22.

King Chilperic, having seized cities belonging to his brother, appointed new counts and ordered that all the tribute of the cities be paid to him. And we know that this was done. In these days two men were seized by Nunnichius, count of Limoges, who were carrying letters in the name of Charterius, bishop of Perigueux, which contained many insults against the king; and among the rest it was put as if the bishop were complaining that he had gone down from paradise to hell, because forsooth he had been transferred from Gunthram's rule to the dominion of Chilperic. The count just named sent these letters and these men to the king under strict guard. The king patiently sent for the bishop to come to his presence to tell whether the charges against him were true or not. The bishop came and the king confronted him with the men and the letters. He asked the bishop if they had been sent by him. He said they had not. The men then were asked from whom they had received them. They said it was Frontonius the deacon. The bishop was asked about the deacon. He replied that he was his greatest enemy and there could be no doubt that this was his wickedness since he had often set wicked plots going against him. The deacon was brought at once and questioned by the king. He testified against the bishop saying: " It was I wrote this letter at the bishop's order." But the bishop cried out and said that this man had often devised clever tricks to cast him out from his office, and the king was moved with pity and commending his cause to God he let them both go, interceding with the bishop for the deacon and begging the bishop to pray for him. And thus the bishop was sent back with honor to the city. But after two months count Nunnichius who started this scandal died from an apoplectic stroke and as he was without children his property was granted to several persons by the king.

[23. On account of the birth of a son king Chilperic releases prisoners and remits taxes. 24. Gundovald, who claims to be a son of of Clothar, returns to Gaul from Constantinople and is received by bishop Theodore of Marseilles who is thereupon seized and held prisoner by king Gunthram. 25. Prodigies. 26. Gunthram Boso is charged with bringing Gundovald to he says that Mummolus is guilty of this and promises to bring him to king Gunthram.]

26.

.... Now duke Gunthram took with him the men of Clermont and Le Velay and went off to Avignon. But by a stratagem of Mummolus rotten boats were ready for them at the Rhone. They embarked on them without suspicion and when they came to the middle of the river the boats filled and sank. Then being in danger, some escaped by swimming and a number tore planks from the boats and reached the shore. But a good many who had less presence of mind were drowned in the river. Duke Gunthram however reached Avignon. Now Mummolus on entering the city had seen to it that as only a small part was left which was not guarded by the Rhone, the whole place should be protected by a channel into which he led water from the river. Here he had dug holes of great depth and running water concealed the traps he had made. Then upon the coming of Gunthram Mummolus cried from the wall: "Since we are men of good faith, let him come to one bank and to the other, and let him say what he wants." When they had come Gunthram said from the other side-it was this arm of the river that was between them-"If you please I will cross, because there are some things to speak of in secret. " Mummolus answered: " Come, don't be afraid." Thereupon he entered the water with one of his friends - he was wearing a heavy coat of mail-and immediately when they reached the hole in the river the friend sank under the water and did not reappear. But while Gunthram was under water and being carried along by the swift current one of the bystanders stretched out a spear to his hand and brought him ashore. And then he and Mummolus abused one another before leaving the place. While Gunthram was besieging this city with king Gunthram's army the news was taken to Childebert. He was angry because Gunthram was doing this without being ordered and sent Gundulf whom I have mentioned before to the place. He put an end to the siege and took Mummolus to Clermont. But after a few days he returned to Avignon.

27.

Chilperic went to Paris the day before Easter was celebrated, and to avoid the curses contained in the compact between him and his brothers that no one of them should enter Paris without the consent of the others, the relics of many saints were carried before him as he entered the city, and he spent Easter amid great mirth, and gave his son to be baptized, and Ragnemod, bishop of the city, received him from the holy font. Chilperic directed them to call him Theodoric.

[28. Marcus the referendary dies, first receiving the tonsure. 29. The piety of the nuns of Poitiers is described. As the result of a vision, one of them acted as follows :]

When the maiden had had this vision she was contrite in heart and after a few days she asked the abbess to get ready a cell in which she could be shut. The abbess got it ready quickly and said: " Here is the cell. What more do you wish ? " The maiden asked to be permitted to be shut in it. This was granted, and the nuns gathered with loud psalmsinging and the lamps were lighted and she was conducted to the place, the blessed Radegunda holding her hand. And so she said farewell to all and kissed each one and became a recluse. And the entrance by which she went in was walled up and she is there now spending her time in prayer and reading.

[**30.** The emperor Tiberius dies and Mauritius succeeds him.]

31.

King Chilperic received legates from his nephew Childebert and am them the leader was Egidius, bishop of Rheims. On being brought before the King they presented their letter and said: "Our master your nephew begs you to keep with especial care the peace you have made with him since he cannot have peace with your brother, who took away his share of Marseilles after his father's death and retains fugitives and is not willing to send them back. Therefore your nephew Childebert wishes to preserve unbroken friendship which he now has with you." Chilperic replied: 'My brother has proven guilty in many particulars. For if my son Childebert would seek the path of reason, he would know at once that it was by my brother's connivance that his father was killed." Upon this bishop Egidius said: "If you would join with your nephew and he with you and take the field, due vengeance would be speedily visited on him." When they had sworn to this agreement and exchanged hostages, they departed. Then relying on these promises Chilperic set the army of his kingdom in motion and went to Paris. And on encamping there he brought great expense to the inhabitants. And duke Berulf went with the people of Tours, Poitiers, Angers, and Nantes to the boundary of Bourges. And Desiderius and Bladast with all the army of their province hemmed in the territory of Bourges on the other side, completely devastating the country through which they came. And Chilperic ordered the army which had come to him to pass through the territory of Paris. And when they passed through, he passed also and went to the town of Melun, burning and wasting all. And although his nephew's army did not come to him, still his dukes and legates were with him. Then he sent messengers to the dukes just mentioned and said: "Enter the territory of Bourges and go right to the city and demand the oath of fidelity in my name." But the people of Bourges gathered at the town of Châteaumeillant to the number of fifteen thousand and there fought duke Desiderius, and there was great slaughter there so that more than seven thousand from each army fell. And the dukes went to the city with the people who were left, plundering and devastating all. And such marauding was done there as was never heard of in old times, so that no house nor vineyard nor tree was left, but they cut, burned, and subdued all. Moreover they carried the sacred utensils from the churches and burned the churches with fire. But king Guntram went with an army against his brother, placing all his hope in the judgment of God. And one evening he sent his army and destroyed a great part of his brother's army. In the morning legates went to and fro and they made peace, promising one another that each would pay for what he had done beyond the limit of the law whatever the bishops and leaders of the people should decide. And so they parted peaceably. And when king Chilperic could not keep his army from plundering he slew the count of Rouen with the sword and thus returned to Paris, leaving all the booty and giving up the captives. And the besiegers of Bourges, on receiving orders to return home, took with them so much plunder that all the district they left was believed to be emptied of men and domestic animals. The army of Desiderius and Bladast went through the land of Tours and burned, plundered, and slew, as is the custom with enemies, and they took captives, the most of whom they spoiled and afterwards let go. There followed upon this disaster a disease among domestic animals so that S scarcely enough remained to make a start with, and it was strange if any one saw an ox or heifer. While this went on king Childebert remained with his army in one place. And one night the army mutinied and the lesser people raised a great murmur against bishop Egidius and the king's dukes, and began to cry aloud and shout in public, saying: "Let those be thrust from the presence of the king who sell his kingdom, give over his cities to the dominion of another, and betray his people to the rule of another prince." While they continued shouting such things the morning came, and they seized their armor and hastened to the king's tent in order to seize the bishop and leaders and crush them by force and beat and wound them. On learning of this the bishop fed on horseback and hastened to his own city. And the people pursued him hurling stones and shouting abuse. And he was saved by the fact that they had no horses ready. The bishop outstripped his companions' horses and hastened on alone so terrified that when one shoe dropped off he did not stop to put it on. And so he arrived at his city and shut himself within the walls of Rheims.

32.

A few months earlier Leudast had come to Tours with the king's command to take his wife back and dwell there. Moreover he brought me a letter signed by the bishops directing that he be admitted to the communion again. But since I saw no letter from the queen, on whose account especially he had been excommunicated, I put off admitting him and said: "When I receive the queen's command then I will not delay to admit him." Meantime I sent to her and she wrote back saying: "I was urged by many and could not help letting him go. But now I ask you not to be reconciled to him nor give him the holy bread from your hand until I consider more fully what I ought to do." But when I read this letter over I was afraid he would be killed, and sending for his brotherinlaw I made it known to him and asked that Leudast be careful until the queen should relent. But he received with suspicion the advice which I gave frankly in God's sight, and since he was my enemy he refused to do what I ordered, and the proverb was fulfilled which I once heard an old man mention: "Always give good advice to friend and foe because the friend takes it and the foe despises it." And so he despised this advice and went to the king, who was then at Melun with his army, and he entreated the people to beg the king to see him. So when all made entreaty the king gave him a hearing. Leudast threw himself at his feet and begged for pardon, and the king replied to him: "Be on guard yet for a little while until I see the queen and make arrangement as to how you are to return into favor with her." But he was reckless and foolish and was confident because he had had a hearing before the king, and when the king returned to Paris he threw himself at the queen's feet in the holy church on the Lord's day and asked for pardon. But she was furious and cursed the sight of him and drove him away and said, bursting into tears: "I have no sons living to avenge the slander against me and I leave it to you, Lord Jesus, to avenge." And she threw herself at the king's feet and added: "Woe is me that I see my enemy and do not prevail over him." Then Leudast was driven from the holy place and the mass was celebrated. The king and queen returned from the holy church and Leudast went to the square having no idea what was going to happen to him; he went around the traders' houses, examined their costly wares, tested the weight of the silver articles and looked at various ornaments, saying: "I'll buy this and this because I still have much gold and silver." As he was saying this the queen's servants came suddenly and wished to bind him with chains. But he drew his sword and struck one of them. Then in a rage they seized their swords and shields and rushed at him. And one of them dealt a stroke that took hair and skin off a great part of his head. And as he fled across the city bridge his foot slipped between two planks of the bridge and his leg was broken and he was taken. His hands were tied behind his back and he was put in prison. The king ordered the physicians to attend him in order that when cured of his wounds he might be executed with prolonged torture. He was taken to one of the estates of the fisc but his wounds putrefied and he was dying when the queen ordered him to be laid on the ground on his back. Then a great bar of iron was placed under his neck and they struck his throat with another. And so after living an always perfidious life he died a just death.

[33. List of Prodigies. 34. Death of Chilperic's infant son Theodoric.]

35.

In the meantime the queen was told that the boy who had died had been taken away by evil arts and enchantments, and that Mummolus the prefect, whom the queen had long hated, had a share in the death of her son Theodoric. And it happened that while Mummolus was dining at home one from the king's court complained that a boy whom he loved had been attacked by dysentery. And the prefect said to him: " I have an herb at hand a draught of which will soon cure a sufferer from dysentery no matter how desperate the case." This was reported to the queen and she was the more enraged. Meantime she apprehended some women of Paris and plied them with tortures and strove to force them by blows to confess what they knew. And they admitted that they practiced magic and testified that they had caused many to die, adding what I do not allow anyone to believe: "We gave your son, O Queen, in exchange for Mummolus the prefect's life." Then the Queen used severer torture on the women and caused some to be drowned and delivered others over to fire, and tied others to wheels where their bones were broken. And then she retired with the king to the villa of Compiègne and there disclosed to him what she had heard of the prefect. The king sent his men and ordered him summoned, and after examining him they loaded him with chains and subjected him to torture. He was hung to a beam with his hands tied behind his back and there asked what he knew of the evil arts, but he confessed nothing of what we have told above. Nevertheless he told how he had often received from these women ointments and potions to secure for him the favor of the king and queen. Now when released from torture, he called a reader and said to him: "Tell my master the king that I feel no ill effect of the tortures inflicted on me." Hearing this the king said: "Is it not true that he practises evil arts if he has not been harmed by these tortures?" Then he was stretched on the wheel and beaten with triple thongs until his torturers were wearied out. Then they put splinters under his finger and toe nails. And when it had come to this, that the sword hung over him to cut his head off, the queen obtained his life; but a disgrace not less than death followed. Everything was taken from him and he was put on a rough wagon and sent to his birthplace, the city of Bordeaux. But on the way he had a stroke of apoplexy and was scarcely able to reach his destination. And not long after he died. Then the queen took all the boy had owned, both garments and costly articles, whether of silk or wool, all she could find, and burned them. They say there were four wagonloads. She had the : things of gold and silver melted in a furnace that nothing might remain as it was to recall the sad memory of her son.

[36. Difficulties of Aetherius, bishop of Lisieux, with a dissolute priest and how he finally triumphed. 37. Abbot Lupentius is falsely accused, tortured, and murdered by Count Innocent. 38. Count Innocent becomes bishop of Rodez. 39. Sulpicius becomes bishop of Bourges. 40. Theological argument between Gregory and a Spanish legate. 41. Chilperic retires to Cambrai. 42. Childebert receives money from the emperor to drive the Lombards out of Italy but fails to do so. 43. Events in Spain. 44. List of prodigies.]

45.

Meantime on the First of September came and a great embassy of Goths came to king Chilperic. He had now returned to Paris. He ordered many households of slaves to be taken from his estates and placed on the wagons; many too who wept and refused to go he ordered to be put under guard, in order to send them more easily with his daughter. They say that many in their grief hanged themselves, fearing they would be taken from their kinsmen. Son was separated from father, mother from daughter, and they departed with loud outcries and curses. There was such a wailing in the city of Paris that it was compared with the wailing of Egypt. Many of the older men who were forced to go made their wills and left their property to the churches, and requested that when the girl had entered the Spains the wills should be opened at once as if they were already buried.

Meantime legates came to Paris from king Childebert and warned king Chilperic not to take anything from the cities he held that belonged to the realm of Childebert's father, [or present his daughter with the treasures in any of them] or dare to touch the slaves or horses or yokes of oxen or anything in them. They say that one of these legates was secretly killed, but it was not known by whom; still suspicion turned to the king. King Chilperic promised that he would touch nothing from these cities, and invited the Frankish nobles and the rest who had sworn fealty and celebrated his daughter's marriage. She was given over to the legates of the Goths and he gave her great treasures. Moreover her mother presented her with a great quantity of gold and silver and garments, so that when the king saw it he thought he had nothing left. The queen noticed he was provoked and she turned to the Franks and said: "Do not think, men, that I have anything here from the treasures of previous kings; for all that you see is taken from my own property, since the most glorious king has given me much and I have gathered a good deal by my own labor, and I have made great gains from houses granted to me, both from the revenues and the tribute. Moreover you have often enriched me with your gifts, and from these sources comes all that you see before you, for there is nothing here from the public treasures." And thus the king's mind was deceived.

There was such a multitude of things that it took fifty wagons to carry the gold and silver and other ornaments. The Franks offered many gifts, some gold, others silver, many horses or garments; each gave such a gift as he could. Finally the girl said farewell after tears and kisses and when she was going out of the gate a wagon axle broke and all said: "Mala hora," which was taken by some as an augury. So she went forth from Paris and ordered the tents pitched at the eighth milestone from the city. And fifty men rose in the night and took a hundred of the best horses with golden bridles and two great chains and fled to king Childebert. Moreover along the whole way when any one could escape, he fled, taking whatever he could lay hands on. Abundantsupplies at the expense of the different cities were gathered along the way; in this the king ordered that nothing should be taken from his own treasury but all from the contributions of the poor.. And as the king was suspicious that his brother or nephew would prepare some ambush against the girl on the way, he directed that she should be guarded by an army. Great warriors were with her, duke Bobo, Mummolinus's son, with his wife as attendant on the bride, Domigisel and Ansovald and the majordomo Waddo who had once been count of Saintes, and also about four thousand common soldiers. The rest of the dukes and chamberlains who started with her turned back at Poitiers. The others journeyed on as they could. And on this journey such spoils and booty were taken as can scarcely be described. For they robbed the huts of the poor, wasted the vineyards, cutting off the vines and carrying them away grapes and all, taking domestic animals and whatever they could come upon and leaving nothing along their road, and the words that were spoken through Joel the prophet were fulfilled, "That which the locust hath left hath the cankerworm eaten, and that which the cankerworm hath left, hath the caterpillar eaten; and that which the caterpillar hath left, hath the palmer-worm eaten." This is what happened on this occasion. What was left by frost the storm destroyed, what was left by the storm the drought destroyed, and what was left by the drought the host carried away.

46.

While they continued on their way with this plunder, Chilperic, the Nero and Herod of our time, went to his villa of Chelles, about one hundred stades distant from Paris and there hunted. One day, returning from the hunt in the dusk, when he was dismounting from his horse and had one hand on a slave's shoulder a certain one came and stabbed him with a dagger under the armpit and repeating the blow pierced his belly. A flood of blood issued at once from his mouth and the open wounds and put his wicked soul to flight. The narratiye before this shows how iniquitous he was. For he frequently laid great districts waste and burned them over, and experienced no pain in this but rather joy, like Nero before him when he recited tragedies as the palace burned. He often punished men unjustly because of their wealth. Very few clerics in his time reached the office of bishop. He was given over to gluttony and his belly was his god. He used to say that no one wiser than he. He wrote two books on the model of Sedulius, but their feeble little verses can't stand on their feet at all, since for lack of understanding he put short syllables for long ones and long for short. He wrote pamphlets also and hymns and masses which can in no wise be received. He hated the causes of the poor. He was always blaspheming the bishops of the Lord, and when he was in retirement ha belittled and ridiculed no one more than the bishops of the churches. He called this one lightheaded, that one vain, another lavish, another wanton, another conceited, another pompous. He hated nothing more than churches. For he often used to say: "Behold our treasury has remained poor, behold our wealth has gone to the churches, no one reigns if not the bishops; our office will perish and be transferred to the bishops of the cities." Going on in this way he would always break wills that were made in favor of churches and he trampled under foot the last directions of his own father, thinking that there was no one left to require the execution of his will. As to lust and wantonness nothing can be found in thought that he did not realize in deed. And he was always looking for new devices to injure the people and of late years if he found any one guilty he would order his eyes torn out. And in the directions he sent to his judges to secure his own advantages he would add this: "If any one disregards our orders let him be punished by having his eyes torn out." He never loved any one sincerely and was loved by no one, and therefore when he died all his people deserted him. But Mallulf bishop of Senlis, who had been sitting in his tent three days and had been unable to see him, came when he heard he was killed, and washed him and put on better garments, and spent the night singing hymns, and took him in a boat and buried him in the church of St. Vincent which is at Paris, leaving queen Fredegunda in the cathedral.

HERE ENDS IN CHRIST'S NAME THE SIXTH BOOK OF THE
HISTORIES. THANKS BE TO GOD. AMEN.

BOOK VII

HERE BEGIN THE CHAPTERS OF THE SEVENTH BOOK

HERE END THE CHAPTERS

HERE BEGINS THE SEVENTH BOOK

1.

Though it is my desire to continue the history which the previous books have left untold, still affection requires me first to tell somewhat concerning the blessed Salvius, who, as is well known, died in this year. [*note: Salvius died Sept 10, 584. Chilperic's death which closes Book VI occurred in 584.*] As he himself was wont to relate he continued for a long time in the secular garb and with secular judges devoted himself to worldly cases, but yet he never entangled himself in the passions in which the mind of the young is usually involved. And finally when the odor of the divine breath had touched his inward parts, he left the warfare of the world and sought a monastery, and being even then devoted to godliness he understood that it was better to be poor with the fear of God than to pursue the gains of the perishing world. In this monastery he continued a long time under the rule established by the fathers. And when he had reached a more mature strength both of understanding and of life, the abbot who was over this monastery died and he took up the task of feeding the flock; and whereas he should have shown himself more commonly among his brethren for their correction, after he had attained this honor he was more retiring; and so he sought for himself a more secluded cell; now in the former, as he himself told, he had changed the skin of his body more than nine times, from scourging himself with too great determination. Then after receiving the office, while he devoted himself to prayer and reading, contented with this abstinence, he kept considering whether it was better for him to be hidden among the monks or to take the name of abbot among the people. Why say more? He said farewell to his brethren and they to him, and was immured. While thus immured he continued in all abstinence more than before; and in his love of charity he sought when any Strangers came to bestow his prayers on them and administer the grace of the blessed bread abundantly, which brought sound health to many who were infirm. And once he lay panting on his bed worn out by a high fever, and behold his cell was suddenly brightened by a great light and quivered. And he lifted his hands to heaven and breathed out his spirit while giving thanks. With mingled cries of mourning the monks and his mother took the dead man's body out [of the cell], washed and clothed it and placed it on a bier and spent the night in weeping and singing psalms. In the morning while preparations for the funeral went on the body began to move on the bier. And behold his cheeks regained color and, as if roused from a deep sleep, he stirred and opened his eyes and lifted his hands and said: " Merciful God, why hast Thou allowed me to return to this gloomy place of life on earth, since Thy mercy in heaven would be better for me than vile life in this world." His people were wonderstruck and asked what such a prodigy could mean, but he made no answer to their questions. He rose from the bier, feeling no harm from the painful experience he had suffered, and continued for three days without the support of food or drink. On the third day he called the monks and his mother and said: "Listen, dear ones, and understand that what you look upon in this world is nothing but it is like the prophet Solomon's song, 'All is vanity.' Happy is he who can live in the world so as to deserve to see the glory of God in heaven." Having said this he began to doubt whether to say more or be silent. When he said no more he was beset by the entreaties of his brethren to tell what he had seen, and he went on: " Four days ago when my cell quivered and you saw me lifeless, I was seized by two angels and carried up to the high heavens, so that I thought I had under my feet not only this filthy world but the sun also, and the moon, the clouds and the stars. Then I was taken through a door brighter than this light into that dwelling in which all the pavement was like shining gold and silver, a brightness and spaciousness beyond description, and such a multitude of both sexes was there that the length and breadth of the throng could not be seen. A way was made for me through the press by the angels who guided me, and we came to a place which I had already seen from a distance; a cloud hung over it brighter than any light, in which no sun or moon or star could be seen, but excelling all these it gleamed more brightly than the light of nature, and a voice came out of the cloud like a voice of many waters. Then I, a sinner, was humbly greeted by men in it, priestly and worldly dress who, my guides told me, were martyrs and confessors whom we worship here with the greatest reverence. I stood where I was bidden and a very sweet odor enveloped me so that I was refreshed by this sweetness and up to the present I have wanted no food or drink. And I heard a voice saying: 'Let him return to the world since he is necessary to our churches.' It was only the voice that was heard, for it could not be seen who spoke. And I threw myself on the pavement and said with loud weeping: 'Alas, Alas, Lord, why didst Thou show me this if I t; was to be deprived of it. Behold today Thou wilt cast me out t: from Thy face to return to the sinful world and never be able to return here again. I beseech Thee, Lord, not to take Thy mercy from me but permit me to stay here and not fall thither and perish.' And the voice which spoke to me said: 'Go in peace, for I am your keeper until I bring you back to this place.' Then I was left alone by my companions and departed weeping by the gate by which I entered and returned here." When he had said this and all present were wonderstruck, God's saint began to weep and say: "Woe is me who have dared to reveal such a mystery. For the pleasant odor which I brought from the holy place, by which it I have been supported the last three days without eating or drinking, has gone. My tongue too is covered with grievous sores and swollen so that it seems to fill the whole of my mouth. And I know that it was not well pleasing to my Lord God to make these secrets known. But Thou knowest, Lord, that I did this in simplicity of heart, not in boastfulness. I beg Thee, be kind and do not abandon me, according to Thy promise." After this he said no more and took food and drink. Now as I write this I am afraid that some reader may not believe it, according to what Sallust the historian says: "When you speak of the virtue and fame of good men each calmly believes what he thinks it easy for himself to do; beyond that he considers it falsely invented." For I call all-powerful God to witness that I learned from his own lips all that I have told. A long time after, the blessed man was taken from his cell, chosen bishop, and ordained against his will. And when he was, I think, in his tenth year as bishop, the plague grew worse in Albi, and the greatest part of the people had now died and few of the citizens remained, but the blessed man, like a good shepherd, never consented to leave the place, but he continually urged those who were left to devote themselves to prayer and to keep watch continually and to be engaged always in good works and profitable thought, saying: "Do this so that if God wishes you to go from this world you can enter not into judgment but into rest." And when by God's revelation, as I suppose, he recognized the time of his calling, he made himself a tomb and washed his body and clothed it; and thus always intent upon heaven he breathed out his blessed spirit. He was a man of great holiness and not greedy at all; he never wished to possess gold. If he took it under compulsion he at once paid it out to the poor. In his time when Mummolus the patrician took many captives from that city he followed him and ransomed them all. And the Lord gave him such favor with that people that the very men who took the captives made him concessions in the price and also gave him gifts. And so he restored the captives taken from his country to their former liberty. I have heard many good things about this man, but as I desire to return to the history I have undertaken I pass them over for the most part.

2.

Now when Chilperic had died and had found the death he had long been looking for, the men of Orleans united with those of Blois made an attack on the people of Châteaudun and defeated them, taking them off their guard; they burned their houses and crops and whatever they could not carry away conveniently, and they plundered flocks and herds and carried off all that was not fast. Upon their departure the men of Châteaudun with the rest of the men of Chartres pursued them closely and treated them in the same way as they were treated, leaving nothing in their houses or outside their houses or of their houses. And while they were still abusing one another and raging, and the men of Orleans were ready to fight the men of Chartres, the counts intervened and at a hearing before them peace was made, on condition that on the day when court was to be held the side which had flamed out wrongfully against the other should make payment according to justice. And thus the war was ended.

[**3.** Vidast is slain in a quarrel with the Saxon Childeric, who settles for it by a payment to Vidast's sons. **4.** Fredegunda takes refuge in a church. Childebert gets some of her treasures. **5.** Fredegunda invites Gunthram to take Chilperic's kingdom and become guardian to her son. He goes to Paris. Childebert also approaches the city]

6.

When the people of Paris refused to admit Childebert he sent legates to king Gunthram, saying: "I know, most righteous father, that it is not unknown to your goodness how up to the present time the enemy has defrauded us both so that neither of us could find justice for what was due him. Therefore I humbly beg you now to keep the agreement that was made between us after my father's death." Then king Gunthram said to the legates: "O wretches, always faithless, you have no truth in you and you, do not stick to your promises; behold, you failed in all your promises to me and entered into a new compact with king Chilperic to drive me from my kingdom and divide my cities between you. Here is your compact; here are your very signatures by which you connived together. With what face do you now ask me to receive my nephew Childebert whom you wished to make my enemy by your perversity ? " To which .the legates said: " If you are so possessed with anger as not to keep your promises to your nephew, at least cease taking what is due to him from Charibert's kingdom." But he replied: "Here is the agreement entered into with my brothers that whoever entered Paris without his brother's consent should lose his part, and Polioctus the martyr and Hilarius and Martin the confessors were to be his judges and punishers. After this my brother Sigibert entered, who died by the judgment of God and lost his part. So did Chilperic. Now they lost their parts by these wrongdoings. Therefore since they have died by the judgment of God in accordance with the curses in the compact, I will subject all Charibert's kingdom with its treasures to my rule by right of law, nor will I grant anything to any one from it except of my own free will. Away with you then, you everlasting liars and traitors, and take this word to your king."

7.

They departed, but legates came again from Childebert to the king I have mentioned, demanding queen Fredegunda, and saying: "Give up that murderess who strangled my aunt [*note: Galesuenta, see p. 90 (Book IV:28)*] and killed my father and uncle and also slew my cousins with the sword." But he answered: " In the court which we hold we decide everything and consider what ought to be done. " For he was supporting Fredegunda and used often to invite her to dinner promising that he would be her strongest defender. And one day when they were dining together the queen rose and said farewell but was detained by the king, who said: "Eat something more" But she replied: "Pardon me, pray, my lord, for according to the custom of women I must rise because of having conceived." Upon hearing this he was amazed, knowing that it was the fourth month since she had borne a son, but he permitted her to rise. Now the leading men of Chilperic's kingdom, like Ansoald and the rest gathered about his son, who, as we have stated, was four months old and was named Clothar, and they exacted oaths in the cities that formerly looked to Chilperic to be faithful to king Gunthram and his nephew Clothar. And king Gunthram by process of justice restored all that king Chilperic's followers had wrongfully taken from various sources, and he himself gave much to the churches, and he gave effect to the wills of the dead which had contained bequests to churches and had been broken by Chilperic, and he was generous to many and gave much to the poor.

8.

But inasmuch as he had no trust in the men among whom he had come, he guarded himself with armed men, and never went to church or to the other places he took pleasure in visiting without a strong guard. And so one Lord's day, when the deacon had called for silence among the people for the hearing of the mass, the king rose and addressed the people: "I adjure you, men and women who are present, to think it worth while to keep unbroken faith with me, and not to kill me as you lately did my brothers, and to allow me for three years at least to help my nephews who have become my adopted sons. For it may perchance happen if I die while they are little that you will perish at the same time-may the eternal Deity not allow it-since there will be no one of our family strong enough to protect you. " When he said this all the people poured forth prayers to the Lord for the king.

9.

While this was going on, Riguntha, king Chilperic's daughter arrived at Toulouse with the treasures described above. And seeing she was now near the Gothic boundary she began to contrive excuses for delay, and her people told her also that she ought to remain there for a time since they were wearied with the journey and their clothing was rough, their shoes torn, and the harness and carriages which had been brought on wagons were not yet put together. They ought first to make all these preparations with care and then set out on the journey and be received in all elegance by her betrothed, and not be laughed at by the Goths if they appeared among them in a rough condition. While they were delaying for these reasons, Chilperic's death was reported to duke Desiderius. And he gathered his bravest men and entered Toulouse and finding the treasures took them from the queen's control and put them in a certain house sealed up and under the guard of brave men, and he allowed the queen a scanty living until she should return to the city.

[10. Gundovald is proclaimed king. 11. A list of prodigies pointing to Gundovold's death. 12. Tours is forced to become subject to Guntram. 13. Poitiers also comes under Gunthram's control.]

14.

Now when court was held, bishop Egidius, Gunthram Boso, Sigivald, and many others were sent by king Childebert to king Gunthram, and they went in to him and the bishop said: "Most righteous king, we thank the allpowerful God that he has retored you after many toils to your own land and kingdom." And the king said to him: "Yes, it is to the King of kings and Lord of lords who in his mercy thought it right to accomplish this, that due thanks should be given. For it is certainly not to you, whose treacherous counsel and perjuries my land was burned over a year ago; you never kept good faith with any man; your crooked dealings are everywhere; it is not a bishop, but an enemy of my kingdom that you show yourself to be." At these the bishop, though enraged, was silent; But one of the legates spoke: "Your nephew Childebert begs you to order the cites which his father held to be given back to him." At this he replied: "I told you before that our compacts give them to me and therefore I refuse to restore them." Another of the legates said: "Your nephew asks you to order the sorceress Fredegunda, through whom many kings have been killed, to be surrendered to him, so that he can avenge the death of his father, uncle and cousins." "She shall not be given into his power," said Gunthram, "because she has a son who is king. Besides I do not believe that what you say against her is true." Then Gunthram Boso approached the king as if he were going to make some request. But since it had been certainly reported that he had raised Gundovald up as king, Gunthram spoke before him and said: " You enemy of my country and kingdom, who went a few years ago to the East for the express purpose of bringing Ballomer"-so he used to call Gundovald-"into my kingdom, you who are always treacherous and never perform what you promise." Gunthram Boso replied: "You are lord and king and sit on a royal throne and no one ventures to make answer to what you say. Now I say that I am innocent of this charge. And if there is any one of my rank who secretly makes this charge against me, let him come now openly and make it. Then, most righteous king, I will leave it to the judgment of God to decide when he sees us fighting on a level field." At this all were silent and the king added: "All ought to be eager to drive from our territories an adventurer whose father was a miller; and to tell the truth his father was in charge of the combs and wove wool." And although it is possible for one man to be master of two trades, still one of them answered in ridicule of the king: "Therefore, as you say, this man had two fathers at the same time, one a worker in wool, the other a miller. Fie on you, king, to say such an outlandish thing. For it is an unheard of thing that one man should have two fathers at the same time except in a spiritual sense." Then they laughed without restraint and another legate said: "We bid you goodby, O king. Although you have refused to restore your nephew's cities we know that the ax is still safe that was driven into your brothers' heads. It will soon strike yours." Thus they went off in a quarrelsome spirit. Then the king, inflamed at their insults, ordered his men to throw on their heads as they went rotted horse-dung, chips, hay and straw covered with filth, and the stinking refuse from the city. And they were badly fouled and went off amid unmeasured t insult and abuse.

15.

While queen Fredegunda was living in the church at Paris, Leonard, formerly an officer of the household, who then came from Toulouse, went to her and began to tell her of the abuse and insults offered to her daughter, saying: ' At your command I went with queen Riguntha and I saw her humiliation and how she was plundered of her treasures and everything. And I escaped by flight and have come to report to my mistress what has happened. " On hearing this she was enraged and ordered him despoiled in the very church and she took away his garments and the belt which he had as a gift from king Chilperic and ordered him out of her presence. The cooks and bakers, too, and whoever she learned of as returning from this journey, she left beaten, plundered, and maimed. She tried to ruin by wicked accusations to the king, Nectar, brother of bishop Baudegysil, and she said he had taken much from the treasury of the dead king. Moreover she said he had taken from the storehouses sides of meat and a great deal of wine, and she requested that he should be bound and thrust into prison darkness. But the king's patience and his brother's help prevented this. She did many foolish things and did not fear God in whose church she was taking refuge. She had with her at the time a judge, Audo, who had assisted in many wrongdoings in the time of the king. For together with Mummolus the prefect he subjected to the state tax many Franks who in the time of king Childebert the elder were free born. After the king's death he was despoiled by them and stripped, so that he had nothing left except what he could carry away. For they burned his house and would have taken his life if he had not fled to the church with the queen.

[16. Praetextatus returns to the bishopric of Rouen.]

17. Promotus had been made bishop in Châteaudun by order of king Sigibert and had been removed after that king's death on the ground that the town was a parish of Chartres - and judgment had been given against him to the effect that he should perform only the functions of a priest. He now came to the king and begged to receive again his ordination as bishop in the town mentioned. But Pappalus, bishop of Chartres, opposed him and said: "It is my parish," pointing especially to the decision of the bishops, and Promotus could obtain nothing more from the king than permission to take again his own property which he had with the territory of the town, on which he lived with his mother who was still living.

21.

After this when king Gunthram returned to Chalon and endeavored to inquire into his brother's death and the queen had put the blame on the chamberlain Eberulf - for she had invited him to reside with her after the king's death but could not prevail upon him to do so - this enmity accordingly broke out and the queen said that the king had been killed by him and that he had taken much from the treasures and so gone off to Tours, and therefore if the king wished to avenge his brother's death he might know that Eberulf was the leader in the matter. Then the king swore to all his nobles that he would destroy not only Eberulf himself but also all his kinsmen to the ninth degree, in order that by their death the wicked custom of killin kings might be ended. On learning this, Eberulf fled to the church of St. Martin, whose property he had often seized. Then upon the pretext of watching him the men of Orleans and Blois came in turn to keep guard, and at the end of fifteen days returned with great booty, taking horses, flocks and herds, and whatever they could carry off. But the men who took away the blessed Martin's horses got into a quarrel and pierced one another with lances. Two, who were taking mules, went to a house near by and asked for a drink. And when the man said he had none they raised their lances to attack him but he drew his sword and thrust them both through and they fell dead; Saint Martin's horses were returned. Such evils were done at that time by the men of Orleans that they cannot be described

22.

While this was going on Eberulf's property was being granted to different persons; his gold and silver and other valuables that he had with him he offered for sale. What he held in trust was confiscated. The herds of horses, swine, and packanimals were taken His house within the walls which he had taken from the possession of the church and which was full of grain, wine, sides of meat, and many other things, was completely cleaned out and nothing but the bare walls remained. Because of this he regarded me with great suspicion although I was running faithfully on his errands, and he kept promising that if he ever regained the king's favor he would take vengeance on me for what he suffered. but God, to whom the secrets of the heart are revealed, knows that I helped him disinterestedly as far as I could. And although in former times he had laid many traps for me in order get St. Martin's property, still there was a reason why I should get them, namely because I had taken his son from the holy font. But I believe it was the greatest drawback to the unlucky man that he showed no respect for the holy bishop. For he often engaged in violence within the very portico that is close to the saint's feet, and was continually occupied with drunkenness and vanities; and when a priest refused to give him wine, since he was plainly drunk already, he crushed him down on a bench and beat him with his fists and with other blows, so that he seemed to be almost dying; and perhaps he would have died if the cupping glasses of the physicians had not helped him. Now because of his fear of the king he had his lodging in the audience chamber of the holy church. And when the priest who kept the door keys had closed the other doors and gone, girls went in with the rest of his attendants by the door of the audience chamber and looked at the paintings on the walls and fingered the ornaments of the holy tomb, which was a wicked crime in the eyes of the religious. And when the priest learned of this he drove nails in the door and fitted bars within. And after dinner when he was drunk he noticed this, and as we were singing in the church on account of the service at nightfall, he entered in a rage and began to attack me with abuse and curses, reviling me, among other things, because I wished to keep him away from the holy bishops' tomb cover. But I was amazed that such madness should possess the man and tried to calm him with soothing words. But as I could not overcome his rage by gentle words I decided to be silent. And finding that I would say nothing he turned to the priest and overwhelmed him with abuse. For he assailed both him and me with vile language and various insults. But when we saw that he was so to speak possessed by a demon, we went out of the holy church and ended the disgraceful scene and the service at the same time, being especially indignant that he had become so abusive before the very tomb, without respect for the holy bishop.

In these days I saw a vision which I told him in the holy church saying: " I thought that I was celebrating mass in this holy church and when the altar with the offerings was now covered with a silk cloth, I suddenly saw king Gunthram entering and he said in a loud voice, 'Drag out the enemy of my family, tear the murderer away from God's sacred altar.' And when I heard him I turned to you and said: 'Wretch, take hold of the altarcloth with which the holy gifts are covered, lest you be cast out of here. ' And although you laid hold of it you held it with a loose hand and not manfully. But I stretched out my hands and opposed my breast against the king's breast, saying: 'Do not cast this man out of the holy church lest you incur danger to your life, lest the holy bishop estroy you by his power Do not kill yourself with your own weapon because if you do this you will lose the present life and the eternal one.' But when the king opposed me you let go the cloth and came behind me. And I was very much annoyed at you. And when you returned to the altar you took hold of the cloth, but again let go. And while you held it without spirit and I manfully resisted the king I woke up in terror, not knowing what the dream meant." Now when I had told it to him he said: "It is a dream that you saw because it strongly agrees with my purpose." And I said to him: "And what is your purpose?" He replied: "I have determined that if the king orders me to be dragged from this place I will hold to the altarcloth with one hand and with the other draw my sword and first kill you and then as many clerks as I can reach. And after this it would not be a misfortune for me to die, if I first took vengeance on this saint's clerks." I heard this and was amazed, and wondered why it was that the devil spoke by his mouth. For he never had any fear of God. For while he was at liberty his horses and flocks were let go among the crops and vineyards of the poor. And if they were driven away by the men whose labor they were destroying these were at once beaten by his men. In this trouble in which he was he often told how many of the blessed bishop's possessions he had taken unjustly. In fact the year before he had urged on a certain foolish citizen and caused him to summon the bailiffs of the church. Then, without regard for justice, he had taken property which the church formerly possessed under pretense of having bought it, giving the man the gold ornament on his belt. Moreover he acted perversely in many other things to the end of his life, which we shall tell of later.

23.

In this year Armentarius, a Jew, with one attendant of his own sect and two Christians, came to Tours to demand payment of the bonds which Injuriosus, exvicar, and Eunomius, excount, had given to him on account of the tribute. And calling on the men, he received a promise to pay the sum with interest, and they said to him besides: "If you will come to our house we will pay what we owe and honor you with presents also, as is right." He went and was received by Injuriosus and placed at dinner, and when the feast was over and night came, they arose and passed from one place to another. Then, as they say, the Jews and the two Christians also were killed by Injuriosus's men, and thrown into a well which was near his house. Their kinsmen heard what ad been done and came to Tours and information was given by certain men and they found the well and took the bodies out, while Injuriosus vigorously denied that he had been involved in this matter. After this it came to trial, but as he denied it with vigor, as I have said, and they had no means of proving him guilty, it was decided that he should take oath that he was innocent. But they were not satisfied with this and they set the trial before king

Childebert However neither the money nor the bonds of the dead Jew were found. Many said at the time that Medard the tribune was involved in this crime, because he too had borrowed money from the Jew. However Injuriosus went to the trial before king Childebert and waited for three days until sunset. But as they dd not come and he was not examined on the case by any one, he returned home.

[24. The territory of Poitiers is devastated and its people are forced to declare their allegiance to Gunthram a second time.]

25.

Marileif, who had been regarded as the chief physician in king Chilperic's household, they attacked most eagerly. And although he had been well plundered already by duke Gararic he was a second time stripped bare by these, so that he had no substance left. They took away his horses, gold, silver, and other valuables alike, and subjected him to the control of the church. For his father's service had been to attend to the mills of the church, and his brothers and cousins and other relatives were attached to the kitchens and mills of their masters.

[26. Gundovald goes about among the southern cities exacting the oath of allegiance. 27. He enters Toulouse and exiles bishop Magnulf. 28. Gunthram's army marches south from Poitiers. 29. Eberulf is slain by Claudius. 30. A legate of Gundovald is captured by Gunthram. 31. Gundovald obtains a piece of the finger bone of the martyr Sergius, hearing that an Oriental king had defeated his enemy by the help of one of Sergius' finger bones. 32. Two legates of Gundovald are taken and tortured. 33. Friendship is reestablished between Gunthram and Childebert. 34. Gundovald takes refuge in Comminges. 35. March of Gunthram's army to Comminges. 36. Gunthram's men outside the wall abuse Gundovald and he answers with an account of his life.]

37..

The fifteenth day of this siege had dawned when Leudeghisel began to make ready new engines to destroy the city, wagons carrying battering rams covered with woven branches, and planks under which the army was to move forward to tear down the walls. But when they came near they were so overwhelmed with stones k that all who got near the wall perished. They threw upon them pots of burning pitch and fat and hurled jars full of stones down on them. And when night ended the contest the army returned to the camp. Now Gundovald had on his side Chariulf, a very rich and powerful man, with whose storerooms the city was very full, and it was on his substance that they were chiefly supported. And Bladast saw what was being done and was afraid that Leudeghisel would win the victory and put them to death, so he set fire to the bishop's house, and when the people shut in the city ran to put the fire out he slipped away and departed. In the morning the army rose again for battle and they made bundles of rods as if to fill the deep trench which lay on the east: but here the engine could do no harm. And Sagittarius the bishop went frequently around the walls in arms and from the wall hurled stones with his own hand at the enemy.

38.

Finally when those attacking the city saw that they could accomplish nothing, they sent secret messages to Mummolus saying: " Recognize your lord and finally give up your perversity. What madness possesses you to become a follower of an unknown man ? For your wife and your daughters have been captured and your sons have been already slain. What end are you coming to ? What do you expect except to perish ? " He received their message and replied:

"Already, as I see, our kingdom has reached its end and its power fails. One thing is left; if I learn that I have security of life, I can relieve you of great trouble." When the messengers left, bishop Sagittarius with Mummolus, Chariulf and Waddo hastened to the church and there they swore to one another that if they should be assured of life they would give up their friendship for Gundovald and betray him to the enemy. The messengers returned and promised them security of life. And Mummolus said: "Let this be done; I will betray him into your hand and I will recognize my master the king and hasten to his presence." Then they promised that if he did this they would receive him to their friendship, and if they could not secure his pardon from the king they would place him in a church that he might avoid the punishment of death. This they promised with an oath and then departed. And Mummolus went to Gundovald with bishop Sagittarius and Waddo and said: "You were present and know what oaths of faithfulness we took to you. But now accept wholesome counsel and go down from this city and present yourself to your brother as you have often desired to do. For we have spoken with these men and they have told us that the king does not wish to lose your support because too few remain of your family." But he understood their treachery and bursting into tears said: "It was at your invitation I came to these Gauls, and of my treasures comprising a great amount of silver and gold and various articles of value, some have been kept in Avignon and some have been taken by Gunthram Boso. And next to God's help I placed all my hope in you, and to you intrusted my counsels and by your help always wished to reign. Now let your settlement be with God if you have lied to me. For he will judge my cause." To this Mummolus replied: "We are not speaking deceitfully to you; and lo ! brave men are standing at the gate awaiting your coming. Now lay down my gilded belt that you are wearing that you may not seem to go forth boastingly and gird on your sword and give me mine back." He answered: "There is a double meaning in what you say since you are taking away the things of yours that I have used as a token of affection." But Mummolus swore that no harm should be done him. Accordingly they went out of the gate and he was received by Ollo, count of Bourges, and by Boso And Mummolus returned into the city with his followers and barred the gate very securely. And when Gundovald saw that he was betrayed into the hands of his enemies he raised his hands and eyes to heaven and said: " Eternal judge, true avenger of the innocent, God from whom all justice comes, whom lying displeases, in whom is no craft or wicked cunning, to Thee I commend my cause, praying that Thou mayst be a swift avenger upon those who have betrayed an innocent man into the hands of his enemies." Having said this he crossed himself and went off with the men I have mentioned. And when they had gone some distance from the gate, as the whole valley around the city is precipitous he was given a push by Ollo and fell, Ollo calling out: "There is your Ballomer, who says he is brother and son of a king." And he threw his lance and wished to pierce him but it was checked by the links of Gundovald's coat of mail, and did him no injury. Then when he rose and attempted to climb the mountain Boso threw a stone and struck his head. And he fell and died. And the whole throng came and thrust their lances into him and tied his feet with a rope and dragged him through all the camp of the armies, and they tore out his hair and beard and left him unburied in the place where he was killed. The next night the leaders secretly carried off all the treasures they could find in the city, together with the church utensils. And in the morning they opened the gates and admitted the army and gave over all the common folk inside to the edge of the sword, butchering also the bishops of the Lord with their attendants at the very altars of the churches. And after they had killed all so that not one remained, they burned the whole city, both churches and other buildings, and left nothing but bare ground.

39.

Now Leudeghisel, on his return to the camp with Mumm0lus, Sagittarius, Chariulf and Waddo, sent messengers secretly to the king to ask what he wished done with them. And he gave orders to put them to death. But Waddo and Chariulf by that time had left their sons as hostages and gone off. When the word about their death had come and Mummolus heard of it, he put on his armor and went to Leudeghisel's hut. And Leudeghisel saw him and said to him: "Why do you come thus as if ready to flee?" And he answered: "The word that was given is not to be kept, I see; for I know that I am close to death." But Leudeghisel replied: "I will go out and settle everything." He went out and immediately by his command the house was surrounded in order that Mummolus might be killed. But he made a long resistance against his assailants and at last came to the door and as he stepped out two with lances struck him on each side, and so he fell and died. On seeing this the bishop was overwhelmed with fear and one of the bystanders said to him: " Behold with your own eyes, bishop, what is being done. Cover your head to escape recognition and make for the woods and hide for a little time, and when their anger passes you can escape." He took the advice, but while he was trying to get away with his head covered, a certain man drew his sword and cut off his head, hood and all. Then each and all returned home, plundering and killing along the way. In these days Fredegunda sent Chuppan to Toulouse to bring her daughter thence as best he could. Now many said that he was sent in case he found Gundovald alive to entice him with many promises and bring him to her. But since Chuppan could not do his he took Rigunda and brought her back from that place amid great scorn and contempt.

[**40.** Mummolus's treasures, amounting to two hundred and fiftytwo talents of silver and a greater value in gold, are taken. **41.** A giant "two or three feet taller than the tallest men" is taken to King Guntrham. **42.** The count of Bourges attempts to fine "St. Martin's men" for not taking part in the expedition against Gundovald. **43.** Desiderius, Waddo, and Chariulf escape.]

44.

There was, at this time, a woman who had a spirit of divination and won great gain for her owners by prophesying and she won such favor from them that she was set free and left to her own devices. And if any one suffered from theft or any wrongdoing would at once tell where the thief had gone, to whom he had given the property, or what he had done with it. She gathered together gold and silver every day and went forth in rich clothing so that she was thought among the people to be something divine But when this was reported to Ageric, bishop of Verdun, he sent to arrest her. When she was arrested and brought to him he perceived, according to that which we read in the Acts of the Apostles, that there was in her an unclean spirit of divination And when he said a formula of exorcism over her and anointed her forehead with holy oil, the demon cried out and revealed to the bishop what it was. But since he could not drive it from the woman she was allowed to go. And the woman saw that she could not dwell in the place and she went off to queen Fredegunda and remained hid.

45.

In this year a severe famine oppressed almost all of the Gauls. Many dried and ground into powder grape seeds and oat k chaff and fern roots and mixed a little flour with it and made bread; many cut straw and did the same. Many who had no flour ate different herbs which they gathered, and in consequence swelled up and died. Many too wasted away and died of starvation. At that time the traders plundered the people greatly selling scarcely a peck of grain or half measure of wine for the third of a gold piece. They subjected the poor to slavery in return for a little food.

[**46.** Christofer, a trader, is killed by his Saxon slaves, one of whom is caught and executed. **47.** Quarrel between two citizens of Tours]

HERE ENDS THE SEVENTH BOOK

BOOK VIII
HERE BEGIN THE CHAPTERS OF THE EIGHTH BOOK

HERE END THE CHAPTERS OF THE EIGHTH BOOK.
THANKS BE TO GOD. AMEN.

IN CHRIST'S NAME HERE BEGINS BOOK EIGHT

1.

Now king Gunthram in the twentyfourth year of his reign started from Chalon and went to the city of Nevers. For he was going to Paris by invitation to receive from the holy font of regeneration Chilperic's son, whom they were already calling Clothar. And he left the territory of Nevers and came to the city of Orleans and at that time appeared much among the citizens. For on receiving invitations he went to their homes and partook of the repasts offered him. He received many gifts from them and bestowed many gifts on them in a very generous way. And when he came to the city of Orleans the day was the festival of the blessed Martin, namely the fourth before the nones of the fifth month [July 4]. And a huge throng of people came to meet him with standards and banners, singing praises. And here the Syrian language, there that of the Latins, and again that even of the Jews, sounded together strangely in varied praises, saying: "Long live the king; may his reign over the people last unnumbered years." And the Jews who were to be seen taking part in these :praises said: "May all the nations honor you and bend the knee and be subject to you." And so it happened that when the king was seated at dinner after mass he said: "Woe to the Jewish tribe, wicked, treacherous, and always living by cunning. Here's what they were after," said he, " when they cried out their flattering praises today, that all the nations were to honor me as master. [They wish me] to order their synagogue, long ago torn down by the Christians, to be built at the public cost; but by the Lord's command I will never do it". O King glorious for wonderful wisdom. He so understood the craft of the heretics that they entirely failed to get from him what they were going to propose later. At the dinner the king said to the bishops who were present: " I beg you to give me your blessing tomorrow in my house and bring me salvation by your coming, so that I may be saved when in my humility I receive your words of blessing." When he said this all thanked him, and as dinner was finished we rose.

2.

In the morning while the king was visiting the holy places to offer prayer he came to my lodging. It was the church of Saint Avitus the abbot, whom I mention in my book of the miracles. I rose gladly, I admit, to go to meet him, and after giving him my blessing begged him to accept St. Martin's holy bread at my lodging. He did not refuse but courteously came in, drank a cup, invited me to the dinner and went away in good humor.

At that time Bertram, bishop of Bordeaux, and Palladius of Saintes were in great disfavor with the king because of their support of Gundovald of which we have told above. Moreover bishop Palladius had especially offended the king because he had repeatedly deceived him. Now they had recently been under examination before the remaining bishops and the nobles as to why they had supported Gundovald and why they had foolishly ordained Faustian bishop of Ax at his command. But bishop Palladius took the blame for the ordination from his metropolitan Bertram and took it on his own shoulders, saying: "My metropolitan was suffering greatly from sore eyes and I was plundered and treated with indignity and dragged to the place against my will. I could do nothing else than obey one who said he had received complete control of the Gauls." When this was told the king hc was greatly irritated so that he could scarcely be prevailed upon to invite to the dinner these bishops whom he had previously refused to see. So when Bertram came in the king asked: "Who is he ? " For it had been a long time since he had seen him. And thc~said: "This is Bertram bishop of Bordeaux." And the king said to him: "We thank you for keeping faith as you have with your own family. For I would have you know, beloved father, that you are my kinsman on my mother's side and you should not have brought a plague from abroad on your own people." When Bertram had been told this and more, the king turned to Palladius and said: " You do not deserve much gratitude either, bishop Palladius. For you perjured yourself to me three times-a hard thing to say of a bishop-sending me information full oi treachery. You excused yourself to me by letter and at the same time you were inviting my brother in other letters. God . Fill judge my cause since I have always tried to treat you as fathers of the church and you have always been treacherous." And he said to the bishops Nicasius and Antidius: "Most holy fathers, tell me what you have done for the advantage of your country or the security of my kingdom." They made no reply and the king washed his hands and after receiving a blessing from the bishops sat at table with a glad countenance and a cheerful behavior as if he had said nothing about the wrongs done him.

3.

Meantime when the dinner was now half over the king asked me to request my deacon who had sung the responsory at the mass the day before, to sing. When he had sung he next asked me to request all the bishops who, at my instance, had come prepared, to appoint each a single clerk from his service to sing before the king. And so I made the request at the king's command, and they sang, each to the best of his ability, a psalm before the king. And when the courses were being changed the king said: "All the silver you see belonged to that perjurer Mummolus, but now by the help God's grace it has been transferred to my ownership. I have already had fifteen of his dishes like the larger one you see yonder smelted down, and I have kept only this one and one other of a hundred and seventy pounds. Why [keep] more than enough for daily use ? It is too bad, but I have no other son than Childebert, and he has enough treasures which his father left him beside what I had sent to him from the property of this wretch which was found at Avignon. The rest must be given for the necessities of the poor and the churches.

4.

"There is only one thing that I ask of you, my lord bishops, namely, to pray God's mercy for my son Childebert. For he is a man of sense and ability so that one so cautious and energetic as he could scarcely be found in many years. And if God would deign to grant him to these Gauls perhaps there would be hope that by turn our race, greatly weakened though it is, can rise again. And I have confidence that this will happen through His mercy because the indications at the boy's birth were of this sort. For it was the holy day of Easter and my brother Sigibert was standing in the church and the deacon was walking in procession with the holy book of the Gospels, and a messenger came to the king, and the words of the deacon as he read from the Gospels and of the messenger were the same, saying: 'To thee a son has been born.' And when they both spoke together all the people cried out: ' Glory to all-powerful God.' Moreover he was baptized on the holy day of Pentecost and was made king also on the holy day of the Lord's birth. And so if your prayers attend him, God willing he will be able to rule." So the king spoke and all prayed the Lord in His mercy to keep both kings safe. The king added: "It is true that his mother Brunhilda threatens my life, but I have no misgiving on this account. For the Lord who has saved me from the hands of my enemies will save me from her plots too."

5.

Then he said much against bishop Theodore, protesting that if he came to the synod he would thrust him off again into exile and saying: "I know it was for the sake of these people [*note:*

Gundovald and his followers.] that he caused my brother Chilperic to be killed. In fact I ought not to be called a man if I cannot avenge his death this year." But I made answer: " And what killed Chilperic, unless it was his own wickedness and your prayers? For he laid many plots for you contrary to justice and they brought death to him. And, so to speak, it was just this that I saw in a dream when I beheld him with tonsured head being ordained bishop, apparently, and then I saw him placed on a plain chair hung only with black and carried along with shining lamps and torches going before him." When I told this the king said: " And I saw another vision which foretold his death. He was brought into my presence loaded with chains by three bishops, of whom one was Tetricus, the second Agricola, and the third Nicecius of Lyons. And two of them said: 'Set him free, we entreat you, give him a beating and let him go.' But bishop Tetricus answered harshly, ' It shall not be so? but he shall be burned with fire for his crimes.' And when they had carried on this discussion for a long time, as if quarreling, I saw at a distance a caldron set on a fire and boiling furiously. Then I wept and they seized unhappy Chilperic and broke his limbs and threw him in the caldron. And he was immediately so melted and dissolved amid the steam from the water that no trace of him at all remained." The king told this story and we wondered at it, and the feast being finished we rose.

6.

Next day the king went hunting. When he returned I brought into his presence Garachar, count of Bordeaux, and Bladast, who, as I have told you before, had taken refuge in the church of Saint Martin because they had been followers of Gundovald. I had previously made intercession for them but had failed, and so at this later time I said: "Hear me, powerful king. Behold I have been sent to you on an embassy by my master. What answer shall I give to him who sent me when you refuse to give me any answer?" And he said in amazement: "And who is your master who sent you?" I smiled and answered: "The blessed Martin." Then he ordered me to bring the men before him. And when they entered his presence he reproached them with many treacheries and perjuries, calling them again and again tricky foxes, but he ; restored them to his favor, giving back what he had taken from them.

7.

When the Lord's day came the king went to church to hear mass. And the brethren and fellow-bishops who were there yielded to bishop Palladius the honor of celebrating it. When he began to read the prophecy the king inquired who he was. And when they told him that it was the bishop Palladius he was angry at once and said: "Is he now to preach the sacred word before me who has always been faithless to me and perjured. I will leave this church immediately and will not hear my enemy preach." So saying he started to leave the church. Then the bishops were troubled by the humiliation of their brother and said to the king: "We saw him present at the feast you gave and we saw you receive a blessing at his hand and why does the king despise him now ? If we had known that he was hateful to you we would have resorted to another to celebrate mass. But now if you permit it let him continue the ceremony which he has begun; tomorrow if you bring any charge against him let it be judged in accordance with the holy canons." By this time bishop Palladius had retired to the sacristy in great humiliation. Then the king bade him be recalled and he finished the ceremony which he had begun. Moreover when Palladius and Bertram were again summoned to the king's table they became angry at one another and reproached one another with many adulteries and fornications and with a good many perjuries as well. At these matters many laughed, but a number who were keener of perception lamented that the weeds of the devil should so flourish among the bishops of the Lord. And so they left the king's presence, giving bonds and security to appear at the synod on the tenth day before the kalends of the ninth month.

[**8.** List of prodigies. **9.** Queen Fredegunda, three bishops and three hundred nobles swear to Gunthram that the young Clothar is Chilperic's son. **10.** Gunthram discovers the bodies of Chilperic's sons, Merovech and Clovis, and gives them due burial. **11.** Gunthram's life is in danger. **12.** Bishop Theodore of Marseilles is forced to appear before Gunthram. **13.** Gunthram sends an embassy to Childebert. **14.** Gregory nearly loses his life in crossing the Rhine but is saved by relics of St. Martin.]

15.

We started on the journey and came to the town of Yvois and there were met by deacon Vulfilaic and taken to his monastery, where we received a very kind welcome. This monastery is situated on a mountain top about eight miles from the town I have mentioned. On this mountain Vulfilaic built a great church and made it famous for its relics of the blessed Martin and other saints. While staying there I began to ask him to tell me something of the blessing of his conversion and how he had entered the clergy, for he was a Lombard by race. But he would not speak of these matters since he was quite determined to avoid vainglory. But I urged him with terrible oaths, first promising that I would disclose to no one what he told and I began to ask him to conceal from me none of the matters of which I would ask. After resisting a long time he was overcome at length by my entreaties and protestations and told the following tale: "When I was a small boy," said he, " I heard the name of the blessed Martin, though I did not know yet whether he was martyr or confessor or what good he had done in the world, or what region had the merit of receiving his blessed limbs in the tomb; and I was already keeping vigils in his honor, and if any money came into my hands I would give alms. As I grew older I was eager to learn and I was able to write before I knew the order of the written letters [before I could read]. Then I joined the abbot Aridius and was taught by him and visited the church of Saint Martin. Returning with him he took a little of the dust of the holy tomb for a blessing. This he placed in a little case and hung it on my neck. Coming to his monastery in the territory of Limoges he took the little case to place it in his oratory and the dust had increased so much that it not only filled the whole case but burst out at the joints wherever it could find an exit. In the light of this miracle my mind was the more on fire to place all my hope in his power. Then I came to the territory of Trèves and on the mountain where you are now built with my own hands the dwelling you see. I found here an image of Diana which the unbelieving people worshiped as a god. I also built a column on which I stood in my bare feet with great pain. And when the winter had come as usual I was so nipped by the icy cold that the power of the cold often caused my toenails to fall off and frozen moisture hung from my beard like candles. For this country is said to have a very cold winter." And when I asked him urgently what food or drink he had and how he destroyed the images on the mountain, he said: "My food and drink were a little bread and vegetables and a small quantity of water. And when a multitude began to flock to me from the neighboring villages I preached always that Diana was nothing, that her images and the worship which they thought it well to observe were nothing; and that the songs which they sang at their cups and wild debauches were disgraceful; but it was right to offer the sacrifice of praise to all-powerful God who made heaven and earth. I often prayed that the Lord would deign to hurl down the image and free the people from this error. And the Lord's mercy turned the rustic mind to listen to my words and to follow the Lord, abandoning their idols. Then I gathered some of them together so that by their help I could hurl down the huge image which I could not budge with my own strength, for I had already broken the rest of the small images, which was an easier task. When many had gathered at this statue of Diana ropes were fastened and they began to pull but their toil could accomplish nothing. Then I hastened to the church and threw myself on the ground and weeping begged the divine mercy that the power of God should destroy that which human energy could not overturn. After praying I went out to the workmen and took hold of the rope, and as soon as I began to pull at once the image fell to the ground where I broke it with iron hammers and reduced it to dust. But at this very hour when I was going to take food my whole body was so covered with malignant pimples from sole to crown that no space could be found that a single finger might touch. I went alone into the church and stripped myself before the holy altar. Now I had there a jar full of oil which I had brought from Saint Martin's church. With this I oiled all my body with my own hands and soon lay down to sleep. I awoke about midnight and rose to perform the service and found my whole body cured as if no sore had appeared on me. And I perceived that these sores were sent not otherwise than by the hate of the enemy. And inasmuch as he enviously seeks to injure those who seek God, the bishops, who should have urged me the more to continue wisely the work I had begun, came and said: ' This way which you follow is not the right one, and a baseborn man like you cannot be compared with Simon of Antioch who lived on a column. Moreover the situation of the place does not allow you to endure the hardship. Come down rather and dwell with the brethren you have gathered.' At their words I came down, since not to obey the bishops is called a crime. And I walked and ate with them. And one day the bishop summoned me to a village at a distance and sent workmen with crowbars and hammers and axes and destroyed the column I was accustomed to stand on. I returned the next day and found it all gone. I wept bitterly but could not build again what they had torn down for fear of being called disobedient to the bishop's orders. And since then I am content to dwell with the brothers just as I do now."

16.

And when I asked him to tell somewhat of the miracles which the blessed Martin worked in that place, he related the following: "The son of a certain Frank of the highest rank among his people was deaf and dumb; he was brought by his kinsmen to this church and I had him sleep on a couch in the holy temple with my deacon and another attendant. And by day he devoted himself to prayer and at night he slept in the church as I have said. And when God pitied him the blessed Martin appeared to me in a vision saying, 'Send the lamb out of the church for he is now cured.' In the morning I was thinking what this dream meant when the boy came to me and spoke and began to thank God, and turning to me said: 'I thank all-powerful God who has restored to me speech and hearing.' After this he was cured and returned home."

[**17.** Peculiar appearances in the heavens from which Gregory expected that "some plague would be sent upon them from the heavens." **18.** Childebert's invasion of Italy and the appointment of various dukes and counts. **19.** The abbot Dagulfus is taken in adultery. **20.** A synod meets at Mâcon.]

20.

Exstitit enim in hac synodo quidam ex episcopis qui dicebat mulierem hominem non posse vocitari. sed tamen ab episcopis ratione accepta quievit: eo quod sacer veteris testamenti liber edoceat, quod in principio deo hominem creante ait, "masculum et feminam creavit eos: vocavitque nomen eorum Adam" (Gen. 5.2), quod est 'homo terrenus'; sic utique vocans mulierem ceu virum: utrumque enim hominem dixit. sed et dominus Iesus Christus ob hoc vocitatur filius hominis, quod sit filius virginis, id est mulieris. ad quam cum aquas in vina transferre pararet, ait: "Quid mihi et tibi est, mulier?" (John 2.4) et reliqua. multisque et aliis testimoniis haec causa convicta quievit.

There came forward at this Council a certain bishop who maintained that woman could not be included under the term "man." However, he accepted the reasoning of the other bishops and did not press his case for the holy book of the Old Testament tells us that in the beginning, when God created man, "Male and female he created them and called their name Adam," which means earthly man; even so, he called the woman Eve, yet of both he used the word "man." And our Lord Jesus Christ is called "Son of man"", but is the son of of virgin, who is a woman.

[-see article by Michael Nolan,, "The Myth of the Soulless Woman," [or here] *First Things, 72* (April 1997): 13-14]

[**21.** Childebert hears a charge of grave robbery against Gunthram Boso. **22.** Various items of the year 585. **2325.** Prodigies. **26.** Eberulf, former duke of Tours and Poitiers, loses his property. **27.** Desiderius is restored to favor with Gunthram. **28.** Relations with the Spanish king. **29.** The plot to assassinate Childebert and its failure. **30.** Gunthram sends two armies to attack Septimania. They plunder his own territories and turn back without success. **31.** Quarrel between Fredegunda and Prætextatus, bishop of Rouen. **32.** Dispute about vineyards between one of Fredegunda's officials and Domnola.]

33.

Now there was in these days in the city of Paris a woman who said to the inhabitants: "O flee from the city and know that t must be burned with fire." And when she was ridiculed by many For saying this on the evidence of lots and because of some idle dream or at the urging of a midday demon, she replied: "It is not is you say, for I say truly that I saw in a vision a man all illumined coming from the church of St. Vincent, holding a torch in his hand and setting fire to the houses of the merchants one after another." Then the third night after the woman made this prophecy, at twilight a certain citizen took a light and went into his storehouse and took oil and other necessary things and went out, leaving the light close by the cask of oil. This was the house next the gate which is towards the south. From this light the house caught fire and burned, and from it others began to catch. Then the fire threatened the prisoners, but the blessed Germanus appeared to them and broke the posts and chains by which they were bound and opened the prison door and allowed all the prisoners to go safe. They went forth and took refuge in the church of St. Vincent in which is the blessed bishop's tomb. Now when the flame was carried hither and thither through the whole city by the high wind end the fire had the complete mastery, it began to approach another gate where there was an oratory of the blessed Martin which had been placed there because he had there cured a case of leprosy with a kiss. The man who had built it of interwoven branches, trusting in God and confident of the blessed Martin's power, took refuge within its walls with his property saying: "I believe and have faith that he who has so often mastered fire and at this place by a kiss made a leper's skin clean, will keep the fire from here." When the fire came near great masses of flame swept along but when they touched the wall of the oratory they were extinguished at once. But the people kept calling to the man and woman: "Run if you wish to save yourselves. For a mass of fire is rushing on you; see, ashes and coals are falling around you like a heavy rain. Leave the oratory or you will be burned in the fire." But they kept on praying and were never moved by these words. And the woman, who was armed with the strongest faith in the power of the blessed bishop, never moved from the window through which the flames sometimes entered. And so great was the power of the blessed bishop that he not only saved this oratory together with his follower's house but he did not permit the flames to injure the other houses which were around. There the fire ceased which had broken out on one side of the bridge. And on the other side it burned all so completely that only the river stopped it. However, the churches with the houses attached to them were not burned. It was said that this city had been as it were consecrated in ancient times so that not only fire could not prevail there but snakes and mice could not appear. But lately when a channel under the bridge had been cleaned and the mud which filled it had been taken out they found a snake and a mouse of bronze. They were removed and after that mice without number and snakes appeared, and fires began to take place.

34.

Inasmuch as the prince of darkness has a thousand arts of doing injury, I will relate what lately happened to recluses vowed to God. Vennoc, a Breton, who had become a priest as we have told in another book, was so given up to abstinence that he wore only garments made of skins and ate wild herbs in the raw state and merely touched the wine to his lips so that one would think he was kissing it rather than drinking. But as the devout in their generosity often gave him vessels of this liquor, sad to say he learned to drink immoderately and to be so given up to it as to be generally seen drunk. And so as his drunkenness grew worse and time went on he was seized by a demon and so violently harassed that he would seize a knife or any kind of weapon or stone or club that he could lay hands on and run after men in an insane rage. And it became necessary to bind him with chains and imprison him in a cell. After raging under this punishment for two years died.

There was also Antholius of Bordeaux. When a boy of twelve years old, it is said, the servant of a merchant, he asked to be allowed to become a recluse. His master opposed him a long time, thinking he would grow lukewarm and that at his age he could not attain to what he wished, but he was at length overcome by his servant's entreaties and permitted him to fulfil his desire. Now there was an old crypt vaulted and very finely built, and in the corner of it was a little cell built of squared stones in which there was hardly room for one man standing. The boy entered this cell and remained in it eight years or more, satisfied with very little food and drink and devoting himself to watching and prayer. After this was seized with a great fear and began to shout that he was being tortured internally. So it happened, by the aid, as I suppose of the devil's soldiers, that he tore away the stones that shut him in, dashed the wall to the ground and cried, wringing his hands, that the saints of God were causing him frightful torture. And when he had continued in this madness a long time and often mentioned the name of Saint Martin and said he caused him more torture than the other saints, he was brought to Tours. But the evil spirit, because, I suppose, of the virtue and greatness of the saint, did not tear the man. He remained in Tours for the space of a year and as he suffered no more he returned, but later on he suffered from the trouble that he had been free from here.

[**35.** An embassy from Spain to king Gunthram.]

36.

By order of king Childebert Magnovald was killed in his presence, for reasons not given, in the following manner: the king staying in his palace in the city; of Metz and was attending a sport in which an animal was surrounded by a pack of dogs and worried, when Magnovald was summoned. He came and not knowing what was to happen he began to look at the animal and laugh heartily with the rest. But a man who had received his orders seeing him intent on the spectacle raised his axe and dashed it against his head. He fell and died and was thrown out by the window and buried by his own people. His property was take at once, as much as was found, and carried to the public treasury Certain persons said that it was because he had beaten his wife to death after his brother died and had married his brother's wife, that he was killed.

[**37.** Birth of a son to Childebert. **38.** Spanish expedition into Gaul. **39.** Death of several bishops.]

40.

There was in the city of Tours a certain Pelagius who w as practiced in every villany and was not afraid of any judge, because he had under his control the keepers of the horses belonging to the fisc. Because of this he never ceased either on land or on the rivers to thieve, dispossess, plunder, murder, and commit every sort of crime. I often sent for him and both by threats and by gentle words tried to make him desist from his wickedness. But it was hatred rather than any reward of justice I got from him, according to Solomon's proverb: Reprove not a fool lest he hate thee.

The wretch so hated me that he often plundered and beat and left halfdead the men of the holy church, and was always looking for pretexts to harm the cathedral or the church of Saint Martin. And so it happened that once when our men were coming and bringing seaurchins in vessels, he beat them and trampled on them and took the vessels. When I learned of this I excommunicated him, not to avenge my wrong but to correct him more easily of this insanity. But he chose twelve men and came to clear himself of this crime by perjury. Though I was unwilling to receive any oath I was compelled by him and my fellowcitizens, and so I sent the rest away and received his oath only, and ordered that he be taken back into communion. It was then the first month. When the fifth month [*note:* *July*] came when the meadows are usually cut, he entered a meadow adjoining his own that belonged to the monks But as soon as he put sickle to it he was seized with fever and died on the third day. He had had a tomb made for him in Saint Martin s church in the village of Candes, but when it was uncovered his people found it broken to bits. He was afterwards buried in the portico of the church. The vessels for which he had perjured himself were brought by his storekeeper after his death. Here the power of the blessed Mary is evident, in whose church the wretch d taken a false oath.

[**41.** Fredegunda is accused of the killing of Prætextatus. **42.** Beppolenus leaves Fredegunda and is made a duke by Gunthram. **43.** Palladius, bishop of Saintes, is forced to appear before Gunthram. **44.** Fredegunda attempts to have Gunthram assassinated. **45.** Death of Duke Desiderius. **46.** Richared succeeds Leuvigild of Spain.]

HERE ENDS THE EIGHTH BOOK

BOOK IX

HERE BEGIN THE CHAPTERS OF THE NINTH BOOK

IN CHRIST'S NAME HERE BEGINS BOOK NINE IN THE TWELFTH YEAR OF KING CHILDEBERT

[**1.** Richared, the new king of Spain, sends legates to Gunthram and Childebert; they are not received by Gunthram. **2.** Death of Radegunda.]

3.

Meantime the festival of Saint Marcellus came, which is celebrated in the seventh month in the city of Chalon, and king Gunthram was present. And when the ceremony was over and he had approached the holy altar for the communion, a certain man came as if to say something. And as he hastened to the king a knife fell from his hand; he was seized at once and they found another knife unsheathed in his hand. He was immediately led from the holy church and put in fetters and subjected to torture, and he confessed that he had been sent to kill the king, saying, "This was the purpose of the man who sent me. " Since the king knew that the hatred of many men was united on him and he feared that he would be stabbed, he had given orders to his men to guard him well and no opportunity could be found to get at him with swords unless he was attacked in the church, where he was known to stand without care or fear. Now the men who had been named were seized and many were executed, but he let this man go alive though severely beaten, because he thought it a crime that a man should be led out of church and beheaded

[**4.** A second son, Theodoric, is born to Childebert. **5.** Prodigies. Among others a village with cottages and men disappeared suddenly.]

6.

There was in that year in the city of Tours a man named Desiderius who claimed to be great and said he could do many miracles. He boasted too that messengers were kept busy going to and fro between him and the apostles Peter and Paul. And as I was not at home, the common folk thronged to him bringing the blind and lame but he did not attempt to cure them by holiness but to fool them with the delusion of necromancy. For he ordered paralytics and other cripples to be vigorously stretched as if he were going to cure by taking pains those whose limbs he could not straighten. by the blessing of the divine virtue. And so his attend ants would lay hold of a man's hands and others his feet, and pull in opposite directions so that one would think their sinews would be broken, and when they were not cured they would be sent off halfdead. And the result was that many died under this torture. And the wretch was so presumptuous that he said he was blessed Martin the younger and put himself on a par with the apostles. And it is no wonder that he compared himself with the apostles when that author of wickedness from whom such things proceed is going to assert toward the end of the world that he is Christ. Now it was known from the following fact that he was versed in the wicked art of necromancy as we have said above, because, as they say who observed him, when any one said any evil of him far away and secretly he would rebuke them publicly and say: "You said so and so about me and it was not right to say such things of a holy man like me." Now how else could he have learned of it except that demons were his messengers? He wore a hood and a goat'shair shirt and in public he was abstemious in eating and drinking, but in secret when he had come to his lodgings he would stuff his mouth so that his servant could not carry food to him as fast as he asked for it. But his trickery was exposed and stopped by our people and he was cast out from the territory of the city. We did not know then where he went, but he said he was a citizen of Bordeaux. Now seven years before there had been another great impostor who deceived many by his tricks. He wore a sleeveless shirt and over it a robe of fine stuff and carried a cross from which hung little bottles which contained as he said holy oil. He said that he came from the Spains and was bringing relics of the blessed martyrs Vincent the deacon and Felix. He arrived at Tours at the church of Saint Martin in the evening when we were sitting at dinner, and sent an order saying: "Let them come to see the holy relics." As the hour was late I replied: "Let the blessed relics rest on the altar and we will go to see them in the morning." But he arose at the first break of day and without waiting for me came with his cross and appeared in my cell. I was amazed and wondered at his hardihood and asked what this meant. He answered in a proud and haughty voice: "You should have given me a better welcome; I'll carry this to the ears of king Chilperic; he will avenge this contemptuous treatment of me." He paid no more attention to me but went into the oratory and said a verse, then a second and a third, began the prayer and finished it, all by himself, then took up his cross again and went off. He had a rude style of speech and was free with disgusting and obscene terms and not a sensible word came from him. He went on to Paris. In those days the public prayers were being held that are usually held before the holy day of the Lord's ascension. And as bishop Ragnemod was walking in procession with his people and making the round of the holy places, this person came with his cross and appearing among the people with his unusual clothing, he gathered the prostitutes and women of the lower class and formed band of his own and made an attempt to walk in procession to the holy places with his multitude. The bishop saw this and sent his archdeacon to say: "If you have relics of the saints to show, place them for a little in the church and celebrate the holydays with us, and when the rites are finished you shall go on your way." But he paid little attention to what the archdeacon said but began to abuse and revile the bishop. The bishop saw that he was an impostor and ordered him shut up in a cell. And examining all he had, he found a great bag full of roots of different herbs and also there were moles' teeth, the bones of mice, the claws and fat of bears. He knew that these were the means of sorcery and ordered them all thrown into the river; he took his cross away and ordered him to be driven from the territory of Paris. But be made himself a second cross and began to do what he had done before, but was captured and put in chains by the archdeacon and kept in custody. In these days I had corne to Paris and had my lodging at the church of the blessed martyr Julian. The following night the wretch broke out of prison and hastened to Saint Julian's Church just mentioned, wearing the chains with which he was bound, and fell on the pavement where I had been accustomed to stand and, overwhelmed with drowsiness and wine, he fell asleep. Unaware of this I rose at midnight to return thanks to God and found him sleeping. And such a stench came from him that that stench surpassed the stenches of all sewers and privies. I was unable to go into the church because of the stench. And one of the clergy came holding his nose and tried to wake him but could not; for the wretch was so intoxicated. Then four of the clergy came and lifted him and threw him into one corner of the church, and they brought water and washed the pavement and scattered sweet-smelling herbs on it and so I went in to offer the regular prayers. But he could not be wakened even when we sang the psalms until with the coming of day the sun's torch climbed higher. There, I surrendered him to the bishop with a request for his pardon. When the bishops assembled at Paris I told this at dinner and bade him be brought to receive correction. And when he stood by, Amelius, bishop of Tarbes, looked at him and recognized him as his slave who had run away. He secured his pardon and so took him back to his native place. There are many who practise these impostures and continually lead the common people into error. It is of these I think that the Lord says in the Gospel that in the latest times false Christs and false prophets shall arise who shall do signs and wonders and lead the very elect into error. Let this suffice for this subject; let us rather return to our task.

[7. Ennodius, duke of Tours and Poitiers, is removed from office. The Gascons make an inroad on Frankish territory, and also the Goths. 8. Childebert desires to punish Gunthram Boso for the insults he had offered to Brunhilda during Childebert's minority. 9. Rauchingus, Ursio, and Bertefred, enemies of Brunhilda, plot Childebcrt's death. Rauchingus is trapped and brutally killed. Ursio and Bertefred take refuge in a stronghold]

10.

While this was going on king Gunthram sent a second time to his nephew Childebert saying: "Let there be no delay; come, that I may see you. For it is surely necessary for your own life as , well as for the public welfare that we see one another." Hearing this he took his mother, sister, and wife and hastened to meet his uncle. Bishop Magneric of the city of Trèves was present also, and Gunthram Boso came, whom bishop Ageric of Verdun had received in custody. But the bishop who had pledged his faith for him was not present, because the agreement was that he should appear before the king without any defender so that if the king decided that he must die he was not to be begged off by the bishop; and if the king granted him life he would go free. Now the kings met and he was judged guilty on various grounds and was ordered to be put to death. When he learned it he flew to Magneric's lodging and shutting the doors and sending the clerks and attendants away he said: "Most blessed bishop, I know that you have great honor with the kings. And now I flee to you to be rescued. Behold, the executioners are at the door, whence you may plainly know that if you do not save me I shall kill you and go outside and die. Let me tell you plainly that either one death overtakes us or an equal life shall protect us. O holy bishop, I know that you share with the king the place of father to his son [*note: Godfather*] and I am sure that whatever you ask you will obtain from him; he will not be able to deny your holiness anything you demand. Therefore either obtain my pardon or we shall die together." He said this with his sword unsheathed. The bishop was alarmed at what he heard and said: "And how can I do it if I am kept here by you. Let me go to beg the king's mercy and perhaps he will pity you." But replied: "By no means, but send abbots and men you trust to carry the message I propose." However, these matters were not reported as they were to the king, but they said that he was being protected by the bishop. And so the king was angry and said: "If the bishop refuses to come out let him die together with that doer of wickedness." The bishop when he was told this sent messengers to the king. And when they had told their story king Gynthram said: "Set fire to the house and if the bishop cannot come out let them be burned together." The clerks on hearing this burst open the door by force and got the bishop out. Then when the wretch saw that he was hemmed in by great flames on every side he approached the door with his sword. But as soon as he left the threshold and set foot outside at once one of the people threw a lance and struck his forehead. He was confused by this stroke and lost his head and tried to throw his sword but he was wounded by the bystanders with such a multitude of lances that with the heads sticking in his body and the shafts supporting him was unable to fall to the earth. A few who were with him were killed and exposed on the field at the same time. And permission to bury them was obtained from the princes only with difficulty. This man was faithless, headlong in avarice, greedy for other men's property beyond limit, swearing to all and fulfilling his promises to none. His wife and sons were sent into exile and his property confiscated. A great quantity of gold and silver and of valuables of different sorts was found in his stores. Moreover what he had concealed underground from a consciousness of wrongdoing did not remain hidden. He often made use of soothsayers and lots , desiring to learn the future from them, but was always deceived.

[**11.** Gunthram and Childebert settle their differences amicably. **12.** Ursio and Bertefred are dislodged from their stronghold and slain. **13.** Baddo is allowed to go free. Dysentery is severe in Metz. Wiliulf's wife marries a third time. **14.** Bishop Egidius of Rheims makes his peace with Childebert.]

15.

Now at that time in Spain king Richard was influenced by the divine mercy and summoned the bishops of his religion and said to them: "Why are quarrels continually going on between you and the bishops who call themselves Catholic , and when they do many miracles by their faith why can you do nothing of the sort? Therefore I beg you let us meet with them and examine the beliefs of both sides and find out what is true; and then either let them take our plan and believe what you say or else you recognize their truth and believe what they preach." This was done and the bishops of both sides gathered and the heretics expounded the doctrines that I have often described them as advocating. Likewise the bishops of our religion made the replies by which, as I have pointed out in the previous books, the heretics have been often defeated. And above all the king said that no miraculous cure of the infirm had been done by the bishops of the heretics, aid when he recalled to mind how in his father's time the bishop who boasted that he could restore sight to the blind by his faith which was not the true one had touched a blind man and [thus] condemned him to perpetual blindness and had come off in confusion I have told this story more fully in the book of *The Miracles* he summoned God's bishops to him separately. And by questioning then, he learned that it was one God that was worshiped with distinction of three persons, namely, the Father, Son, and Holy Ghost, and the Son was not inferior to the Father nor the Holy Ghost, nor the Holy Ghost inferior to the Father nor the Son, but they were equal and alike all-powerful, and in this Trinity they confessed the true God. Then Richared perceived the truth and ending the argument he placed himself under the Catholic law, and receiving the sign of the blessed cross together with baptism he believed in Jesus Christ son of God, equal to the Father and the Holy Ghost, reigning for ages of ages. Amen. Then he sent messengers to the province of Narbonne to tell what he had done and bring the people to a like belief. The bishop of the Arian sect there at the time was Athalocus who caused such trouble to God's churches by his vain doctrines and false interpretations of the Scriptures that he was believed to be the very Arius who, as the historian Eusebius relates, lost his entrails in a privy. But when he did not allow the people of his sect to believe these things and only a few flattered him by agreeing with him he was transported with spite and went to his cell and laid his head on the bed and breathed out his worthless soul. And thus the heretics in the province confessed the inseparable Trinity and departed from error.

[**16.** King Richared sends an embassy to Gunthram and Childebert. It is not received by Gunthram. **17.** An unusually cold spring. **18.** The Bretons ravage the territory of Nantes.]

19.

The feud among the citizens of Tours which, as we have stated above, was ended, burst out again with renewed fury. After slaying Chramsind's kinsmen Sichar had become very friendly with him, and they loved one another so dearly that they often ate together and slept together in one bed. Once Chramsind made ready a dinner towards night and invited Sichar. He came and they sat down together to dinner. And Sichar became drunk with wine and made many boasts to Chramsind, and he is reported to have said at last: "Dearest brother, you owe me great gratitude for killing your kinsmen since you got payment for them and you have much gold and silver in your house, and if that payment had not given you a start you would now be naked and in need." But Chramsind heard Sichar's word with a bitter heart and said within himself: "Unless I avenge my kinsmen's death I ought to lose the name of man and be called a weak woman." And at once he exinguished the lights and plunged his dagger into Sichar's head. Sichar made a little cry and immediately fell and died. The attendants who had come with him rushed away. Chramsind stripped the garments from his lifeless body and hung it on a picket of the fence and mounted his horse and went to the king. He entered the church and threw himself at the king's feet and said: "I beg for my life, O glorious king, because I have killed men who slew my kinsmen secretly and plundered all their property." But when the case was gone into in detail queen Brunhilda was displeased that Sichar, who was under her protection, had been killed in such a way, and she became angry at Chramsind. When he saw that she was against him he went to Bouges, a village in the territory of Bourges where his kinsmen lived, because it was in Gunthram's kingdom. And Tranquilla, Sichar's wife, left her sons and her husband's property in Tours and Poitiers and went to her kinsmen at PontsurSeine and there married again. Sichar was twenty years old when he died. He was in his lifetime a fickle, drunken, murderous person, who offered insults to many when he was drunk. Later Chramsind returned to the king and it was decided that he must prove that Sichar had killed his kinsmen. This he did. But since queen Brunhilda had placed Sichar under her protection, as we have said, she ordered Chramsind's property to be confiscated. But later it was returned by the court official Flavian. In addition he went to Agen and got a letter from Flavian directing that no one should touch him. Flavian had received his property from the queen.

20.

In that year, which was also the thirteenth of king Childebert, I went to visit him at the city of Metz, and received orders to go on an embassy to king Gunthram. I found him at Chalon and said: "O famous king, your glorious nephew Childebert sends you many greetings and offers endless thanks to your goodness because he is continually reminded by you to do the things that please God and are acceptable to you and of advantage to the people. As regards the matters of which you spoke together he promises to fulfil everything and engages not to break any of the agreements which are made in writing between you." And the king said to this: " I do not offer him like thanks, because his promises to me are being broken. My part of Senlis is not surrendered; the men whom I wished to go for my good, since they are my enemies, they have not let go. And in what sense do you mean that my sweet nephew does not wish to break any of his written agreements? " To this I answered: "He wishes to do nothing contrary to those agreements but promises to fulfil them all, so that if you wish to send [men] to divide Senlis there need be no delay; for you shall receive your own at once. And as to the men you mention let their names be given in writing and all that is promised shall be fulfilled." We spoke of these matters and the king ordered the agreement itself to be read over again in the presence of the bystanders.

Copy of the Agreement.

When the most excellent lords, kings Gunthram and Childebert, and the most glorious lady queen Brunhilda met lovingly in Christ's name at Andelot to arrange with full counsel whatever might in any way cause a quarrel among them, it was affectionately settled, resolved upon and agreed between them by the mediation of the bishops and chief men and the help of God, that as long as all-powerful God wished them to live in the present,world they ought to keep faith and affection pure and undefiled for each other. In the same way since lord Gunthram in accordance with the agreement which he had entered into with lord Sigibert of good memory, claimed that the whole share which Sigibert had received from Charibert's kingdom belonged entirely to him and [since] the party of lord Childebert wished to claim from all what his father had possessed, it is definitely and deliberately agreed between them that the third of the city of Paris with its territory and people which had gone to lord Sigibert from Charibert's kingdom by written agreement, with the castles of ChAteaudun and Vendôme and whatever the said king received of the district of Étampes and the territory of Chartres in that direction, with their lands and people, were to remain perpetually under the authority and rule of lord Gunthram, with that which he held before from Charibert's kingdom while lord Sigibert was alive. In like manner king Childebert asserts his right from the present to Meaux and to twothirds of Senlis, Tours, Poitiers, Avranches, Aire, Saint Lizier, Bayonne, and Albi with their territories. The condition being observed that he of these kings whom the Lord wills to survive shall have a perpetual right to the whole kingdom of him who goes from the light of the present world without children, and by God's aid shall leave it to his descendants. It is especially agreed upon to be in every way inviolably observed that whatever the lord king Gunthram has given or by God's favor shall give to his daughter Clodechild in goods and men, both cities, lands, and revenues, shall remain under her ownership and control. And if she wishes of her own free will to dispose of lands belonging to the fisc or valuable articles or money , or to bestow them on any one, let it be kept with a good title forever and not be taken from any one at any time, and let her be under the protection and defense of lord Childebert, since she ought to possess in all honor and security everything that he finds her in possession of at her father's death. Likewise the lord king Gunthram promises that if in the uncertainty of human life lord Childebert should happen to pass from the light while he is living, - may the divine goodness not allow it and Gunthram does not wish to see it he will receive under his protection and guardianship like a good father Childebert's sons Theodobert and Theodoric and any others that God wishes to give him, so that they shall possess their father's kingdom in all security; and he will receive under his protection with a spiritual love lord Childebert's mother, queen Brunhilda, and her daughter Clodosind, sister of king Childebert, while she is in the country of the Franks, and his queen Faileuba like a good sister and daughters, and they shall possess all their property in all honor and dignity with peace and security, namely, cities, lands, revenues, and all rights, and every kind of property, both what they actually possess at the present time and what they are able justly to acquire in the future by Christ's aid, and if they wish to dispose of any of the lands of the fisc or articles or money of their own free will, or to present them to any one, let it be kept with a good title forever, and let their will in this respect not be disregarded by any one at any time. And as to the cities, namely, Bordeaux, Limoges, Cahors, Lescar, and Cieutat, which it is well known that Galsuntha, lady Brunhilda's sister, acquired as dowry or *morganegyba,* that is, morning gift, when she came into Francia, and which lady Brunhilda is known to have acquired by the decision of the glorious lord king Gunthram and of the Franks when Chilperic and king Sigibert were still alive, it is agreed that the lady Brunhilda shall have as her property from today the city of Cahors with its lands and all its people, but the other cities named lord Gunthram shall hold while he lives, on condition that after his death they shall pass by God's favor with every security under the control of the lady Brunhilda and her heirs, but while lord Gunthram lives they shall not at any time or on any pretext be claimed by lady Brunhilda or her son king Childebert or his sons. In the same way it is *agreed that* lord Childebert shall hold Senlis in entirety, and as far as the third therein due to lord Gunthram is concerned he shall be compensated by the third belonging to lord Childebert which is in Ressons. Likewise it is agreed that according to the agreements *entered into* between lord Gunthram and lord Sigibert of blessed memory, the *leudes* who originally took oath to lord Gunthram after the death of lord Clothar, if afterwards they are proved to have gone to the other side, shall be removed from the places where they are dwelling, and in the same manner those who after the death of king Clothar are found guilty of having first sworn allegiance to lord Sigibert and then have passed to the other side shall be removed likewise. Also whatever the kings mentioned have given to churches or to their followers, or in future by God's favor wish to give in accordance with justice, shall be held securely. And whatever is due to any one of their men in either kingdom according to law and justice, he shall not suffer any prejudice, but shall be permitted to take and hold what is due him; and if anything is taken from anyone without fault on his part in an interregnum, a hearing shall be held and it shall be restored. And as regards that which each owned through the generosity of previous kings down to the death of lord king Clothar of glorious memory, let him keep it in security. And whatever has been taken since that from persons who are faithful let them receive it back at once. And since a pure and untainted friendship has been formed in God's name between the kings mentioned, it is agreed that passage shall at no time be denied in either kingdom to the men of either king who wish to travel on public or private business. It is likewise *agreed that* neither shall entice away the others *leudes* or receive them when they come. And if perhaps one thinks that because of some act he has to flee to the other part, let him be excused in regard to the nature of the fault and sent back. It has been decided also to add this to the agreement, that if either party shall at any time transgress the present statute under some clever interpretation, he shall lose all the benefits both prospective and present, and it shall turn to the advantage of him, who faithfully observes all that is written above, and he shall be freed in all details from the obligation of his oath. All these matters having been definitely agreed upon, the parties swear by the name of all-powerful God and the inseparable Trinity and all that is divine and the awful day of judgment that they will faithfully observe all that is written above without any fraud or deceit. This, compact was made four days before the Kalends of December in the twentysixth year of the reign of the lord king Gunthram and in the twelfth year of lord Childebert.

When the agreement was read over the king said: "May I be struck by the judgment of God if I transgress in any one of the matters contained here." And he turned to the legate Felix who had come with us and said: "Tell me, Felix, have you established a close friendship between my sister Brunhilda and Fredegunda t he enemy of God and man? " When he replied " no " I said: " Let the king be sure that the friendship is being kept up between them as it was started many years ago. For you may be certain that the hatred that was once established between them is alive yet, it has not withered up. I wish you, most glorious king, would have less friendship for her. For as we often learn, you receive her embassies with greater state than ours." He answered: "Let me tell you, bishop of God, that I receive her embassies in such a way as not to lose the affection of my nephew king Childebert. For I cannot be friendly. with one who has often sent to take rn~ life." Upon this Felix said: " I suppose it has come to your greatness that Richared has sent an embassy to your nephew to ask for your niece Clodosinda, your brother's daughter, in marriage. But he was unwilling to make any promise without your advice." The king said: "It is not well for my niece to go to a place where her sister was killed. I am not at all pleased that the death of my niece Ingunda is not avenged." Felix replied: "They are very anxious to set themselves right either by oath or on any other terms you suggest; but only give your consent for Clotosinda to be betrothed to him as he requests." The king said: " If my nephew keeps the agreements that he bound himself to in the compact I will do his will in this matter." We promised that he would fulfil all and Felix added: "He begs your goodness to give him help against the Lombards so that they may be driven from Italy and the part which his father claimed when alive may return to him, and the other part be restored by your and his aid to the dominion of the emperor." The king replied: "I cannot send my army to Italy and expose the soldiers to death uselessly. For a very severe plague is now wasting Italy." And I said: "You have told your nephew to have all the bishops of his kingdom meet together since there are many things to be decided. But it was the opinion of your glorious nephew that each metropolitan according to the custom of ,the canons should meet with his provincials, and then what went wrong in each district would be set right by order of the bishops. For what reason is there that so great a number should assemble? The faith of the church is not attacked by any danger; no new heresy is appearing. What need will there be for so many bishops to meet together? " And he said: "There is much to be looked into that has gone wrong, both acts of incest and matters which are in discussion between us. But the most important case of all is that of God, since you must investigate why bishop Praetextatus was slain by the sword in his church. Moreover there ought to be an examination of those who are accused of wantonness so that if found guilty they can be corrected by the bishops' sentence, or if they prove innocent that the falsity of the charge can be publicly recognized." Then he gave orders for the synod to be adjourned to the Kalends of the fourth month. [**note:** *June*] After this conversation we went to church; it was the day of the anniversary of the Lord's resurrection. After mass he invited us to a dinner which was as abundant in dishes as rich in cheer. For the king talked always of God, building churches and helping the poor, and then he made pious jokes and to please us he went on to say this: "I hope my nephew will keep his promises; for all I have is his. Still, if he is disturbed because I receive my nephew Clothar's legates, I'm not so mad, am I, but that I can mediate between them and keep the trouble from going further ? I know it is better to cut it short than to carry it too far. If I decide that Clothar is my nephew I will give him two or three cities in some part, so that he not seem to be disinherited, and what I leave to Childebert will not then disquiet him." After this talk he bade us go on our way, treating us affectionately and loading us with gifts, and telling us always to give king Childebert good advice to live by.

21.

The king himself, as we have often said, was great in almsgiving and unwearied in watches and fasting. It was told at the time that Marseilles was suffering greatly from the bubonic plague and that the disease had spread swiftly as far as the village in the country of Lyons called Octavus. But the king like a good bishop was for providing remedies by which the wounds of the sinful people could be cured, and ordered all to assemble at the church and engage devoutly in prayer. He directed that nothing else than barley bread and clean water should be taken in the way of food and that all without intermission should keep watch. And this was done and for three days he gave alvis with more than usual generosity and he showed such fear for all the people that he was now believed to be not merely a king but a bishop of God, placing all his hope in God's mercy, and in the purity of his faith turning all his thoughts to him by whom he believed that these thoughts could be given effect. It was then commonly told among the faithful that a woman whose son was suffering from a fourday fever and was lying in bed very ill, approached the king's back in the throng of people and secretly broke off the fringe of the royal garment and put it in water and gave to her son to drink, and at once the fever die down and he was cured. I do not regard this as doubtful since I have myself heard persons possessed by demons in their furies call on his name and admit their ill deeds, recognizing his power.

22.

Since we have told above that the city of Marseilles was sick with a deadly plague it seems suitable to give more details of what the city suffered. In these days bishop Theodore had gone to the king to speak to him against the patrician Nicetius. But when he got no hearing from king Childebert on this matter he made ready to return home. Meantime a ship from Spain put in at the port with its usual wares and unhappily brought the seed of this disease. And many citizens bought various merchandise from her, and one household in which were eight souls was quickly left vacant, its inmates all dying of this plague. But the fire of the plague did not at once spread through all the houses, but after a definite time like a fire in standing grain it swept the whole city with the flame of disease. However the bishop went to the city and shut himself within the walls of St. Victor's church with the few who then remained with him, and there devoted himself to prayer and watching while the people of the city perished, praying for God's mercy that the deaths might at length cease and the people be allowed to rest in peace. The plague passed away in two months, and when the people, now reassured, had returned to the city the disease came on again and they who returned perished. Later on the city was many times attacked by this death.

[23. Ageric, bishop of Verdun, dies of chagrin because Gunthram Boso, whose safety he had pledged, had been killed, and because Bertefred had been killed in his oratory. 24. Phronius the new bishop, of Vence. 25. Childebert makes war on the Lombards and suffers a defeat " the like of which in former times is not recalled." 26. Gregory assists queen Ingoberga in making her will.]

27.

Duke Amalo sent his wife to another estate to attend to his interests, and fell in love with a certain free-born girl. And hen it was night and Amalo was drunk with wine he sent his men to seize the girl and bring her to his bed. She resisted and they brought her by force to his house, slapping her, and she was stained by a torrent of blood that ran from her nose. And even the bed of the duke mentioned above was made bloody by the stream. And he beat her, too, striking with his fists and cuffing her and beating her otherwise, and took her in his arms, but he was immediately overwhelmed with drowsiness and went to sleep. And she reached her hand over the man's head and found his sword and drew it, and like Judith Holofernes struck the duke's head a powerful blow. He cried out and his slaves came quickly. But when they wished to kill her he called out saying: "I beg you do not do it for it was I who did wrong in attempting to violate her chastity. Let her not perish for striving to keep her honor." Saying this he died. And while the household was assembled weeping over him the the girl escaped from the house by God's help and went in the night to the city of Chalon about thirtyfive miles away; and there she entered the church of Saint Marcellus and threw herself at the king's feet and told all she had endured. Then the king was merciful and not only gave her her life but commanded that an order be given that she should be placed under his protection and should not suffer harm from any kinsman of the dead man. Moreover we know that by God's help the girl's chastity was not in any way violated by her savage ravisher.

[**28.** Brunhilda's messenger to the Spanish king is detained by Gunthram. **29.** Childebert sends an army against the Lombards.]

30.

King Childebert at the invitation of Bishop Maroveus sent assessors to Poitiers, namely, Florientian, the queen's majordomo, and Romulf, count of the palace, to make new tax lists in order that the people might pay the taxes they had paid in his father's time. For many of them were dead and the weight of the tribute came on widows and orphans and the weak. And they made an orderly examination and released the poor and sick and subjected to the public tax those who should justly pay. And so they came to Tours. But when they wished to impose the payment of taxes on the people, saying they had the book in their hands, showing how they had paid in the time of previous kings, I answered saying: "It is well known that the city of Tours was assessed in the time of king Clothar and those books were taken to the presence of the king, but the king was stricken with fear of the holy bishop Martin and they were burned. After king Clotbar's death this people swore allegiance to king Charibert and he likewise swore that he would not impose new laws or customs on the people but would thereafter maintain them in the status in which they lived in his father's reign, and he promised that he would not impose any new ordinance which would tend to despoil them. And count Gaiso in the same time began to exact tribute, following a capitulary which we have said was written at a more ancient time. But being stopped by bishop Euphronius he went with the little he had collected to the king's presence and pointed to the capitulary in which the tributes were contained. But the king uttered a groan and fearing the power of Saint Martin he had it burned, and sent back the gold coins that had been collected to the church of Saint Martin, asserting that no one of the people of Tours should pay tribute. After his death king Sigibert ruled this city and did not lay upon it the weight of any tribute. Moreover in the fourteen years of his reign from his father's death up to now Childebert has demanded nothing, and this city has not groaned with the burden of tribute. It is now for your decision whether to assess tribute or not; but be careful lest you do some harm if you plan to go against his oath." When I had said this they answered: "Behold, we have the book in our hands in which a tax was imposed on this people." But I said: "This book was not brought from the king's treasury and it has had no authority for many years. it is no wonder, considering the enmities among these citizens, if it has been kept in some one's house. God will give judgment on those who have brought out this book after so long a time to despoil our citizens." And while this was going on the son of Audinus, who had brought out the book, was seized with a fever on the very day and died three days after. We then sent messengers to the king asking him to send his commands on this matter. And they at once sent a letter ordering that out of respect for Saint Martin the people of Tours should not be assessed. Upon receipt of the letter the men who had come for this purpose returned home.

[31. An expedition of king Gunthrarn against Septimania is defeated. 32. Misunderstanding between Childebert and Gunthram. 33. Quarrel between Ingytrude, head of the convent within St. Martin's walls, and her daughter.]

34.

Rigunda, daughter of Chilperic, often made malicious charges against her mother and said that she was mistress and that her mother ought to serve her, and often attacked her with abuse and sometimes struck and slapped her, and her mother said to her: "Why do you annoy me, daughter? Come, take your father's things that I have and do as you please with them." And she went into the storeroom and opened a chest quite full of necklaces and costly jewels. For a long time she took them out one by one and handed them to her daughter but finally said: "I am tired; you put in your hand and take what you find." And she thrust in her arm and was taking things from the chest when her mother seized the lid and slammed it down on her head. And she was holding it down firmly and the lower board was pressing against her daughter's throat so that her eyes were actually ready to pop out when one of the maids who was within called loudly: "Run, I beg you, run; my mistress is being choked to death by her mother." And those who were awaiting their coming outside rushed into the little room and saved the girl from threatening death and led her out. After that their enmity was more bitter and there were continual quarrels and fighting between them, above all because of the adulteries Rigunda was guilty of.

35.

Beretrude, when dying, appointed her daughter heir, leaving certain property to the nunneries she had founded and to the cathedrals and churches of the holy confessors. But Waddo, whom we mentioned in a former book, complained that his horses ,had been taken by her soninlaw, and he proposed to go to an estate of hers which she had left to her daughter and which was within the territory of Poitiers, saying: "He came from another kingdom and took my horses and I will take his estate." Meantime he sent orders to the bailiff that he was coming and to make everything ready for his use. The bailiff on hearing this gathered all the household and got ready to fight, saying: "Unless I'm killed Waddo shall not enter my master's house." Waddo's wife heard that warlike preparations were being made against her husband, and she said to him: "Do not go there, dear husband; for you will be killed if you go and my children and I will be miserable." And she laid hold of him and wished to detain him, and her son also said: " If you go, we will be killed together and you will leave my mother a widow and my brothers orphans." But these words altogether failed to hold him back and he was enflamed with madness at his son, and calling him cowardly and soft he threw his ax and almost crushed his skull. But the son dashed it partly aside and escaped the stroke. Then they mounted their horses and went off, sending word again to the bailiff to sweep the house and spread covers on the benches. But he paid little attention to the order and stood with his throngs of men and women before his master's door, as we have said, awaiting Waddo's coming. He came and at once entered the house and said: "Why are these benches not spread with covers and the house swept?" And he raised his hand with his dagger in it and struck the man's head and he fell and died. Upon seeing this the dead man's son hurled his lance from in front against Waddo and pierced the middle of his belly with the blow, and the spearhead came out of his back and he fell to the ground, and the multitude which had gathered drew near and began to stone him. Then certain of those who had come with him rushed up amid the showers of stones and covered him with a cloak and the people were calmed, and his son, uttering mournful cries, got him upon his horse and took him back home still living. But he died soon amid the laments of his wife and sons. And so his life was unhappily ended and his son went to the king and obtained his property.

[**36.** Childebert sends his son Theodobert to represent him in Soissons. **37.** Bishop Droctigisil goes insane from excessive drinking or because evil arts had been practiced on him. **38.** A plot ,against Brunhilda and Childebert's wife. **3943.** The story in detail of the secession of forty nuns from the convent at Poitiers, with documents involved in the case. **44.** The weather.]

HERE ENDS THE NINTH BOOK.

BOOK X

HERE END THE CHAPTERS OF THE TENTH BOOK

THE NAME OF OUR LORD JESUS CHRIST
HERE BEGINS THE TENTH BOOK

1.

In the fifteenth year of king Childebert our deacon returned from Rome with relics of the saints and related that in the ninth month of the previous year the river Tiber so flooded the city of Rome that ancient temples were destroyed and the storehouses of the church were overturned and several thousand measures of wheat in them were lost. A multitude of snakes, among them a great serpent like a big log, passed down into the sea by the channel of this river, but these creatures were smothered among the rough and salty waves of the sea and cast up on the shore. Immediately after came the plague which they call *inguinaria. [**note:** affecting the groin (inguen)]* It came in the middle of the eleventh month and according to what is read in the prophet Ezekiel: "Begin at my sanctuary," it first of all smote the pope Pelagius and soon killed him. Upon his death a great mortality among the people followed from this disease. But since the church of God could not be without a head all the people chose Gregroy the deacon. He belonged to one of the first senatorial families and from his youth was devoted to God and with his own means had established six monasteries in Sicily and a seventh within the Roman walls; and giving to these such an amount of land as would suffice to furnish their daily food, he sold the rest and all the furniture of his house and distributed the money among the poor in the city; and he who had been used to arrayed in silken robes and glittering jewels was now clad in cheap garments, and he devoted himself to the service of the Lord's altar and wasassigned as seventh levite to aid the pope. And such was his abstinence in food, his sleeplessness in prayer, his determination in fasting that his stomach was weakened and he could scarcely stand upright. He was so versed in grammar, dialectic, and rhetoric that he was believed second to none in the city. He strove earnestly to avoid this high office for fear that a certain pride at attaining the honor might sweep him back into the worldly vanities he had rejected. And so he sent a letter to the emperor Mauricius whose son he had taken from the holy font, adjuring him and entreating him with many prayers never to grant his consent to the people to raise him to this place of honor. But Germanus, prefect of Rome, forestalled the messenger and had him arrested and the letter destroyed, and himself sent to the emperor the choice which the people had made. And the emperor on account of his friendship with the deacon thanked God that he had found a place of honor and sent his command to appoint him. . . .

[Because of the plague Gregory makes an address to the people of Rome to meet it by prayer.]

When he spoke these words bands of clergy gathered and he bade them sing psalms for three days and pray for God's mercy. Every three hours choirs of singers came to the church crying through the streets of the city "Kyrie eleison." Our deacon who was there said that in the space of one hour while the people uttered cries of supplication to the Lord eighty fell to the ground and died. But the bishop did not cease to urge the people not to cease from prayer. It was from Gregory while he was still deacon that our deacon received the relics of the saints as we have said.

And when Gregory was making ready to go to a hiding place he was seized and brought by force to the church of the blessed apostle Peter and there he was consecrated to the duties of bishop and made pope of the city. Our deacon did not leave until Gregory returned from the port to become bishop, and he saw his ordination with his own eyes.

2.

Grippo returned from the emperor Maurice and reported that in the preceding year he and his companions had taken ship and landed at an African port and gone on to Carthage the Great. While they were remaining there, awaiting the orders of the prefect who was in the city as to how they were to reach the emperor's presence, one of the men belonging to Evantius, who had gone out with him, snatched an article of value from a trader's hand and took it to their lodging. The owner of the article followed him and demanded his property back. But the man put him off and the quarrel grew greater from day to day, and one day the trader met the man on the street and took hold of his clothes and held fast saying: "I'll never let you go until you return to my possession what you took by violence." But the other after trying to shake him off did not hesitate to snatch his sword and kill the fellow, and he at once returned to the lodging but did not disclose to his comrades what had happened. Now as I have said the legates were Bodigisel, son of Mummolinus of Soissons, and Evantius, son of Dinamius of Arles, and this Grippo, a Frank, and they had arisen from dinner and retired to rest and sleep. But when the act of their man was reported to the ruler of the city he gathered soldiers and all the people put on their armor and he sent them to their lodging. But the legates were amazed on being wakened to see what was going on, having had no expectation of it. Then the leader cried out saying: "Lay your arms aside and come out to us, that we may peaceably learn how the homicide happened." On hearing this they were alarmed as they did not yet know what had happened, and they asked for a pledge so that they could go out safely without arms. The men swore that they could but their hastiness did not allow them to keep their oath. But soon after Bodigisil went out they killed him with the sword and likewise Evantius. And when they lay before the door of the lodging Grippo seized his armor and went out to them with the men he had with him, saying: "We do not know what has happened and behold here are the comrades of my journey who were sent to the emperor lying slain by the sword. God will avenge our wrong and will atone for their death by your destruction, since you butcher us in this way when we do not harm you but come in peace. There shall not be peace any longer between our kings and your emperor. It was for peace we came and to bring aid to your state. Today I call God to witness that it is your crime that has caused the promised peace to be kept no longer between the princes." When Grippo had spoken these words and more to the same effect, this Carthaginian troop dispersed and each returned to his home. The prefect went to Grippo and attempted to calm m as to these occurrences and arranged for his going to the presence of the emperor. He went and told the business on which he had been sent and described the fate of his comrades. At this the emperor was greatly annoyed and promised to avenge their death in accordance with the judgment king Childebert should give. Then Grippo received gifts from the emperor and returned without being molested.

3.

These matters were related by Grippo to king Childebert, who at once commanded his army to march into Italy and sent twenty dukes to conquer the Lombards. I have not thought it necessary to set their names down here in order. But duke Audovald with Wintrio set the people of Champagne on the march and when he came to the city of Metz which is on the way he plundered, slew, and mistreated the inhabitants in such a manner that it might have been thought that he was leading an army against his own country. Moreover the other dukes did the same with their phalanxes and ravaged their own country and the people who remained behind, before they won any victory over the enemy. When they reached the Italian boundary Audovald with six dukes invaded the right side and reached the city of Milan, and there they pitched their camp at a distance on the plain. And duke Olo went rashly to Bellinzona, a stronghold of this city, situated on the plains called *Canini,* and was wounded with a dart under the nipple and fell and died. Moreover when they went out to plunder in order to get food, they were slain by the Lombards who rushed upon them everywhere. There was a lake in the territory of Milan called *Ceresium [**note:** Lugano]* out of which a small but deep stream flowed. Upon the shore of this lake they heard that the Lombards were encamped. They came to it, but before they could cross the stream we have mentioned one of the Lombards standing on the shore, armed with a coat of mail and helmet and carrying a lance in his hand, shouted against the army of the Franks, saying, "Today it shall appear to whom the Divinity will grant a victory." It may be understood that the Lombards had arranged this as a sign. Then a few crossed and fought this Lombard and slew him. And behold the whole army of the Lombards took to flight. Our men crossed the river but found none of them, seeing only the camp arrangements, where they had their fires and pitched their tents. And when they could capture none of them they returned to their own camp and there the emperor's legates came to them bringing the news that an army was at hand to help them, and saying, "After three days we will come with it, and this shall be a sign for you: when you see the houses of this village which is on the mountain burn with fire and the smoke rising up to heaven, be assured that we are close at hand with the army which we promised." However they waited according to agreement six days and saw none of them come.

And Chedinus with thirteen dukes entered Italy on the left and took five strongholds and exacted oaths of fealty. But dysentry affected his army severely because the air was new to his men and disagreed with them and many died of it. But when e wind rose and it rained and the air began to freshen a little it brought health in place of sickness. Why more? For about three months they wandered through Italy without accomplishing anything or being able to take vengeance on their enemies, since they were shut up in strongholds, or to capture the king and take vengeance on him, since he was shut up within the walls of Pavia, and then the army sickened as we have said because of the unhealthfulness of the air and grew weak from hunger and prepared to return home after exacting oaths of fidelity and subjecting to the king's rule the people of the country which his father had held before and from which they took captives and other booty. And returning thus they were so starved that they sold their armor and clothing to buy food before they came to their native place. . . .

4.

Maurice caused the Carthaginians who had killed king Childebert's legates the previous year, to be bound and loaded with chains and sent them to Childebert's presence, twelve in number, under these conditions, that if he wished to put them to death he should have permission; or if he would allow them to be ransomed he should receive three hundred gold pieces for each and be content; and thus he was to choose whichever he wished, that the disagreement might be more readily forgotten and no further cause of enmity arise between them. But king Childebert refused to accept the bound men and said: "It is uncertain in my mind whether these men you bring are the homicides or others, perhaps slaves of somebody or other, whereas our men who were killed in your country were free born." Grippo in particular, who had been legate at the time with the men who were killed, was present and said: "The prefect of the city with two or three thousand men whom he had gathered made an attack on us and killed my comrades; and I would have perished with them if I hadn't been able to make a brave defence. I can go to the place and identify the men. It is these that your emperor ought to punish if, as you say, he proposes to keep peace with our master." And so the king decided to send to the emperor for the guilty men and he bade these depart.

5.

In these days Chuppa, who had once been king Chilperic's constable, made an inroad into the territory of Tours and desired to take flocks and other property as if he were taking booty. But the inhabitants had warning and a multitude gathered and began to pursue him. He lost his plunder and two of his men were killed: he escaped with nothing and two other men were captured; they were sent in fetters to king Childebert. He ordered them to be thrown into prison and examined as to who it was by whose aid Chuppa escaped from being captured by his pursuers. They answered that it was through a stratagem of the vicar Animodus, who had the power of a judge in that district. At once the king sent a letter and ordered the count of the city to send him in chains to the king's presence; and if he should attempt resistance he was to crush him by force and even kill him, if he wished to gain the king's favor. But Animodus made no resistance but gave sureties and went as he was told, and finding Flavian the court-official he pleaded together with his companion and was not found guilty , they were acquitted and ordered to return home. However he first gave presents to the courtofficial. Chuppa a second time roused some of his people and purposed to carry off the daughter of Badigysel, former bishop of Mans, to marry her. He made a night attack with a band of his companions on the village of Mareil to fulfil his purpose, but Magnatrude, the mother of the girl and head of the household, had warning of him and his treachery ; she went out against him with her slaves and repelled him by force, killing many of his men; and he did not come off without disgrace.

[**6.** Miraculous deliverance of prisoners in a jail in Auvergne.]

7.

In the same city king Childebert most piously remitted all the tribute of the churches as well as of the monasteries and of the clergy who were attached to a church and of whoever were engaged in cultivating the church land. For the collectors of the tribute had suffered great losses, since in the course of long time and succeeding generations the estates had been divided into small parts and the tribute could be collected only with difficulty, and Childebert by inspiration of God directed that the trouble should be remedied and the amount which was due to the fisc from these should not be exacted from the collectors, and that arrearage should .not deprive any tiller of church land of his benefice.

8. Where the territories of Auvergne, Gévaudan, and Rouergue meet, a synod of bishops was held to hear the case against Tetradia, widow of Desiderius, from whom count Eulalius claimed the property which she had taken with her when she fled from him. I think that I ought to relate this case in full detail and how she left Eulalius and fled to Desiderius. Eulalius, as a young man will, had behaved in several matters in a senseless fashion, and so it came about that he was often reproached by his mother and began to hate when he should have loved her. Now she used frequently to devote herself to prayer in the oratory of her house and to spend the watches of the night in prayer and tears while her servants slept, and at last she was found strangled in the hair shirt in which she prayed. And though no one knew who had one this nevertheless her son was charged with the murder. When Cautinus, bishop of Clermont, heard of this, he excommunicated him. But when the citizens gathered with the bishop at the festival of the blessed martyr Julian, Eulalius threw himself at the feet of the bishop complaining that he had been excommunicated without a hearing. Then the bishop permitted him to attend the service of the mass with the others. But when the time for communion came and Eulalius went forward to the altar the bishop said: "Common talk among the people declares that you are a murderer. Now I do not know whether you have done this crime or not: therefore I leave it to the judgment of God and the blessed martyr Julian. You then, if you are fit to do so, as you say, approach and take a share of the Eucharist and put it in your mouth. For God will know your conscience." Eulalius received the Eucharist and had communion and departed. He had a wife, Tetradia by name, noble on her mother's side, of low rank by her father. And in his house he took the maidservants for concubines and began to neglect his wife, and when he returned from these harlots he would often beat her severely. Moreover because of his many illdeeds he contracted a number of debts and often used his wife's jewels and gold for these. Finally when his wife was in this hard situation since she had lost all the honor she had in her husband's house, and he was gone to the king, Virus, this was the man's name her husband's nephew, fell in love with her and wished to marry her since he had lost his wife. Virus however was afraid of his uncle's enmity and sent the woman to duke Desiderius with the intention of marrying her later on. And she took with her all her husband's substance both in gold and silver and garments and all she could take, together with her older son, but she left the younger son at home. Eulalius returned from his journey and learned what had happened. And when his grief was lessened and he had taken a little rest he rushed upon his nephew Virus and killed him in a narrow valley of Auvergne. And Desiderius who had lately lost his wife heard that Virus had been killed and married Tetradia. But Eulalius took a girl by force from the convent at Lyons and married her. But his concubines impelled by envy, as some say, made her insane by evil arts. A long time after Eulalius secretly attacked and killed Emerius, cousin of this girl. In like manner he killed Socratius, brother of his halfsister whom his father had had by a concubine. He committed also many other crimes, too many to tell. John, his son, who had gone off with his mother ran away from Desiderius's house and went to Auvergne. And Innocent being now a candidate for the bishopric of Rodez, Eulalius sent a message to him that he could recover by Innocent's aid the property that was rightfully his in the territory of this city. Innocent replied: "If I receive one of your sons to make a cleric of and to keep to help me, I will do what you ask." Eulalius sent the boy named John and received his property back. And Innocent received the boy and shaved the hair of his head and put him in the care of the archdeacon.of his church. And he became so abstemious that he ate barley instead of wheat, drank water instead of wine, used an ass instead of a horse, and wore the meanest garments. And so the bishops and leading men met, as we have said, at the confines of the cities mentioned, and Tetradia was represented by Agyn and Eulalius appeared to speak against her. When Eulalius asked for the things she had taken from his home when she went to Desiderius, Tetradia was ordered to repay what she took fourfold, and the children that she had by Desiderius were declared illegitimate; they also directed that if she paid Eulalius what she was ordered to pay him, she would have the liberty of going to Auvergne and of enjoying without disturbance the property which had come to her from her father. This was done.

[**9.** Gunthram sends an expedition against the Bretons which proves a failure.]

10.

In the fifteenth year of king Childebert which is the twenty-ninth of Gunthram, while king Gunthram was hunting in the Vosges forest he found traces of the killing of a buffalo. And when he harshly demanded of the keeper of the forest who had dared to do this in the king's forest, the keeper named Chundo the king's chamberlain. Upon this he ordered Chundo to be arrested and taken to Chalon loaded with chains. And when the two were confronted with each other in the king's presence and Chundo said that he had never presumed to do what he was charged with, the king ordered a trial by battle. Then the chamberlain offered his nephew to engage in the fight in his place and both appeared on the field; the youth hurled his lance at the keeper of the forest and pierced his foot; and he presently fell on his back. The youth then drew the sword which hung from his belt but while he sought to cut his fallen adversary's throat he himself received a dagger thrust in the belly. Both fell dead. Seeing this Chundo started to run to Saint Marcellus's church. But the king shouted to seize him before he touched the sacred threshold and he was caught and tied to a stake and stoned. After this the king was very penitent at having shown himself so headlong in anger as to kill hastily for a trifling guilt a man who was faithful and useful to him.

[**11.** King Clothar is dangerously ill. **12.** Ingytrude, abbess of a convent attached to St. Martin's church, dies, directing that her disobedient daughter should not even be allowed to pray at her tomb. **13.** One of Gregory's priests is "infected with the malignant poison of the Sadducean heresy." [note: *Denying the resurrection of the body.*]] He is overcome in argument by Gregory. **14.** Story of the drunken priest Theodulf who falls off the wall of Angers and is killed.]

15.

The scandal which by the help of the devil had arisen in the monastery at Poitiers was growing worse every day and Chrodield [***note:*** *Daughter of king Charibert. She had seceded from the monastery with a large following of nuns and was at this time at St. Hilary's church in Poitiers.*] was sitting all prepared for strife, having gathered to herself, as I have said above, murderers, sorcerers, adulterers, runaway slaves and men guilty of all other crimes. And so she gave orders to them to break into the monastery at night and drag the abbess from it. But the latter heard the uproar coming and asked to be carried to the chest containing the relics of the holy cross [***note:*** *The monastery was called the monastery of the Holy Cross*] for she was painfully troubled with gout thinking that she would be kept safe by their aid. Accordingly when the men had entered and lit the candles and were hurrying with weapons ready here and there through the monastery looking for her, they went into the oratory and found her lying on the ground before the chest of the holy cross. Thereupon one who was fiercer than the rest, having come on purpose to commit this crime, namely, to cleave the abbess in two with the sword, was given a knife stab by another, the divine providence aiding in this, I suppose. The blood gushed out and he fell to the ground without fulfilling the vow he had foolishly made. Meantime Justina, [***note:*** *Gregory's niece*] the prioress, and the other sisters had taken the cloth of the altar which was before the Lord's cross and covered the abbess with it, putting the lights out at the same time. But the men came with drawn swords and spears and tore the nuns' clothes and almost crushed their hands and seized the prioress instead of the abbess, since it was dark, and pulled her robes off and tore her hair down and dragged her out and carried her off to place her under guard at St. Hilary's Church; but, as the dawn was coming on, they perceived when near the church that it was not the abbess, and presently they told the woman to return to the monastery. They returned, too, and seized the abbess and dragged her away and confined her near St. Hilary's Church in a place where Basina [*note: One of Chrodield's faction, daughter of king Chilperic.*] lodged, setting guards at the door so that no one should give aid. to the captive. At the next twilight they entered the monastery and when they found no candles to light they took a cask from the storehouse which had been pitched and left to dry and set fire to it, and there was a great light while it burned, and they made plunder of all the furniture of the monastery, leaving only what they were unable to carry off. This happened seven days before Easter. And as the bishop was distressed at all this and could not calm this strife of the devil, he sent to Chrodield, saying: "'Let the abbess go, so that she shall not be kept in prison during these days; otherwise I will not celebrate the Lord's Easter festival nor shall any catechumen receive baptism in this city unless you order the abbess to be set free from the confinement in which she is held. And if you refuse to let her go, I will call the citizens together and rescue her." When he said this, Chrodield appointed assassins, saying: " If any one tries to carry her off by violence, give her a thrust with the sword at once." Now Flavian came in those days; he had lately been appointed *domesticus,* and by his aid the abbess entered St. Hilary's Church and was free. Meantime murders were being committed at the holy Radegunda's [*note: Daughter of Berthar, a Thuringian king, and wife of Clothar I*] tomb, and certain persons were hacked to death in a disturbance before the very chest that contained the relics of the holy cross. And since this madness increased daily because of Chrodield's pride, and continual murders and other deeds of violence, such as I have mentioned above, were being done by her faction, and she had become so swollen up with boastfulness that she looked down with lofty contempt upon her own cousin Basina, the latter began to repent and say: "I have done wrong in supporting haughty Chrodield. Behold I am an object of contempt to her and am made to appear a rebel against my abbess." She changed her course and humbled herself before the abbess and asked for peace with her; and they were equally of one thought and purpose. Then when the outrages broke out again, the men who were with the abbess, while resisting an attack which Chrodield's followers [*note: Chrodieldis scola.*] had made, wounded one of Basina's men who fell dead. But the abbess' men took refuge behind the abbess in the church of the confessor, and on this account Basina left the abbess and departed. But the men fled a second time, and the abbess and Basina entered again into friendly relations as before. Afterward many feuds arose between these factions; [*note: scolas.*] and who could ever set forth in words such wounds, such killings, and such wrong-doings, where scarcely a day passed without a murder, or an hour without a quarrel, or a moment without tears. King Childebert heard of this, and sent an embassy to king Gunthram to propose that bishops of both kingdoms should meet and punish these actions in accordance with the canons. And king Childebert ordered my humble self [*note: Mediocritatis nostriae personam*] to sit on this case, together with Eberegisel of Cologne and Maroveus himself, bishop of Poitiers; and king Gunthram sent Gundigisil of Bordeaux with his provincial s, since he was the metropolitan of this city. But I began to object, saying: "I will not go to this place unless the rebellion which has arisen because of Chrodield, is forcibly put down by the judge." [*note: the count is meant*] For this reason a command was sent to Macco, who was then count, in which he was ordered to put the rebellion down by force if they should resist. Chrodield heard of this and ordered her assassins to stand armed before the door of the oratory, thinking they would fight against the judge, and if he wished to use force, they would resist with equal force. So it was necessary for this count to go there with armed men and to beat some with clubs and pierce others with spears, and when they resisted fiercely he had to attack and overwhelm them with the sword. When Chrodield saw this, she took the Lord's cross, the miraculous power of which she had before despised, and came out to meet them saying: "Do no violence to me, I beg of you, for I am a queen, daughter of one king and cousin of another; don't do it, lest a time may come for me to take vengeance on you." But the throng paid little heed to what she said but rushed, as I have said, upon those who were resisting and bound them and dragged them from the monastery and tied them to stakes and beat them fiercely and cut off the hair of some, the hands of others, and in a good many cases the ears and nose, and the rebellion was crushed and there was peace. Then the bishops who were present sat on the tribunal of the church, and Chrodield appeared and gave vent to much abuse of the abbess and many charges, asserting that she had a man in the monastery who wore woman's clothes and was treated as a woman although he had been very clearly shown to be a man, and that he was in constant attendance on the abbess herself, and she pointed her finger at him and said: "There he is himself." And when this man had taken the stand before all in woman's clothes, as I have stated, he said that he was impotent and therefore had put these clothes on; but he did not know the abbess except by name and he asserted that had never seen her or spoken with her, as he lived more than forty miles from the city of Poitiers. Then as she had not proved the abbess guilty of this crime, she added: "What holiness is there in this abbess who makes men eunuchs and orders them to live with her as if she were an empress." The abbess, being questioned, replied that she knew nothing of this matter. Meantime when Chrodield had given the name of the man who was a eunuch, Reoval, the chief physician, appeared and said: "This man when he was a child was diseased in the thigh and was so ill that his life was despaired of ; his mother went to the holy Radegunda to request that he should have some attention. But she called me and bade me give what assistance I could. Then I castrated him in the way I had once seen physicians do in Constantinople, and restored the boy in good health to his sorrowing mother; I am sure the abbess knows nothing of this matter." Now when Chrodield had failed to prove the abbess guilty on this charge also, she began fiercely to make others. But I have decided that it is better to insert the charges and the rebuttals of each in my narrative just they are contained in the decision which was given as regards these same persons.

16.

Copy of the Decision.

To the most glorious kings the bishops who are present [***note:*** *reading* Adfuerunt *for* adferunt.][send greetings]. By God's favor religion properly discloses her causes to the pious and orthodox kings who are given the to people and to whom the country is granted, knowing well that through the mediation of the holy spirit she is made a partner in the decree of the rulers and is supported by it. And whereas in accordance with the command of your majesties we are assembled at Poitiers on account of the situation in the monastery of Radegunda of holy memory, in order to take cognizance at first hand of the disputes between the abbess of the said monastery and the nuns who left the flock for no sound reason; we summoned the parties and interrogated Chrodield and Basina as to why they had so boldly departed contrary to the rule, breaking the doors of the monastery, and why the united congregation had at this time been broken in two. In answer they asserted that they could not endure any longer the risk of starvation, nakedness, and above all of beating; and they added also that several men had bathed in their bath contrary to decency, and that the abbess played games, and that worldly persons dined with her, and that a betrothal had actually taken place in the monastery; that she had impiously made a dress for her niece out of a silk altar cloth, and that she had frivolously taken the golden leaves which were on the border of the altar cloth and sinfully hung them about her niece's neck; and she had made a fillet with gold ornaments for her niece without any need for it, and that she had a masquerade [***note:*** Barbaturias. *Cf. Du Cange,* barbaloria.] in the monastery. We asked the abbess what she had to answer to this, and she said that as to the complaint about starvation, they had never endured too great privation considering the poverty of the time. And as to clothes, she said that if one were to examine their boxes, [he would find] they had more than was necessary. And as to the charge about the bath, she related that the bath had been built in the time of Lent and that on account of the disagreeable smell of the limestone, in order that the newness of the building might not do harm to the bathers, lady Radegunda had given orders for the servants of the monastery to use it as a common thing until all harmful odor had disappeared. It had been in common use by the servants through Lent and until Pentecost. To this Chrodield answered: "And later on in the same way many men bathed at different times." The abbess replied that she did not approve of what they reported but she did not know whether it was true; moreover she found fault with them for not informing the abbess if they had seen it. As to the games she played, she answered that she had played when lady Radegunda was alive and it was not regarded as a sin, and she said that neither in the rule nor the canons was there any reference in writing to their prohibition. However at the order of the bishops she promised that she would bow her head and do whatever penance should be demanded. As to the dinners, she said she had introduced no new custom but had merely offered the blest bread to orthodox Christians as had been done under lady Radegunda, and it could not be proved against her that she had ever dined with them. As to the betrothal, she said that she had received the earnest money [*note*: Arrhae. *Cf. P. 97 (Book: IV:42)*] in behalf of her niece, an orphan girl, in the presence of the bishop, the clergy and the leading men, and if this was a sin, she ask would for pardon in the presence of all; however not even on that occasion had she made a feast in the monastery. In answer to the charge about the altar cloth, she brought forward a nun of noble family who had given her as a gift a silk robe she had received from her relatives, and she had cut off a part of this to do what she wished with it, and from the rest, which was sufficient, she had made a suitable cloth to adorn the altar, and she used the scraps left over from the altar cloth to trim her niece's tunic with purple; and she said she gave this to her niece when she was serving in the monastery. All this was confirmed by Didimia who had given the robe. As to the leaves of gold and the fillet adorned with gold, she offered Macco your servant, who is here, as a witness, since it was by his hand that she received twenty pieces of gold from the betrothed of the said girl her niece, from which she had purchased these articles openly, and the property of the monastery was not involved in it at all.

Chrodield and Basina were asked whether perchance they imputed adultery to the abbess, which God forbid, or whether they could say she had committed a murder or a sorcery or a capital crime for which she should be punished. They replied they had nothing to say to this; they only asserted that she had acted contrary to the rule in the matters they had mentioned. Finally they said that nuns whom we believed to be innocent were with child because of these faults, namely, that the doors were broken open and the wretched women were at liberty to do what they would for many months without discipline from their abbess.

When we had discussed these charges in order and had found no wrongdoing for which to degrade the abbess, we gave her a fatherly admonition for the pardonable faults she had committed, and urged her not to incur any reproof later. Then we inquired into the case of the opposing party who had committed greater crimes, that is to say, who, when within the monastery, had despised the warning of their bishop not to go forth in despite of their bishop and had left him in the monastery under the greatest contempt and had broken the bars and doors and foolishly departed, involving other nuns in their sin. Moreover when the archbishop Gundigisil with his provincials had received notice of this case and come to Poitiers by order of the king and had summoned them to a hearing at the monastery, they disregarded his summons, and when the bishops went to them at the church of St. Hilary the Confessor where they were staying, going to them as is seemly for anxious pastors to do; while they were receiving the admonition of the bishops a disturbance arose, and they attacked the bishops and their attendants with clubs, and even shed the blood of deacons within the church. Then when the venerable priest Teuthar by command of the princes came to judge this case, and the time for rendering the judgment had been fixed, they did not wait for it but attacked the monastery like rebels, setting fire to casks in the courtyard and breaking the doors with crowbars and axes, and setting fire, and beating and wounding nuns in the very oratories within the walls, and plundering the monastery, and stripping the clothes off the abbess and tearing her hair and dragging her violently through the streets in derision and thrusting her into a place where, although not in fetters, she was not free. And when the festival of Easter came, which is always honored, the bishop offered a ransom for the prisoner so that she could aid in baptism, but his entreaty could not secure this for any consideration, Chrodield answered that she had neither known of such a crime nor ordered it, adding further that it was at a sign from her that the abbess was not killed by her people, from which we may be confident in inferring that they were becoming more cruel and they had killed a slave of their own monastery who was fleeing to the blessed Radegunda's tomb, and instead of improving had gone deeper into crime; and later they entered the monastery and took possession of it; and at the order of the kings to produce the rebels in public they refused to obey, and rather took up arms against the king's command and wickedly rose with arrows and lances against the count and the people. Then lately when they appeared for a public hearing they took the holy and most sacred cross secretly and wrongfully, which they were later forced to store to the church.

Having taken cognizance of so many capital crimes and of a wickedness that was not restrained but continually increased, we told them that they should beg the abbess for pardon for their sin and restore what they had wrongfully taken. But they were unwilling to do this but talked rather of killing her, a design they admitted in public. Then we opened and read the canons, and it seemed most just that until they made a suitable repentance they should be excommunicated and the abbess should continue permanently in her place. This is what we suggest should be done in accordance with your command, as far as the interests of the church are concerned, having read the canons and having made no distinction of persons. For the rest, as to the property of the monastery and the deeds given by the kings your kinsmen which have been stolen, and which they say they have but disregard our orders and fail to return, it belongs to your piety, your power and royal authority to compel them to be returned to their place, in order that your reward and that of the previous kings may continue for ever. Do not permit them to return or think of returning again to the place which they so impiously and sacrilegiously destroyed, lest worse may come. With the aid of the Lord let all be wholly restored and returned to God under the catholic kings; let religion lose nothing; let the decision of the fathers and the canons be maintained and be of profit to us for worship and bring you gain. May Christ the Lord support and guide you, may He bestow on you a long reign and the blessed life.

17.

After this when the decision was made known and they were excommunicated and the abbess restored to the monastery, they went to king Childebert, adding crime to crime, naming forsooth certain persons to the king who not only lived in adultery with the abbess but also sent messengers daily to his enemy Fredegunda. On hearing this the king sent men to bring them in chains. But when they were examined and no wrongdoing was found, they were let go.

[18. Attempt on the life of Childebert. 19. Bishop Egidius is removed from office. 20. Basina and Chrodield are pardoned. 21. Waddo's sons are punished. 22. Death of Childeric.]

23.

In this year there was such a light shed over the earth in the night that one would think it mid-day moreover balls of fire were frequently noticed at night speeding across the sky and lighting the world. There was doubt about Easter for the reason that Victor wrote in his cycle that Easter came on the fifteenth day of the moon. But to prevent Christians from celebrating this festival at the same time of the moon as the Jews, he added: "But the Latins [place it] on the twentysecond of the moon." For this reason many in Gaul celebrated on the fifteenth of the moon but we celebrated on the twentysecond. We made careful inquiry but the springs in Spain which are filled by a divine power were filled at our Easter.

There was a great earthquake on the eighteenth day before the Kalends [*note: June 14*] of the fifth month, being the fourth day [of the week], early in the morning when dawn was coming. The sun was eclipsed in the middle of the eighth month and its light was so diminished that it scarcely gave as much light as the horns of the moon on the fifth day. There were heavy rains, loud thunders in the autumn and the streams were very full. The bubonic plague cruelly destroyed the people of Viviers and Avignon.

[24. An Armenian bishop visits Tours and tells the story of the destruction of Antioch.]

25.

Now in the Gauls the disease I have mentioned attacked the province of Marseilles, and a great famine oppressed Angers, Nantes, and Mans. These are the beginning of sorrows according to what the Lord says in the Gospel: "There shall be pestilence and famines and earthquakes in different places and false Christs and false prophets shall arise and give signs and prodigies in the heavens so as to put the elect astray" as is true at the present time. For a certain man of Bourges, as he himself told later, went into the deep woods to cut logs which he needed for a certain work and a swarm of flies surrounded him, as a result of which he was considered crazy for two years; whence it may be believed that they were a wickedness sent by the devil. Then he passed through the neighboring cities and went to the province of Arles and there wore skins and prayed like one of the devout, and to make a fool of him the enemy gave him the power of divination. After this he rose from his place and left the province mentioned in order to become more expert in wickedness, and entered the territory of Gévaudan, conducting himself as a great man and not afraid to say that he was Christ. He took with him a woman who passed as his sister to whom he gave the name of Mary. A multitude of people flocked to him bringing the sick, whom he touched and restored to health. They who came to him brought him also gold and silver and garments. These he distributed among the poor to deceive them the more easily, and throwing himself on the ground and praying with the woman I have mentioned and rising, he would give orders to the bystanders to worship him in turn. He foretold the future and announced that disease would come to some, to others losses and to others health. But all this he did by some arts and trickeries of the devil. A great multitude of people was led astray by him, not only the common ilk but bishops of the church. More than three thousand people followed him. Meantime he began to spoil and plunder those whom he met on the road; the booty, however, he gave to those who had nothing. He threatened with death bishops and citizens, because they disdained to worship him. He entered La Velay and went to the place called Puy and halted with all his host at the churches near there, marshalling his line of battle to make war on Aurilius who was then bishop, and sending messengers forward, naked men who danced and played and announced his coming. The bishop was amazed at this and sent strong men to ask what his doings meant. One of these, the leader, bent down as if to embrace his knees and check his passage and [the impostor] ordered him to be seized and spoiled. But the other at once drew his sword and cut him into bits and that Christ who ought rather to be named antiChrist fell dead; and all who were with him dispersed. Mary was tortured and revealed all his impostures and deceits. But the men whom he had excited to a belief in him by the trickery of the devil never returned to their sound senses, but they always said that this man was Christ in a sense and that Mary had a share in his divine nature. Moreover through all the Gauls many appeared who attracted poor women to themselves by trickery and influenced them to rave and declare their leaders holy, and they made a great show before the people. I have seen some of them and have rebuked the m and endeavored to recall them from error.

[26. A Syrian trader, Eusebius, becomes bishop of Paris.]

27.

Among the Franks of Tournai a great feud arose because the son of one often angrily rebuked the son of another who had married his sister, for leaving his wife and visiting a prostitute. And when reform on the part of the guilty man did not follow, the anger of the youth became so great that he rushed upon his brotherinlaw and killed him and his men, and was himself killed by his opponents, and there was only one left from both parties who lacked a slayer. Upon this the kinsmen on both sides raged at one another, but were frequently urged by queen Fredegunda to give up their enmity and become friends lest their persistence in the quarrel might cause a greater disturbance. But when she failed to reconcile them with gentle words she tamed them on both sides with the ax. For she invited many to a feast and caused these three to sit on the same bench, and when the dinner had been prolonged until night covered the earth, the table was taken away according to the custom of the Franks and they sat on the bench in their places. Much wine had been drunk and they were so overcome by it that the slaves were intoxicated and were lying asleep in the corners of the house, each where he fell. Then by the woman's order three men with axes stood behind these three and while they were talking together the hands of the men flashed in a single blow, so to speak, and they were struck down and the banquet ended. Their names were Charivald, Leodovald, and Valden. When this was told to their kinsmen they began to watch Fredegunda closely and sent messengers to king Childebert to seize her and put her to death. The people of Champagne were angry because of this matter, but while Childebert was interposing delay she was saved by the help of her people and hastened to another place.

[**28.** Baptism of Clothar. **29.** Miracles of the abbot Aridius. **30.** The plague. **31.** The bishops of Tours from the beginning to Gregory.]

The nineteenth was I, unworthy Gregory, who found the church of Tours, in which the blessed Martin and the other bishops of the Lord were consecrated in the pontifical office, shattered and ruined by fire. I rebuilt it larger and higher, and dedicated it in the seventeenth year after being ordained; and in it as I learned from the old priests the relics of the blessed Maurice and his companions had been placed by the ancients. I found the very box in the treasury of the church of St. Martin, and in it the relics, greatly decayed, which had been brought because of their miraculous power. And while vigils were being kept in their honor I wished to visit them again by the light of a torch. And I was examining them intently when the keeper of the church said to me: "Here is a stone with a cover, but I don't know what it has in it and I haven't been able to learn from my predecessors who have had charge here. Let me bring it and you look carefully to see what it contains." I took it and opened it of course, and found a silver box containing relics of the witnesses of the blessed legion as well as of many saints both martyrs and confessors. We also found other stones hollow like this one, containing relics of the holy apostles and the rest of the martyrs. I wondered at this bounty divinely given and after, giving thanks, keeping vigil, and saying mass, I placed them in the cathedral. I placed the relics of the holy martyrs Cosmas and Damian in St. Martin's cell close to the cathedral. I found the walls of the holy church consumed by fire and ordered skilful workmen to repaint and adorn them with their er splendor. I had a baptistery built close by the church, where I placed the relics of the holy martyrs John and Sergius, and in what had been the baptistery I placed the relics of the martyr Benignus. And in many localities in the territory of Tours I dedicated churches and oratories and glorified them with relics of the saints, but I think it tiresome to speak of them in order.

I wrote ten books of Histories, seven of Miracles, one on the Lives of the Fathers; a commentary in one book on Psalms; one book also on the Services of the Church. And though I have written these books in a style somewhat rude, I nevertheless conjure you all, God's bishops who are destined to rule the lowly church of Tours after me, by the coming of our Lord Jesus Christ and the judgment day, feared by the guilty, if you will not be condemned with the devil and depart in confusion from the judgment, never cause these books to be destroyed or rewritten, selecting some passages and omitting others, but let them all continue in your time complete and undiminished as they were left by us. And bishop of God, whoever you may be, if our Martianus has trained you in the seven disciplines, that is, if he has taught you by means of grammar to read, by dialectic to apprehend the arguments in disputes, by rhetoric to recognize the different meters, by geometry to comprehend the measurement of the earth and of lines, by astrology to contemplate the paths of the heavenly bodies, by arithmetic to understand the parts of numbers, by harmony to fit the modulated voice to the sweet accents of the verse; if in all this you are practiced so that my style will seem rude, even so I beg of you do not efface what I have written. But if anything in these books pleases you I do not forbid your writing it in verse provided my work is left safe.

I am finishing this work in the twenty-first year after my ordination.

Although in what I have just written of the bishops of Tours I have told their years, still this calculation does not agree with the [total] number of years, because I have not been able to learn accurately the length of time between the different ordinations. Now the grand total of years of the world is as follows:

From the beginning to the flood	2242 years
From the flood to the crossing of the Red Sea by the children of Israel years.	1404 years
From the crossing of this sea to the resurrection of the Lord.	1538 years
From the resurrection of the Lord to the death of St. Martin	412 years
From the death of St. Martin to the year mentioned above, namely, the twentyfirst year after my ordination, which is also the fifth of Gregory, pope of Rome, the thirtyfirst of king Gunthram, and the nineteenth of Childebert the second .	197 years
The grand total of which is	5792 years

HERE ENDS IN CHRIST'S NAME THE TENTH BOOK OF THE HISTORIES